Educating for Justice Around the World

Legal education, legal practice and the community

Edited by
LOUISE G. TRUBEK
Clinical Professor of Law, University of Wisconsin-Madison

JEREMY COOPER
Professor of Law and Dean of Law Faculty, Southampton Institute

Routledge
Taylor & Francis Group
LONDON AND NEW YORK

First published 1999 by Dartmouth and Ashgate Publishing

Reissued 2018 by Routledge
4 Park Square, Milton Park, Abingdon, Oxon, OX14 4RN
605 Third Avenue, New York, NY 10158

Routledge is an imprint of the Taylor & Francis Group, an informa business

A Library of Congress record exists under LC control number: 99075460

ISBN 13: 978-1-138-31270-8 (hbk)
ISBN 13: 978-0-429-45807-1 (ebk)

Contents

List of Contributors

JEREMY COOPER is Dean of the Law Faculty, and Professor of Law, at Southampton Institute. He is also a Barrister, and worked previously at a community law center in London. Co-editor of *Public Interest Law* (Basil Blackwell, 1986); Author of *Public Legal Services* (Sweet and Maxwell, 1983); *Keyguide to Information Sources in Public Interest Law* (Mansell, 1991); *The Legal Rights Manual* (Ashgate, 1994); *Disability and the Law* (Jessica Kingsley, 1996) with Stuart Vernon.

KENNETH S. GALLANT is Director of Clinical Programs and visiting Professor of Law, University of Arkansas, Little Rock School of Law. Previously he worked at the University of Idaho School of Law. He was also a Fulbright Scholar and Visiting Professor at the National Law School of India, Bangalore.

WOUTER T. DE GROOT is Professor of Environmental Studies at the University of Nijmegen and Associate Professor at the University of Leiden, the Netherlands.

LENY E. DE GROOT-VAN LEEUWEN is Assistant Professor at the Law Faculty of the University of Utrecht and at the University of Nijmegen, the Netherlands. She has published several books and articles in the field of the Sociology of Law, primarily on the Legal Profession.

GOTARO ICHIKI is the Director of the Tokyo branch of the Japanese legal Aid Association.

WEIDONG JI is Professor of Law, at Kobe University Japan and concurrent Professor of Law, at Peking University, China. He was Visiting Scholar at the Stanford University Law School, 1991-1992. His recent publications include, *A Hypermodern Law, the Structure of Chinese Legal Order in the Depths*, Minerva Press, Kyoto, 1999, and *Constructing Rule of Law*, China University of Law and Political Sciences Press, Beijing, 1999.

ELIANE BOTELHO JUNQUEIRA is Professor at the Catholic University of Rio de Janeiro and Director of the Instituto Direito e Sociedade (IDES), Brazil. She has published books and articles on Law and Literature, Legal Education and Cause Lawyering.

LINDA A. KELLY is Associate Professor of Law, at the Saint Thomas University School of Law, Miami, Florida. She has written numerous articles on the issues raised by the intersection of Gender and Immigration with a particular interest in Domestic Violence.

STEPHEN MEILI is Clinical Associate Professor and Director of the Consumer Law Litigation Clinic, University of Wisconsin Law School, Madison. Of-Counsel, Center for Public Representation, Madison, Wisconsin.

SETSUO MIYAZAWA holds degrees from Hokkaido University in Japan as well as from Yale University. After teaching at Hokkaido University, he became a Professor of Law at Kobe University in Japan. He has also been a Visiting Professor at York University (Canada), the University of Washington, Harvard University, the University of California at Berkeley, UCLA and New York University. His current research interests include Public Interest Lawyering. He is heavily involved in the ongoing debate on judicial reform in Japan.

MALEE PRUEKPONGSAWALEE holds degrees from Thammasat University, and Yale University. Now Assistant Professor, she has been a faculty member of Thammasat Law School since 1973. Active in the faculty legal aid services program during her student time, she is currently a committee member of the Law Center, the Faculty unit in charge of legal aid services, and a founding member of the Friends of Women Foundation, an NGO working to promote the equality and the quality of life of women in Thailand. She holds several positions related to women's issues, including Chairperson of Thammasat University Women and Youth Studies Program. Her teaching subjects are Labor Law and Law and State Policies on Women.

JANE E. SCHUKOSKE is Associate Professor of Law, and Director of the Community Development Clinic, at the University of Baltimore School of Law, in Maryland. She has worked with law teachers, working in communities in India, Sri Lanka, and Nepal.

LOUISE G. TRUBEK is Clinical Professor of Law, University of Wisconsin Law School and Clinical Director, Center for Public Representation, Madison, Wisconsin. Co-author of *Poverty Law: Theory and Practice* (West Publishing, 1996), she teaches Health Law, Poverty Law, and Lawyering in the Public Interest. She is currently directing a series of conferences and publications on Providing Legal Services for Underrepresented Groups in East and Southeast Asia, with meetings in Thailand and Japan.

TETSUO OHISHI is the Vice-Secretary of the Japanese Legal Aid Association.

DAE-KYU YOON is Professor of Law at Kyungnam University and Vice-Director of its Institute for Far Eastern Studies. He holds degrees from Seoul National University College of Law, Kyungnam University in Masan, Korea, and from the University of Washington School of Law Asian Law Program. He has published many articles on Constitutional Law, Comparative Law and the Sociology of Law.

Acknowledgements

This volume is the second in a series on 'Educating for Justice'. The series reflects the collaborative work of scholars and activists dedicated to social values in law. In the first volume, *Educating for Justice: Social Values and Legal Education,* published by Ashgate in 1997, we examined ways in which, in various parts of the world, the law school experience influences the desire and the capacity of law students and law activists to engage in social action lawyering in poor and marginalized communities. We tried to show, in the words of Duncan Kennedy, 'that law schools can, and sometimes do, fulfill a mission beyond educating hired guns for the corporate bar' and via 'an eclectic group of experiments' showed how it is possible (to quote Howard Erlanger) to 'get out of the box that defines contemporary legal education'.

This second volume continues further reflection on the importance of legal education contained in the first volume and affirms again the importance of global networks in sharing ideas and strategies. The chapter on East and Southeast Asia reflects the initiative of the University of Wisconsin East Asian Legal Studies Center, particularly Professor Charles Irish, and of the Japan Foundation Center for Global Partnership in sponsoring a workshop in Summer, 1998, in Bangkok, Thailand, on 'Lawyering for the Underrepresented in East and Southeast Asia'. That workshop produced papers, which formed the basis for chapters two, three, four, five, and six of this volume. The interchanges initiated in Bangkok will continue at a second meeting in Kobe and Tokyo, Japan, in December, 1999. Chapters eleven and twelve, on India and South Asia, are based upon papers presented at the Fourth International Clinical Conference in India, in 1998. The other chapters derive from the continued work of scholars in the United States, Latin America, and Europe studying the interaction of legal education, legal practice, and the community.

Many organizations and individuals assisted in the development, editing, and production of this volume. In particular, we wish to acknowledge the important contributions of Sara E. Zeman, at the University of Wisconsin Law School, and Mike Foster and Irene Clark, at Southampton Institute. We would also like to thank John Irwin, of Ashgate Publishing Company, for his unerring willingness to support this project.

1 Rethinking Lawyering for the Underrepresented Around the World: An introductory essay

LOUISE G. TRUBEK AND JEREMY COOPER

Introduction

This volume is dedicated to exploring the relationship between social values and law.[1] Lying at the core of this project is a belief in the central importance of transnationalism in linking together groups of people and ideas with a reliance on the capacity of legal education, in its broadest sense, to underpin this activity. What is distinctive about this volume is the detailed discussion of efforts in different nations and regions to develop lawyering for the underrepresented, highlighting in particular the continuing importance played by the comparative study of law.[2] We are especially interested in tracking how formal legal culture has served as both a barrier and a goal to the development of a consciousness to work for the underrepresented in areas of the world where such a concept is relatively untried. The volume also reflects the considerable impact of globalization on the legal field, with particular reference to marginalized groups and to training of lawyers and law personnel. The chapters indicate the incorporation of the consequences of globalization in a broad range of legal activities.[3]

The volume contributes to a context: the relationship of comparative scholarship to action and its capacity to give meaning to disparate activities that might previously have seen themselves as isolated and unrelated. The dispassionate and critical external study of a system of law, at which the comparative method aims, enables us to form some estimate of the relative value of various parts or principles of our law in its function as a social institution.

We use the comparative method to distinguish accidental differences and similarities among jurisdictions from those which are structural, rooted in a particular legal culture. In this context, we take legal culture to include the whole complex of beliefs, values, and modes of reasoning that typify a given society (Savigny, 1831). Lawyering for social change presents a rich and fertile library of pioneering and imaginative scholarship which has been developed extensively in the American context. A number of studies demonstrate this approach, beginning with the classic article in the Yale Law Journal, by Edgar and Jean Cahn, published in 1964, entitled 'The War on Poverty' (Cahn and Cahn, 1964), and typified in the subsequent work of Handler, Hollingsworth, and Erlanger (1978). The massive volumes by Cappelletti *et al*, (1972; 1978-9), built upon these pioneering analytic methodologies to study access to justice across much of the world. They provided a series of detailed accounts of the development of legal aid systems in Australia, Austria, Bulgaria, Canada, Chile, Holland, Hungary, Indonesia, Israel, Italy, Japan, Mexico, Poland, the Soviet Union, Spain, the United States, and Uruguay. This series also identified key global trends such as the development of class actions designed to protect specified groups with common interests, e.g. civil rights groups working with black communities, and the movement to develop law and legal processes to protect groups with diffuse interests across generic themes, e.g. consumer and environmental groups. Richard Abel pioneered a further series of incisive and scholarly studies of the role and politics of informal justice across a series of countries (Abel, 1982). The same scholar published, three years later, a monumental study of legal aid in advanced capitalist countries, in which he sought to provide answers to the key questions: Why does legal aid emerge where it does and when it does? What are the true politics behind legal aid? (Abel, 1985).

Richard Abel and Philip Lewis carried out a parallel study of the legal profession across a number of different countries around the same period (Abel and Lewis, 1988; 1995). Splitting their analysis into two volumes: *The Common Law World* and *The Civil Law World,* they attached particular importance to the role of the civil/common law distinction in explaining variation among countries (Abel and Lewis, 1988). They also emphasized the importance of the single bar versus the barrister and solicitor organization of the legal professions in influencing the specific cost, role, and attitude of lawyers (Abel and Lewis, 1988, vol. 1, 23). In contrast, the Cappelletti volumes concentrated on the social role of lawyering for the underrepresented, emphasizing the wide variety of possible styles and strategies, whether through simplification of legal institutions (small claims), traditional individual representation for the indigent (legal aid), or lawyering for diffuse interests (environmental and consumer policy and court challenges). All this comparative work was of great value; it created a body of information that was available throughout the world and created networks of people who worked together in writing about their own societies. These scholars contributed insights about their own legal professions and also learned about the ways other societies operated.

Our volume demonstrates substantial differences from those earlier series, brought about by important changes in the world since the 1970s and 1980s. For example, many of the earlier sets did not discuss the developing world or the communist countries in anything but passing detail. Legal education was barely mentioned. There was little discussion of the movement of people and ideas between different societies. In contrast, these themes are central to our project; there are substantial contributions relating to what used to be called developing countries and countries emerging from authoritarian regimes. Furthermore, the framing concept of our book is legal education. Although this volume pays little attention to the relevance of the civil versus common law distinction,[4] it has some goals simliar to those of the earlier studies. The first goal of the organizers of the previous massive research undertakings was the desire to share knowledge about different societies. The Abel and Lewis volumes attempted to use this knowledge to promote understanding of the role of lawyers in their society while Cappelletti's volumes had a reformist and aspirational vision, as expressed in his three 'Access to Justice' waves (Cappelletti *et al*, 1978-9). In the words of Cappelletti, writing in 1993 (Cappelletti, 1993, 283), 'The access to justice movement... tends toward a vision more faithful to the complexity of human society.... The primary element is the *people, with all their cultural, economic and psychological features*'. The contributors to the present volume share this aspirational goal for exchange of knowledge.

The second goal of the earlier studies was to bring together researchers to form networks. For example, the Abel and Lewis books were an outgrowth of the longstanding, *Working Group on the Legal Profession*.[5] The scholars, activists, and government officials involved in the Cappelletti project met over an extended period of time, forming contacts that continued.[6] Similarly, our project includes a vision of a network of scholars and practitioners who can continue to meet and exchange ideas and visions.[7]

This volume thus brings together discussions of contemporary lawyering in different nations throughout the world and descriptions of formal interchanges between different societies.[8] This introductory essay outlines and explores some of the themes emerging from the chapters. In particular, three themes that appear in the local accounts are discussed: the role of communities, legal professional values, and legal education. Thereafter, we discuss the issue of transnational effects and conclude with a vision for future projects.

Communities, Legal Professional Values, and Legal Education

The contributions to this volume show how the tension between broader community participation and individual client representation continue to influence provision of services for the underrepresented. The tension between the two creates an uncertain tightrope, which programs for the underrepresented must navigate.[9] In addition to this tension, legal professionalism reflects the paradox of the need for a higher status for lawyers in order to advance their participation in society while remaining responsive to community equity. Legal education, to a certain extent, reflects both the tension in allocating resources and the paradox of legal professionalism. Its major contribution to educating for justice can be to expose students to these contradictions. The continued interest in legal clinics, with their relevance to societal issues and actual practice, may reflect the ability of legal education to provide this grounding.

Communities

The connection between law and community life is complex. Which social structure or community network should provide the building blocks for legal assistance programs? This volume illustrates a widespread tension in lawyering for the underrepresented, one that transnational analysis reinforces: Should lawyering for the indigent primarily be about ensuring representation in confrontations with a court or agency, or is it to be more about proactive, community lawyering? An aspect of this tension that emerges from these studies, and one that is a longstanding issue in lawyering for the underrepresented, is the choice between using limited resources for individual representation or broader group initiatives (Cappelletti and Garth, 1983). As Cappelletti wrote in 1978:

> More and more frequently the complexity of modern societies generates situations in which a single human action can be beneficial or prejudicial to large numbers of people, thus making entirely inadequate the traditional scheme of litigation as merely a two-part affair (Cappelletti *et al*, 1978-9).

The tension between these two approaches has been apparent in many countries, for example the United States, the United Kingdom, and Australia, for most of the past 50 years, or even longer (see Cooper, 1983; Basten *et al*, 1983; Noone, 1997, 257; Grossberg, 1997). The difficulty of providing preventive and proactive legal work for the underrepresented is an ongoing theme.[10] In fact, it is probably *the* major continuing issue of legal services jurisprudence.

The complexity of this tension is reflected in many of the contributions. The discussions of India and Thailand are positive stories of the ability to relate community needs and legal services. Gallant, for example, discusses the close interaction between rural community life and customs, and the importance of extending legal services and legal understandings to clients based in those communities (Gallant, chapter 12). He discusses how Indian law school clinics are providing services to rural communities integrating legislative enactments and court decisions in the field. This observation is further reenforced by the contribution of Schukoske who demonstrates that 'in addition to community education and individual counselling in villages and urban slums, ...comparative clinical work involves learning through experiencing cultures as well as through study of comparative law and legal systems' (Schukoske, chapter 11). In the Thammassat Law School Clinic, in Thailand, a rural community focus is a central component in the development of a program that is capable of bringing about change in the community through legal intervention with an educational basis (Pruekpongsawalee, chapter 6). Though not examined in this volume, the Community Law Centre (CLC), based in Natal, South Africa, illustrates another version of the approach of passing back to the community itself the choice of which model to adopt at any given time (Baekey and Gabriel, 1994). The CLC is an independent, privately-funded, nonprofit NGO (non governmental organization) set up to work within the poor, rural communities of Natal on issues of development, civil society, and self sufficiency through legal education and the development, by law, of local resources. CLC has adopted an alternative strategy, premised ultimately upon the twin principles of community legal education and self help, with the community itself driving the decision-making process. The CLC has eschewed both a legal advice/individual case approach and a group advocacy approach in an attempt to side-step the previously described tensions. These community-based legal programs present one way of resolving the tension of how to use limited resources to advance social equity.

Ji's discussion of the survival of community-based informal mediation systems in China presents another approach to resolving the tension between individualized rights and representation and community and group approaches.

The informal mediation systems continue to retain an important place in Chinese rural society despite China's slow shift from a culture of 'communism with Chinese characteristics', to a flirtation with the free market (Ji, chapter 5). These mediation systems are based in villages and involve community participation. Ji indicates that this system is co-existing in a satisfactory manner with the newly developing legal aid system based on the more traditional Western model for legal aid provision (Ji, chapter 5). Furthermore, the Chinese government is showing no signs of wishing to rush into imposing a Western style model of legal aid onto a system that is deeply rooted in community-based mediation, exploring the widest possible range of options through a series of dialogues with legal service policy makers and analysts in a number of foreign countries (Cooper, 1999). By this process, the Chinese are hoping to find a way of maintaining an informal, local community-based law and mediation program while embarking on the introduction of a parallel legal aid system.[11]

The discussion of legal aid in Japan presents a fascinating study of an effort to create a system of representation for the disadvantaged that combines an expansion of individual representation with a continuation of group and community advocacy. The Japanese have a longstanding history of promoting group interests based on individual lawyers' political commitments and the mission of their Bar Associations (Sarat and Scheingold, 1997). This commitment has allowed them to provide important litigation and organizing services. However, representation for individual clients and legal educational programs have been less developed. Ichiki and Ohishi indicate that there is difficulty in conceptualizing how an expanded legal aid program, now being considered by the Japanese government, should include any functions beyond representation of clients in court proceedings. For example, there is skepticism about an advice and consultation function, which might take the form of community legal education for the expanded legal aid program. (Ichiki and Ohishi, chapter 3). Moreover, it is possible that the suggested reforms may undercut the ability to provide cause lawyering because the proposed simultaneous increase in the size of the legal profession may reduce the income of lawyers (Miyazawa, chapter 2).

Legal Professional Values

All professions are located somewhere upon a continuum from total regulation at one end, to total deregulation at the other end. The deregulation of a service profession can take one of two forms: 'soft deregulation' and 'hard deregulation'. The 'soft' form of deregulation merely removes state regulation and replaces it with self regulation, via an autonomous professional body. Under this model, any state legislation controlling the use of professional titles and training programs, defining monopoly activities, fixing professional fees and other costs, and so forth is replaced by a system of professional self-regulation, normally through a centralized professional body, such as a bar association. The 'hard' form of deregulation either removes regulation altogether or never allows it to exist in the first place. This would mean, in the case of lawyers, that *anybody* would have the right to offer legal advice and assistance or to 'practice law', whether or not they had obtained the formal qualification of a 'lawyer'. Models for such an approach can be found in other professions including journalism, counselling, financial advising, surveying, and a whole range of therapeutic and analytical services that might be loosely described as the 'ologies'.

The normal *quid pro quo* for lawyers agreeing to be a *regulated* profession is a quasi-monopoly of legal representation and advice to clients. The monopoly, however, is not total. For example, *pro se* litigants are allowed in many court systems. Many tribunals and some courts allow representation from nonlawyers in defined circumstances, and the giving of legal advice is not normally proscribed either by law or in practice. Another justification for self-regulation, with an associated quasi-monopoly on the provision of legal services offered by the legal profession itself, is the reenforcement of a professional responsibility, to provide legal services to all. There are, however, elements of the lawyer-client relationship, enshrined in professional ethics, that mitigate against this ideal of legal assistance for all: lawyer autonomy, client confidentiality, and conflicts of interest can present barriers to achievement of the altruistic goals (Trubek, L. 1999; De Groot van Leeuwen, 1997). This contradiction is a consistent dilemma in longstanding liberal, democratic societies (Economides, 1997). It is also starting to appear in societies that are emerging from a previous authoritarian regime (Argentina, Chile and Brazil); in societies in transition (China, and the Czech Republic); and in the East Asian model (Japan, Korea). The role of the Brazilian and Japanese Bar Associations as arenas for social activity by lawyers, are shining achievements. The Brazilian Bar Association played a very positive role in the move from military to democratic government in the 1980s. The Japanese Bar Association has provided extensive cause lawyering as well as individual assistance to the poor since the 1940s. Both Bar Associations are now facing a changing society that requires them to confront the contradiction between professional status and social needs. In Brazil, a democratic, capitalistic society is increasing the importance of the lawyer in the business role, and creating disincentives to speak out for the underrepresented (Junqueira, chapter 8). In Japan, the small size of the legal profession has allowed firms to make a living, while providing controversial representation for underrepresented groups and individuals. The small number of lawyers is now a problem for the corporate firms searching for lawyers and for the provision of individual representation, in everyday legal matters for poor people. Thus, the Bar is confronting the dilemma between expanding the legal profession to meet business needs and designing a new system to provide lawyering for the poor. Korea and China also display a struggle over the size and mission of the profession that could significantly affect the provision of legal services (Yoon, chapter 4; Cooper, 1999). Developing an autonomous legal profession is viewed as essential to the emergence of a liberal society. How that move will be merged with the provision of needed legal services is under debate.

The problems surrounding codes of professional ethics are discussed in the description of teaching and developing judicial ethics codes in the Czech Republic (De Groot van Leeuwen and De Groot, chapter 9). Judicial codes can provide minimum provisions that protect the public from abuses. They can also contain aspirational goals for the role of judges in society. In nations emerging from authoritarian regimes, putting in place fair judges uncorrupted by bribery or politics may be the prime goal for the legal profession. However, a goal for the judiciary of access to justice for all may contradict the neutral role of the judge; ethics codes can serve as arenas for this struggle.

Legal Education

Clinics and curricula design were central to the studies on social values in law and the linkages with legal education contained in the first volume (Cooper and Trubek, 1997, 4,7). They retain a crucial role in the systems under review in this book. Clinics have been an important element in legal education in India, Thailand, and the United States since the 1960s. Interest in clinics is growing in Argentina and Chile. The close relationship between some Indian law school clinics and community legal services has been noted since the 1980s (Block and Ishar, 1990; Menon, 1998). The spread of clinics is based on their effectiveness in providing a social justice mission for the law schools, allowing students and teachers to participate in the life of the community, and developing legal skills and information to meet community and client needs. The National Law School of India, based in Bangalore, has clinic work as a compulsory component in its law curriculum for all students, and moves are underway to extend this provision to all Indian law schools (Menon, 1998). The Thai clinic is an especially poignant story of how law students involved in the move to democracy in the 1960s developed a clinic to serve clients and reform legal education and of how that clinic continues to be a valued part of the community, law school, and university (Pruekpongsawalee, chapter 6).

The importance of clinics in legal education varies with social context, curriculum design, and the attitude of government towards legal aid. The story of the St. Thomas immigration clinic in Florida reflects the increasing emphasis on international human rights and immigration issues, as well as the continuing importance of feminist issues in law schools in the United States (Kelly, chapter 10).[12] In Japan, the government's interest in expanding legal aid is contributing to the exploration of clinic development; it is thought that exposure to the legal problems of the underrepresented, via clinical work, might serve to foster wider social concerns in students (Miyazawa, chapter 2). Clinical skills and values also can be incorporated into the more general curriculum, if the importance of the link to community and clients is supported by the government and the legal profession; the Bar Council of India's recent requirement is seeking to mandate courses on skills and legal aid (Schukoske, chapter 11).

Transnational Interpenetration

Transnational flows of people and ideas is not a new phenomenon.[13] The Abel and Lewis and the Cappelletti studies aimed to encourage sharing of information and contacts among people throughout the world who were interested in the legal profession. A notable theme of this volume is the increased importance of transnational effects on the national provision of lawyering for the underrepresented.

This is not to understate the crucial importance of nation-state actions. Understanding the shift from military regimes to more democratic regimes in Thailand, Argentina, Brazil, and Chile is essential to understanding the changing roles of legal education and the profession. Even more subtle changes, such as those in Japan, reflect government policy; for the Japanese government to become more open, the legal profession and law schools must change.[14] On a more mundane level, the attitude of national governments towards government support of legal aid versus private bar control influences the way lawyering will occur in a nation, as is clear in the studies of Japan, China, and Korea.[15] Moreover, local conditions will persist as factors influencing the social role of law. Pruekpongsawalee (chapter 6) notes the importance of Buddhism in understanding the role of law in Thailand. The Thammassat clinic, for Pruekpongsawalee, is an outcome of both the violence in the transition to democracy and the spirituality of the religious tradition. Nonetheless, the case studies contained in this volume strikingly note the role of transnational interpenetration. This interpenetration is demonstrated through three mechanisms: external funding, transplanting of laws, and global law firms.

External Funding

The interest in law on the part of international funding agencies such as the World Bank, USAID, and EU is relatively new. However, private foundations such as the Ford Foundation and Asia Foundation have been funding law projects since the 1960s.[16] In India and Thailand, the community link to legal education initiated the development of legal clinics but funding from the Ford Foundation and Asia Foundation was essential to the sustainability and status of these clinics (Gallant, chapter 12; Pruekpongsawalee, chapter 6). A number of projects working on raising the profile of women's rights in the Indian sub-continent receive significant funding from such organizations as the Asia Foundation and the World Bank. External funding has advantages. It encourages interchange of people and ideas, as shown by the important influence of Indian legal services models and approaches to clinical legal education in the United States. United States clinicians, inspired by their experiences in Indian law schools, are rethinking their work, as demonstrated in the contributions to this volume by Gallant (chapter 12) and Schukoske (chapter 11). However, the provision of funding from external sources, while seductive, comes with a cost. The difficult struggle to raise domestic sources of funding, so familiar to United States legal services programs, encourages institutional independence and alliances with unexpected sources. This search for domestic funding requires interaction with government, local business, and the legal profession, which may result in positive strategies. The availability of external funding relieves these programs from these potentially positive interactions and leaves them vulnerable to external funding trends and international conflicts. It is interesting to note that the projects described in India and Thailand appear to be utilizing both domestic and external sources of funding.

Transplanting of Laws

Another aspect of transnational interpenetration and the comparative approach is the transplanting of laws (Kahn-Freund, 1966; Kamba, 1974; Markesenis, 1990). 'No lawyer would embark upon a comparative legal study without intending that his (her) endeavors should be utilized either by him (her) or by others' (Schmitthoff, 1939). As Sir Henry Maine, the 'founder' of comparative law wrote, 'the chief function of comparative law is to facilitate legislation and the practical improvement of the law' (Maine, 1907). The story of the Dutch judicial ethics code and the effort to transplant it to the Czech Republic is instructive in this regard (De Groot van Leeuwen and De Groot, chapter 9). The De Groots describe how this effort revealed the limitations of both the Czech and Dutch legal cultures. The close connection between acceptance of a code of judicial ethics and the role of law in each society is clearly and somewhat amusingly presented. Jane Schukoske discusses the earlier effort by United States lawyers in the 1960s at transplanting laws and legal institutions (Schukoske, chapter 11). One effect of that endeavor was on United States scholars and policy, contributing to the development of critical legal studies and a withdrawal of the United States from legal outreach, until just recently. Transplanting must be done with care, cultural sensitivity, and perhaps a sense of humor.

Global Law Firms

The development and spread of United States style law firms also is appearing as an influence on both provision of legal services and legal training (Trubek, D. and Dezelay *et al*, 1994). In Japan and Korea, this influence is seen in the perceived need for the legal profession to provide more lawyers for corporate law services to multinational corporations. The proposed increase in size may have an effect on the provision of lawyers for the underrepresented. In Japan, the services have been underwritten by the monopoly power of the small Bar. As the Bar grows, there will be a need to reconsider how to provide the services. There may be more lawyers willing to earn less and represent middle income persons without subsidy, and the government may increase support for legal aid.

The global law firms may influence ethics and professionalism. One effect may be a spread of a commitment to *pro bono*. A number of the recent 'death row' appeals from Trinidad to the Privy Council (House of Lords) in the United Kingdom have been conducted *pro bono*, to a very high level of expertise, by high flying young city lawyers in global law firms based in London. The rise of multinational accounting firms is now having a major influence on the practice of law within the United States. These firms offer comprehensive services to clients and wish to offer integrated management, accounting, and legal services.

Multidisciplinary practices, however, are largely prohibited in the United States. The American Bar Association Commission on Multidisciplinary Practice has just released a report, which recommends substantial changes in ethics to allow global law firms to engage in multidisciplinary practice in the United States. The report specifically urges the maintenance of the *pro bono* obligation for *all* attorneys (American Bar Association, 1999).

Global law firms also are having an influence on legal education. Meili indicates that professors in Argentina and Chile note a desire of law students to seek jobs in the high status corporate firms, undercutting a desired social mission role for law students and the profession (Meili, chapter 7). The diminution of social commitment due to the status and income of the corporate practice has been long noted in United States legal education. Overcoming this effect in the United States has required reform of law school curricula and career counselling as well as establishment of *pro bono* ethics for law firms (Stover, 1989). The challenge global law firms present to the social mission commitment within law schools may be the source of focused development of local curriculum reforms and clinics in Argentina and Chile.

Conclusion

In 1981, the two general editors of the Florence Access to Justice Project, reflected on their work to date in the following terms (Cappelletti and Garth, 1981):

> Ambiguities and pitfalls pervade the access to justice movement. It is the task of interdisciplinary and comparative scholarship and empirical research to clarify these problems, monitor developments relevant to access to justice, and facilitate creative efforts to respond to the social problems that to a great extent inspired the access to justice movement in the first place... The great mass of work remains to be done.

These words ring as true today as they did almost 20 years ago; this book continues the processes that they map. The complexity of these processes requires looking at particular stories and analyses, as well as at broader trends. The stories follow different paths in their struggle to include social values in law. Transnational flows are evident, but local conditions are still crucial.

How do we understand the role of outsiders in our local society? Can the movement of people across borders open up our societies? Will our definition of community change? The stories of transnational gender issues and the influence of the India experience on some United States clinicians and social action lawyers demonstrate the emergence of a broad view of community, one that includes people outside our own local neighborhood or nation. Kelly's discussion of transnational gender issues in the immigration of African women to the United States raises the issue of international norms (Kelly, chapter 10). This development of a transnational 'legal consciousness' may be accompanied by institutional developments that create new types of law and legal institutions for open borders. This influence can be seen in the European Union, where new types of law and legal institutions are emerging. These new law making and enforcement bodies are able to create new forums for law that cross boundaries (Joerges, 1997).

Movement of people and ideas and creation of new forums require and construct changes in the legal profession. Legal education can encourage law students to look at how the legal system works to empower or disempower underrepresented people. Thus, in addition to values, legal education should include pedagogy that explores a wide variety of techniques and strategies for assisting underrepresented people, including transnational forums. These discussions should note the importance of the legal profession, both individually and as a group, in creating the conditions for such advocacy. The story of judicial ethics in Holland and in the Czech Republic and the story of the Japanese and Brazilian Bar Associations reveal how legal institutions can create the conditions for equity.

Social activists are having to become increasingly 'more global about the local'. Everywhere, the challenges thrown down by the 'globalization effect' are as great as any challenges people of the world have faced this century. The potential for incisive, interventionist social action lawyering, generated at the interface between education, training, and legal practice, is greater than ever. Transnational advocacy networks[17] are new vehicles for bringing together groups dedicated to advocacy for the underrepresented. These groups enable improvement in national programs and create transnational forums and norms. This volume is an example of the ability of scholars and practitioners around the world to share and to build on their knowledge. This effort is aided by funding sources, law schools, and bar associations that recognize the importance of the enterprise. The need for such networks, always important, is now essential.

Notes

1 The International Working Group on Social Values in Law (IWGSVIL) was the original group formed to explore this topic. For a discussion on the history of this group, see Cooper and Trubek, 1997, 1. Also, see the preface to this volume.

2 The use of the word 'underrepresented' is contested. It is a word that attempts to include people who cannot find legal services because of indigence, and those that cannot locate services because their interest is 'collective', i.e. many people are affected but one person cannot afford to pay for the vindication of that collective interest. This book discusses both types of legal needs. The authors use various words to describe the need.

3 Several of the authors participated in the 1999 Law and Society Meeting in Chicago, where there was extensive discussion of the effect of globalization as reflected in Japan, Korea, Chile, and Argentina. The discussion reflected the tension between local legal and societal factors and global phenomenon, as explored later in this introduction.

4 Duncan Kennedy, in a recent volume, discusses the debunking of the traditional understanding of the distinction between the civil law and common law. See Kennedy, 1997, 75.

5 See the Preface to the three volumes that discusses the importance of the Working Group, Abel and Lewis, 1988, vol. 1, *xi-xii.*

6 See, for example, the volume Cappelletti, 1981b, a series of essays on access to justice issues that arose from a conference in Florence to mark the publication of the outcomes of the Access to Justice Project.

7 *IWGSVIL* was formed in 1992, at the end of a special seminar to explore the themes that were to bring about the group's formation. Since its inception in 1992, members of the *IWGSVIL* network have met and exchanged ideas in a number of locations including Baltimore (1993), Bangalore (1993), Chicago (1993), Toronto (1995), Glasgow (1996), St Louis (1997), Bangkok (1998) Kobe and Tokyo (1999).

8 Our book emphasizes Asia and Latin America, with some discussion of Europe and the United States. South Africa and the Middle East, where there is substantial interesting work, are not included, due only to current funding

and networking constraints, and not to any observation on where the interesting projects can be found!

9 It is sobering to note in this respect that Brent Community Law Centre, the foremost proponent of the proactive community based model of public legal services delivery in the United Kingdom, which has been in existence providing such services for the past 29 years, is at the time of writing about to be closed down, and transformed into a reactive telephone advice agency, largely as a result of the caprice of the dominant political party in the local funding authority.

10 In the first volume (Cooper and Trubek, 1997, 13) we discussed in more detail, the importance of proactiveness in legal services while stressing the barriers: low status, outreach requirements, and unconventional skills.

11 In January, 1998, Jeremy Cooper attended a five day closed conference in Beijing, as one of four 'foreign experts' invited by the Chinese Ministry of Justice, to address China's slowly growing cadre of legal aid practitioners and policy makers on the range of options available to them, drawn from a number of comparative models. The Chinese delegates asked many questions and made extensive notation of all that they heard, but gave no indication as to which approach they might finally adopt. The slow process of consideration, assimilation, and adaptation continues.

12 This issue is addressed in more detail in Cooper and Trubek, 1997, in particular in chapters 1 and 4.

13 An interesting discussion of transnational interpenetration is to be found in an article describing the influence of German legal aid on Russian legal aid in the early twentieth century (Pomeranz, 1996).

14 In the United States, the contrary is being seen. The United States government is cutting back on government support for legal services (Trubek, 1996).

15 See Miyazawa, chapter 2; Ichiki and Ohishi, chapter 3; Yoon, chapter 4.

16 For example, the Florence Access to Justice Project received major funding from the Ford Foundation (Cappelletti, 1978-8).

17 There is discussion of transnational networks in works by Keck and Sikkink, 1998, and Santos, 1995.

References

Abel, R. (ed.) (1982) *The Politics of Informal Justice* (vol. 2), Academic Press, New York.

Abel, R. (1985), 'Law without Politics: Legal Aid under Advanced Capitalism', *UCLA Law Review*, vol. 32 (3), 474.

Abel, R. and Lewis, P. (eds) (1988), *Lawyers in Society* (Three Volumes), University of California Press, Berkeley.

Abel, R. and Lewis, P. (eds) (1995), *Lawyers in Society: an Overview*, University of California Press, Berkeley.

American Bar Association (1999), *Commission on Multidisciplinary Practices*, Chicago, Illinois.

Baekey, C. and Gabriel, A. (1994), 'Community Law Centre: Empowering Rural South African Communities', *Maryland Journal of Contemporary Legal Issues*, vol. 5 (2), 399.

Basten, J. Graycar, R. and Neal, D. (1983), 'Legal Centres in Australia', *University of New South Wales Law Journal*, vol. 6, 163.

Block, F.S. and Ishar, I.S. (1990), 'Legal Aid, Public Service, and Clinical Legal Education: Future Directions From India and the United States', *Michigan Journal of International Law*, vol. 1, 92.

Cahn E. and Cahn, J. (1964), 'The War on Poverty: a Civilian Perspective', *Yale Law Journal*, vol. 73, 1317.

Cappelletti, M. and Gordley, J. (1972), 'Legal Aid: Modern Themes and Variations', *Stanford Law Review*, vol. 28, 347.

Cappelletti, M. *et al* (eds) (1978-9), *Access to Justice: a World Survey* (Four Parts, Six Volumes), Sijthoff and Noordhoff, Alphen aan den Rijn.

Cappelletti, M. and Garth, B. (1981a), 'Access to Justice as a Focus for Research', *Windsor Yearbook of Access to Justice*, vol. 1, ix.

Cappelletti, M. (ed.) (1981b) *Access to Justice in the Welfare State*, Sijthoff and Noordhoff, Alphen aan den Rijn.

Cappelletti, M. and Garth, B. (1983), 'Finding an Appropriate Compromise: a Comparative Study of Individualistic Models and Group Rights in Civil Procedure', *Civil Justice Quarterly*, April, 111.

Cappelletti, M. (1993), 'Alternative Dispute Resolution Processes within the Framework of the World-Wide Access-to-Justice Movement', *Modern Law Review*, vol. 56 (3), 282.

Cooper, J. (1983) *Public Legal Services: a Comparative Study of Policy, Politics and Practice*, Sweet and Maxwell, London.

Cooper, J. (1999), 'China's Lawyers and the Rule of Law', *International Journal of the Legal Profession*, vol. 6 (1), 71.

Cooper, J. and Trubek, L. (eds) (1997), *Educating for Justice: Social Values and Legal Education*, Ashgate, Aldershot.

De Groot van Leeuwen, L. (1997), 'The Lawyer poised Between Client and Society', in Cooper, J. and Trubek, L. (1997), 39.
Economides, K. (1997), 'Cynical Legal Studies' in Cooper, J. and Trubek, L. (1997), 26.
Grossberg, M. (1997) 'The Politics of Professionalism: the Creation of Legal Aid and the Strains of Political Liberalism in America, 1900-1930', in Halliday and Karpik (1997).
Halliday, T. and Karpick, L. (eds) (1997), *Lawyers and the Rise of Western Political Liberalism*, Clarendon Press, Oxford.
Handler, J. Hollingsworth, J. and Erlanger, H. (1978) *Lawyers and the Pursuit of Legal Rights,* Academic Press, New York.
Joerges, C. (1997), 'The Impact of European Integration on Private Law: Reductionist Perceptions, True Conflicts, and a New Constitutionalist Perspective', *European Law Journal*, vol. 3 (4), 378.
Kahn-Freund. O. (1966), 'Comparative Law as an Academic Subject', *Law Quarterly Review,* vol. 82, 40.
Kamba, W. (1974), 'Comparative Law: a Theoretical Framework', *International and Comparative Law Quarterly*, vol. 23, 485.
Keck, M. and Sikkink, K. (1998), *Activism Beyond Borders: Advocacy Networks in International Politics*, Cornell University Press, Ithaca, New York.
Kennedy, D. (1997), *A Critique of Adjudication*, Harvard University Press, Cambridge, Mass.
Maine, H. (1907), *Village Communities in the East and West* (7th Edition), Murray, London.
Markesinis, B. (1990), 'Comparative Law - a Subject in Search of an Audience', *Modern Law Review*, vol. 53, 1.
Menon, M. (ed) (1998), *A Handbook on Clinical Legal Education,* Eastern Book Company, Lucknow.
Noone, M. (1997), 'Australian Community Legal Centres-The University Connection', in Cooper, J. and Trubek, L. (1997), 257.
Pomeranz, W. (1996), 'Legal Assistance in Tsarist Russia: The St. Petersburg Consultation Bureaus', *Wisconsin International Law Journal*, vol. 14, 586.
Santos, B. de S. (1995), *Toward a New Common Sense*, Routledge, New York, New York, London.
Sarat, A. and Scheingold, S. (eds) (1997), *Cause Lawyering: Commitments and Professional Responsibilities,* Oxford University Press, Oxford.
Savigny, F. (1831), *Of the Vocation of our Age for Legislation and Jurisprudence,* Arno Press, New York.
Schmitthoff, C. (1939), 'The Science of Comparative Law', *Cambridge Law Journal*, vol. 7, 94.
Stover, R. (1989), *Making It and Breaking It: The Fate of Public Interest Commitment During Law School*, University of Illinois Press, Urbana and Chicago, Illinois.

Trubek, D. and Dezelay, Y. *et al* (1994), 'Global Restructuring and the Law: The Internationalization of Legal Fields and the Creation of Transnational Arenas', *Case Western Reserve Law Review*, vol. 44 (2).
Trubek, L. (1999), 'Context and Collaboration: Family Law Innovation and Professional Autonomy', *Fordham Law Review*, vol. 67 (5).
Trubek, L. (1996), 'Embedded Practices: Lawyers, Clients and Social Change', *Harvard Civil Rights-Civil Liberties Law Review*, vol. 31 (2), 415.

2 Lawyering for the Underrepresented in the Context of Legal, Social, and National Institutions: The case of Japan

SETSUO MIYAZAWA

Introduction[1]

This chapter discusses how the provision of legal services to the indigent and other under-represented people can be affected by the specific legal, social, and institutional context of a given country, and how it can be altered by changes in the political environment. The case study is Japan, and I will draw partly on my previous research on public interest lawyering in Japan. In spite of the limitation of this chapter to a single country, I hope that it will nonetheless raise issues relevant to different national contexts.

The Background of Legal Services in Japan

Law as an Instrument of the Government

Law is fundamentally an instrument of the government in authoritarian countries. In such countries, law is not designed to provide ordinary people with opportunities to challenge the government and the powerful. Such countries have the rule *by* law, not the rule *of* law. Pre-war Japan was such a country.[2]

When the Meiji government started to develop a modern legal system in Japan in the late 19th century, the immediate purpose was to abolish unequal treaties with western powers signed by the Tokugawa Shogunate by creating a western-looking legal system. The long-term purpose was to establish authoritarian control over the entire country. Prussia was chosen as the model because it was a rising authoritarian country in Europe. Legal education was mainly designed for training bureaucrats and professional legal training was provided only to future government lawyers, namely judges and prosecutors (Miyazawa, 1997). Providing legal services to the indigent and other underrepresented people was not a consideration for the pre-war government.

The situation had no fundamental changes until a few years ago. The legal system, which mainly empowers the government and reduces legal risks to the government and businesses, served the post-war elite just as it did their pre-war counterparts.

Of course, an innumerable number of laws are passed by the legislature every year. Under a parliamentary cabinet system, most laws are drafted by government agencies and presented by the cabinet. Such laws are designed mainly to provide governmental agencies with jurisdiction and discretionary powers in certain policy areas. Since such laws grant wide discretionary powers to governmental agencies, agencies can exercise their powers informally. This is what is commonly known as administrative guidance (gyosei shido). However, such informal administrative guidance is not exactly informal. Governmental agencies have an extensive arsenal of licensing powers, and such licensing power has been used to back up apparently toothless, informal guidance. A common tactic has been to use implied threats to deny licenses or permissions on unrelated matters in order to obtain consent from the private party on the matter under consideration (Upham, 1987).

Although a revisionist view has been presented more recently that argues that governmental agencies were forced to use informal methods of persuasion because they were denied legally binding authority (Haley, 1991), such ostensibly extra-legal, informal methods had a clear benefit for governmental agencies - such methods do not give private parties legal bases to challenge them. Thus, governmental agencies need not be legally accountable, and regulatory processes need not be transparent. That must be one of the reasons why governmental agencies vehemently opposed the Administrative Procedure Act (Gyosei Tetsuzuki Ho) of 1994, which required governmental agencies, among other things, to provide written explanations for their decisions upon request from the affected private party, and prohibited discrimination against private parties who did not comply with administrative guidance. It is easy to imagine what had happened before the enactment of this law, although it is still doubtful that many private parties have the courage to demand written explanations or defy administrative guidance.

Under such a system, legal services to the indigent and other under-represented people had to be provided by non-governmental organizations. In Japan, attorneys (bengoshi) and attorneys' associations (bengoshi-kai) have provided such services. It is important to examine the background of their commitment to legal aid in spite of the lack of laws requiring them to take legal aid cases.

Professional Ideology of the Japanese Bar

The Practicing Attorneys Act (Bengoshi Ho) of Japan was enacted not as a cabinet bill, but as a member bill in the Japanese parliament (Diet), and became effective in 1949 as part of the postwar reform under the support of the Supreme Commander of Allied Powers. It was resisted by judges and prosecutors. Its Article 1 proudly proclaims that '[T]he mission (shimei) of the practicing attorney (bengoshi) is the protection of human rights and the realization of social justice (shimei)'. This is an expression of a professional ideology which reflects the prewar status of practicing attorneys.[3]

Before the war, practicing attorneys were qualified by an examination which was different from, and considered less demanding, than that for judges and prosecutors. Law graduates of Imperial Universities could be qualified as practicing attorneys without taking any examination until 1923. Apprenticeship was not required until 1936. Attorneys were placed under the supervision of the head of the district prosecutor's office until 1933 when they were placed under the direct supervision of the Justice Minister.

Because most attorneys were actually engaged in civil disputes for most of their time, their self-concept evolved as 'opposition lawyers' (zaiya hoso), as opposed to judges and prosecutors as 'government lawyers' (zaicho hoso). When attorneys found an opportunity to change this situation and improve their professional status in the postwar reform, this self-concept naturally provided the most powerful guiding ideology. Article 1 of the Act rectifies it.

Under the postwar system, those who wish to become attorneys take the single national law examination (shiho shiken) along with those who wish to become judges or prosecutors. Those who pass the examination spend two years in the Judicial Research and Training Institute (Shiho Kenshujo), while receiving a salary from the government. The examination is still administered by the Justice Ministry, while the Institute is administered by the Supreme Court. In other words, future attorneys are simply allowed to join programs mainly designed for future judges and prosecutors. The postwar system clearly represents an elevation of the professional status of attorneys.

Moreover, attorneys have become independent from the Justice Minister, and obtained professional autonomy in terms of admission of new members and disciplinary actions. Attorneys are organized at both national and local levels. Nationally, they are required to be admitted to the Japan Federation of Bar Associations (JFBA). Locally, each prefecture has its own bar association, with the exception of Tokyo, which has three associations. In addition to the JFBA, attorneys must be admitted to one of these local bar associations. While these associations use the word 'bar' in English translations of their names, judges and prosecutors are not members. Former judges and prosecutors are required to obtain admission at these two levels if they wish to practice as attorneys. Furthermore, since the JFBA is the only legally designated organization to represent attorneys nationally, it holds the position in the Japanese corporatist political structure to participate in policy-making processes regarding the law and judiciary along with the Justice Ministry and the Supreme Court.[4]

One should note that Article 1 of the Practicing Attorneys Act does *not* define the attorney's 'mission' in terms of the legal representation of a client's interest. It clearly defines an attorney's mission in terms of commitment to the promotion of the human right clauses of the new Constitution. Given the hostility to these clauses among the conservative elite in Japan, the organizational commitment of Japanese attorneys to human rights and social justice represents a clearly political position. More neutral and day-to-day functions such as the representation of clients in judicial and administrative proceedings and the provision of other forms of legal services are identified in Article 3 as an attorney's professional 'function' (shokumu).

Article 1 of the Act appears to have actually generated tangible commitments to human rights issues by a substantial number of attorneys. A good example is the activity of the Human Rights Protection Committee of the JFBA and its local counterparts. Japan does not have well-funded human rights organizations comparable to the NAACP, the ACLU, the National Lawyers Guild, etc. in the United States' Human rights committees of bar associations have been their functional equivalents in Japan. While these committees do not represent individual clients, they receive complaints from individuals about human rights violations, present specific opinions and recommendations to alleged violators, make general policy recommendations, provide networking channels for activist attorneys, and probably most importantly, tend to dominate the internal policy-making processes of bar associations at both national and local levels. Indeed, it has been the case that unless a presidential candidate expresses commitment to human rights issues, he is not likely to be elected in either national or local bar associations.

As a more concrete example, the Japanese version of the duty solicitor scheme (toban bengoshi) is a good recent illustration. Japanese law does not provide free defence counsel until the accused is indicted. In other words, indigent people do not have access to free legal counsel during the crucial stages of police investigation and prosecution where they may be detained at a police station and interrogated for up to 23 days for each count. Learning from the British scheme of duty solicitors, a local bar association in Kyushu began to provide free legal counselling at the pretrial stage in 1990 as a *pro bono* activity. It has quickly spread nation-wide. Now every local bar association has its own scheme, the Japan Legal Aid Association provides limited financial assistance, and the JFBA charges a special monthly fee to every member to support the system. The JFBA has been negotiating with the Justice Ministry to change it into a publicly-funded program, but the Ministry is extremely reluctant to do so, arguing, among other things, that aggressive lawyering by some defence lawyers is unacceptable interference with police investigation (Tokushu, 1998).

It is possible to find many other examples which indicate Japanese attorneys' sincere commitment to the ideal of Article 1. Provision of legal services to under-represented groups is a good example. Organizational effort is expressed as legal aid; individual effort is expressed as cause lawyering.[5]

The Problematic Aspect of the Official Commitment to Public Interest and Politics over the Number of Attorneys

Like everything else, the Japanese bar's official commitment to public interest is not always positive. Before moving on to discuss legal aid and cause lawyering, one should pay some attention to the negative or problematic effects of the dominant professional ideology of Japanese attorneys. These effects include the extremely high entry barrier, the remarkably restrictive internal regulation of the bar, and the intense reluctance to expand the number of attorneys, which would increase public access to attorneys.

Regarding the entrance barrier, only 500 out of 20,000 applicants were allowed to pass the national law examination until 1990. The pass rate has been gradually increased, and 812 applicants passed in 1998. Yet, the percentage change is so minuscule that the average age of a successful applicant has been stable at around 27 years old. This means that on average, a 'successful' applicant has waited 5 years after finishing his 4-year undergraduate legal education.[6]

In terms of internal regulation, individual advertisement is strictly limited to forms which are virtually meaningless as a means of providing information to potential clients. Specialisms may not be mentioned, and an attorney may not even say that a potential client can visit or call at any time. Attorneys may not have more than one office, and law firms may not open branch offices. A standard fee schedule has also been set and published by the JFBA as a guideline, including both upper and lower limits. Moreover, while I use the word 'service' in this chapter to refer to an attorney's professional work, many attorneys actually claim that their work is not a 'service', which they feel implies selling ones' skill for money.

The entrance barrier and prohibition of competition have been justified by many Japanese attorneys in terms of their commitment to the protection of human rights and the realization of social justice. They argue that only those who are both intellectually well-qualified and strongly committed to those ideals should be admitted to the bar. They further contend that if the number of attorneys is increased, the quality of legal services would decline, and that increased competition would make it financially more difficult to maintain their commitment to those ideals. When you speak to Japanese attorneys, particularly those who spend time in public interest lawyering, it is surprising how many sincerely believe the validity of these arguments.

This apparently contradictory combination of Japanese attorneys' commitment to public interests and their tremendous hostility to increasing the number of attorneys, which would expand public access to legal services, is at least partly understandable if the lack of economic incentives for public interest lawyering in Japan is considered. Japan does not have punitive damages nor statutory recovery of attorney's fees. Attorney's fees are usually not recoverable from the losing party. There are no organizations like public defender offices, poverty law centers, the ACLU Legal Defence Fund, etc. that employ attorneys on a salary basis, allowing them to devote themselves to their areas of interest. With a per-capita budget that is even smaller than that of Korea, the legal aid system in Japan is extremely weak. Therefore, many attorneys argue that any proposal to lower entry barriers or to increase competition would decrease their income and thus, must be rejected.

The result has been an extremely small bar relative to the size of the population and economy. For a population of 125 million with the world's most developed economy, Japan still has only 16,000 attorneys. The population-attorney ratio of Japan must be the lowest among developed countries.

Therefore, as far as the size of the bar is concerned, there was a curious harmony between the basically anti-government bar on the one hand, and the conservative government and big business on the other hand. This situation has ultimately served the interests of the government and big business since many ordinary citizens have been forced to abandon their cases against them or have been unable to raise effective defences due to the lack of access to attorneys.

That harmony was broken by the Justice Ministry in the late 1980s.[7] Facing the difficulty of recruiting a sufficient number of new graduates of the Judicial Research and Training Institute to fill prosecutorial positions, the Justice Ministry proposed to increase the number of applicants passing the national law examination and to introduce a limitation on how many times an applicant may take the examination. This latter point is related to the bureaucratic structure of the Justice Ministry where prosecutors are expected to stay until retirement. In such a structure, seniority differences should also reflect age differences, and, thus, it is desirable to recruit the youngest graduates. The Supreme Court agreed with the Justice Ministry's proposal since the Japanese judiciary is also structured as a career bureaucracy (Miyazawa, 1994). The JFBA immediately opposed the proposal.

The Justice Ministry has consistently taken the initiative at every step of the debate with the JFBA, and has wisely framed its proposal in more neutral, universal terms. The Justice Ministry supports its proposal by expressing sympathy for the large number of people who ultimately fail to pass the examination after spending all of their productive years in futile efforts to pass the exam. It also cites the expanding gap between the need for legal services under a rapidly growing economy and the extremely limited access to attorneys. In other words, the Justice Ministry has most effectively used the symbolic capital of these apparently acceptable arguments. The Supreme Court has always agreed with the Justice Ministry.

This situation has put the JFBA in the minority position. While it represents the largest group of lawyers in Japan, it has constantly found itself in a defensive position. The JFBA has criticized the true motive of the Justice Ministry and the Supreme Court, as well as their failure to reform their internal structures to attract more graduates of the Judicial Research and Training Institute. It has, of course, utilized its traditional justification for keeping the bar small in terms of the quality of lawyers and the danger of competition. It has even relied upon Japan's allegedly 'unique legal culture' which had been a favored weapon of conservatives in preventing the development of legally enforceable rights. Like conservatives who argued that 'we should not become like the United States' in preventing the strengthening of antitrust laws and the enactment of product liability laws, attorneys have argued that 'we should not become like the United States which is rife with frivolous suits and ambulance chasers'.

A temporary compromise was struck in 1990. The three parties agreed to increase the number of applicants passing the examination from 500 to 700 in 1993. They also agreed to follow the development until 1995 to see whether certain numerical standards would be met in terms of the proportion of applicants who pass the examination within a certain number of times. If these standards were not met, they consented to introduce a reform which would give priority to those applicants who have taken the exam for three or fewer years.

Unfortunately for the JFBA, those standards were not met in 1995. The Justice Ministry and the Supreme Court quickly proposed to double the number of applicants passing the examination to 1500 so that there would be no need to treat applicants differently on the basis of the number of times they have taken the examination. In addition, they proposed to halve the length of training as a paid Judicial Trainee to one year so that the reform would not cost more than the present system. The JFBA opposed both measures. In response, the Justice Ministry and the Supreme Court decided to introduce differential treatment of applicants depending on the number of years they have taken the examination.

In 1996, 500 applicants passed the examination totally according to their points. Another 200 applicants were chosen from among those who had taken the examination for three or fewer years.

The JFBA is currently trying to realign its battle plan. Its present position is to expand the capacity of the judiciary along with the expansion of the bar so that an increased number of attorneys would find places to work. It also wants the government to expand legal aid and to maintain the training system which is paid for by the government. As will be explained later, there has been significant progress on legal aid, but the paid training period will be reduced to one and a half years starting in 1999.

The problem is whether attorneys can obtain agenda-setting status in the near future. It is at least promising that increasingly more attorneys seem to understand the contradiction between their official commitment to public interest and their opposition to the expansion of the size of the bar. I am hopeful that attorneys will eventually present a comprehensive and more progressive plan for changing themselves so that they will begin to lead discussions on the reform of the judicial and legal system as a whole.

Cause Lawyering

Let us return to the discussion of the provision of legal services to the indigent and other under-represented people by individual attorneys and by bar associations. Individual attorneys will be more willing to provide legal services for free or for reduced fees if they are committed to certain political causes and if they deem that a particular case will make positive contributions to their causes. This form of public interest lawyering is called cause lawyering. As I studied cause lawyering in the Kinki region, namely in areas including Osaka, Kobe, and Kyoto (Miyazawa, 1996), let me first discuss cause lawyering in Japan.

The first stage of my study was questionnaire surveys of members of three bar associations in the Kinki region which were carried out from January to May 1994. The second stage was interviews of selected members of the Kobe Bar Association which were conducted during November 1994 to January 1995. This stage was interrupted by the Great Earthquake on January 17, 1995. The third stage was interviews of selected members of the Osaka and Kyoto Bar Associations during February to March 1995. I shall explain each stage in more detail.

The purpose of the questionnaire surveys was to obtain a rough estimate of the degree of actual engagement of Japanese attorneys in cause lawyering and to locate attorneys who were appropriate for intensive interviews. The bar associations of Osaka, Kobe, and Shiga were selected for this purpose because they are examples of large, medium, and small bar associations respectively: Osaka had 2,088 members, Kobe 328, and Shiga 36. A two-page questionnaire was mailed to a random sample of 410 attorneys in Osaka, as well as to all the attorneys in Kobe and Shiga. The response rates were 37.3 per cent, 47.9 per cent, and 52.8 per cent respectively. A total of 329 attorneys returned the questionnaire.

The questionnaire defined cause lawyering as

> activities of the attorney (bengoshi) to take charge of litigation, participate in a movement, or otherwise make use of the knowledge, ability, or qualification as a lawyer (horitsuka), not simply for the immediate purpose of the protection or realization of rights or interests of the client or party, but rather out of one's own sympathy or support of the social cause, namely some value, ideal, principle, or purpose which the given litigation or movement is deemed to realize.

The questionnaire also provided the following explanatory notes:

(a) In accordance with the definition of an attorney's mission by Article 1 of the Practicing Attorneys Act, the respondent might deem any activity of the attorney as cause lawyering in its most abstract and general sense. Therefore, the respondent is requested to understand cause lawyering in this questionnaire not in terms of such abstract and general values or ideals, but in terms of more concrete and specific values or ideals.

(b) Cause lawyering may include any political positions.

(c) Cause lawyering may include both paid and unpaid activities.

(d) Cause lawyering may include activities in committees of the local bar association or the JFBA if the respondent participates in them not simply as a duty for a member, but rather with the purpose to make them adopt certain policies or actions.

(e) Cause lawyering may include activities as a court-appointed defence counsel in a criminal case if the respondent deliberately takes charge of the case not simply as a duty as a member of the bar, but rather for its significance with regard to certain values, ideals, principles, doctrines, or movements.

52.9 per cent of the Osaka respondents, 52.9 per cent of the Kobe respondents, and 42.1 per cent of the Shiga respondents answered that they were engaged in cause lawyering. The overall rate of participation in cause lawyering was 52.3 per cent. While it is very likely that those who were engaged in cause lawyering were more likely to respond to my survey, I may still conclude that participation in cause lawyering was fairly widely distributed among Japanese attorneys.

Combining these three respondent groups, women (77.8 per cent) were more likely to engage in cause lawyering than men (50.8 per cent); attorneys in their 30s or younger were most likely (67.1 per cent), while those in their 70s were least likely (16.7 per cent); those who have been an attorney for 11 to 20 years were most likely (62.0 per cent), while those with 41 years or longer experience were least likely (20.0 per cent); former judges were less likely (19.4per cent) than others (55.7 per cent); former prosecutors were less likely (32.1per cent) than others (54.2 per cent); and those belonging to two-attorney offices were most likely (71.7 per cent), while solo practitioners were least likely (37.6 per cent).

Among the 159 attorneys who replied that they were engaged in cause lawyering, the proportion of their time spent for cause lawyering varied from less than 5 per cent (18.3 per cent) to more than 35 per cent (15.7 per cent). The most frequent response in this regard was between 5-10 per cent (23.5 per cent).

When they were asked about the proportion of their income earned through cause lawyering, the most frequent response was 0 (45.3 per cent); only 8.7 per cent of the respondents engaged in cause lawyering answered that more than 10 per cent of their income was earned through cause lawyering. One response included an interesting story regarding the recent settlement of the Minamata mercury poisoning cases that concerned cause lawyering. The largest victims' organization demanded that money should be paid not only to individual victims, but also to victims' organizations in order to pay their attorneys. This story illustrates that when cause lawyering results in a large money award to the client, it can also provide income to involved attorneys. Generally speaking, however, cause lawyering in Japan is a *pro bono* activity. There was no significant correlation between the time spent for cause lawyering and the income earned through cause lawyering.

The second and third stages of the research were based on the data about the time spent for cause lawyering. I wanted to interview all the respondents who replied that they spent 30 per cent or more of their time on cause lawyering. In the rest of this paper, the interviewed attorneys will be identified by ID numbers.

In Kobe (second stage), I interviewed 15 attorneys before the Great Earthquake. Interviews were mostly conducted by myself, took one to two hours each, and were tape recorded. At least one student accompanied me to each interview and the tapes were transcribed by that student.

In Osaka (third stage), interviews were carried out by Stuart Scheingold. He arrived at Kobe only two weeks after the quake, and stayed in Japan until the first week of March 1995. I put him in a hotel in Osaka near the law firm which became our base, and commuted from Kobe to Osaka by ferry to work as his interpreter. Seven attorneys were interviewed according to my original plan (Nos. 9, 14, 15, 17, 18, 19, and 29). Two attorneys (Nos. 25 and 30) were added as examples from corporate law firms who reported lesser commitment to cause lawyering. Moreover, two attorneys (Nos. 3 and 22) were added from outside the surveyed respondents because they were attorneys of the firm which was our base in Osaka. One more Osaka attorney (No. 1) was also added from outside the surveyed respondents because he was known for his activities in an international

NGO and for his innovative litigation to protect endangered species of animals. Furthermore, some attorneys in Kyoto expressed their interest in our research. Thus, three attorneys in Kyoto (Nos. 4, 8, and 24) were also interviewed. The interviews in Osaka and Kyoto also took one to two hours each and were tape recorded. However, these tapes were not transcribed, but were summarized by a student.

Age Groups

There were approximately the same number of attorneys in the 3 age groups of 36-40, 41-45, and 46-50. They accounted for the vast majority of my interviewees. Since there is no guarantee that my interviewees' form a representative sample of most active cause lawyers in Osaka, Kobe, and Kyoto, it is difficult to draw any implications from this pattern only, except that they may belong to the age groups who are most active anyway, whether they are progressive cause lawyers or conservative corporate lawyers.

There are two generations who experienced highly politicized university campuses. One is those in their early 60s. They were university students in the late 1950s when there was an extensive student movement against the 1960 renewal of the United States-Japan Securities Treaty. The other is those in their 40s. They were students when there were riots on many university campuses in the late 1960s or when the effects of the riots were still felt in subsequent years.

Among my interviewees in their early 60s, No. 3 was actually a national leader of a Communist-related student organization against the Treaty. This experience clearly provided him with a basic motivational background for his engagement in cause lawyering. He has served as the chairperson of the JFBA Human Rights Protection Committee and is widely regarded as a leading cause lawyer in Osaka particularly in the field of domestic application of international human rights.

The student riots in the late 1960s were characterized by the leadership of radical students who criticized not only the conservative elite, but also the centralized and allegedly authoritarian structure of the Communist Party. They were called New Left and were close to the then-Socialist Party. Among my interviewees in their 40s, Nos. 9, 15, 17, 18, and 19 can be classified in this New Left group.

The difference between these two generational groups could be more meaningfully discussed in terms of differences in political positions.

The Political Positions and the Prospect of Cause Lawyering

The largest political group in my Osaka-Kyoto attorneys was New Left or those closer to the then-Socialist Party. Most of them were in their 40s. As the Socialist Party has abandoned its traditional progressive positions when it became a partner of a coalition government with conservative parties, changed its name to the Social Democratic Party, and has been rapidly disintegrating, these attorneys appear to be losing their political base. Another serious problem for this group of attorneys appears to be the difficulty of recruiting new attorneys with similar views.

On the other hand, my Kobe attorneys were dominated by those who belonged to or supported the Communist Party. There was no clearly New Left attorney in my Kobe interviewees. While the Communist Party is not likely to control the government, neither does it have the problem of disintegration of the former Socialist Party, and it is even increasing its popularity due to a more clearly anti-government position. Compared to New Left or socialist attorneys, communist attorneys appear to have better chances to maintain their organizational cohesion and to recruit new attorneys.

However, there is at least one commonality between these two groups of progressive attorneys. If they were leaders of progressive student organizations, they were not likely to be hired by business corporations. If they were less active, they may have been hired. However, as the experience of No. 17 indicates, their experience in business corporations could become unbearable. For these students, the national law examination provides an ideal escape route. Admission to the Judicial Research and Training Institute has always been determined solely on the basis of points in the examination. As long as this meritocratic nature of the national law examination remains, it will continue to provide this route to future generations of progressive students who will also form future generations of cause lawyers in Japan.

Then the question becomes whether present or future generations of university students will include as many progressive students as in those earlier generations. Nos. 3, 21, 24, 25, and 26 were clearly skeptical about the prospect of cause lawyering both in terms of the ideological inclinations of younger generations and in terms of economic conditions. Nos. 4, 6, 8, 15, and 19 were less pessimistic, and No. 22 was most optimistic. Generally speaking, however, cause lawyers seem to be skeptical about the future of cause lawyering in Japan.

The Time Spent for Cause Lawyering and Its Environment

Several attorneys responded that they spend half or more of their time on cause lawyering. They include Nos. 6, 7, 10, 11, 18 (two thirds of his time), 21, 23, 27, and 29. Since Japan does not have organizations which enable attorneys to focus on their chosen areas on a salary basis, these attorneys are the closest things we have in Japan to salaried attorneys in the United States who are employed by public defender's offices, poverty law centers, labor unions, and various non-profit organizations. Four of them (Nos. 6, 7, 10, and 27) were solo-practitioners, while five (Nos. 11, 18, 21, 23, and 29) were members of firms with three or more attorneys. Except one attorney who earned a net annual income of 30 million yen (No. 7), their income was relatively modest, ranging between seven million yen (No. 29) and 15 million yen (No. 6).

One possible implication of this pattern is the benefit of belonging to a multiple-attorney firm. Another possible implication is that even solo-practitioners have been able to maintain their cause lawyering if they have chosen a relatively modest life style. In either case, it appears that gross revenues of Japanese attorneys have been large enough to sustain some level of cause lawyering.

The exception is No. 7 who earns a net income of 30 million yen. In fact, his office was the most elaborate among the solo-practitioners in my interviewees. This reflects his cause, 'minbo', the involvement of organized crime in civil disputes. His clients in his cause lawyering are business corporations and property owners. In order to protect his clients from organized crime, he also maintains a good relationship with the police. Indeed, the police have actively campaigned to organize local businesses, residents, and attorneys into various anti-organized crime associations. Therefore, there has been a general tension between 'minbo' cause lawyers and criminal justice cause lawyers while they both participate in bar association activities in human right protection committees. The latter does not regard the former as a progressive cause, but as a disguised form of effort to expand markets for business-oriented attorneys. Since my interviewees do not include any clearly conservative cause lawyers, this 'minbo' area seems, relatively speaking, to be the most conservative cause for my interviewees.

An interesting question may be whether more conservative, clearly business-oriented firms can provide an environment conducive to cause lawyering. My interviewees include two examples from such firms (Nos. 25 and 30). Thirty-nine-year-old No. 25 earned a net income of 30-40 million yen, while

28-year-old No. 30 earned a net income of 9-10 million yen. No. 25's income was largest among my interviewees, while No. 30's income was larger than those of No. 26, No. 27, No. 28, and No. 29 who were 4 to 10 years older than No. 25. No. 25 has participated in the Osaka airport and other environmental cases, while No. 30 was participating only in totally free legal counselling and duty solicitor activities organized by the bar association. Among these two, No. 25 is apparently the more interesting case. If one earns 30 million yen a year and can still spend 10 per cent of his time on environmental litigation, further commodification of lawyering in Japan is not necessarily a bad idea.

Yet, as No. 25 said, the possibility of cause lawyering in corporate firms will fluctuate depending on economic conditions. Moreover, as in the case of No. 30, corporate firms may impose some limitations on the types of causes. Considering these factors, attorneys in solo practice or in smaller firms will remain the main force of cause lawyering in Japan through the near future, although efforts should certainly be made to recruit members of corporate law firms.

The Cause and the Purpose of Cause Lawyering

Cause lawyering by my interviewees takes place in two settings. One is through committees and other projects organized by the JFBA or regional or local bar associations. The other is through activities outside formal projects of bar associations. These two areas are mutually related because the same attorneys participate in both, and because bar association activities provide cause lawyers with forums for their networking or policy-oriented activities. Nevertheless, they can be distinct, since participation in bar association activities may be taken as a matter of general duty for a bar member, while other activities require a stronger commitment to specific causes.

Among bar association activities, the most frequently mentioned areas were human rights protection committees and related activities (Nos. 3, 4, 5, 11, 12, 18, 24, and 28), criminal defence and other criminal justice issues (Nos. 4, 8, 9, 13, 15, 28, and 30), and children's rights and juvenile law (Nos. 10, 12, 19, 21, 23, and 30). Environmental protection (Nos. 17, 19, 20, and 25), consumer issues (Nos. 6, 27, and 29), and training of lawyers (Nos. 13, 27, and 28) follows them. Although there is some overlap, one gets the impression that Communist-related attorneys tend to prefer human rights protection committees, while New Left and Socialist-related attorneys tend to prefer criminal justice activities.

Among activities outside the bar associations, the most frequently mentioned areas were environmental cases and issues (Nos. 1, 8, 11, 12, 13, 20, 22 (including the Minamata mercury poisoning and Kadena-air-base noise-pollution cases), 23, 25, 26, 27, and 28), including seven attorneys (Nos. 12, 13, 20, 23, 26, 27, and 28) who had been involved in the air pollution case which I studied with Robert Kidder (Kidder and Miyazawa, 1993); criminal defence and criminal justice issues (Nos. 3, 4, 7, 9 (including defence of radical students), 10, 11, 14, 22, 23, 26 (seeking to overturn a conviction with death penalty), 27, and 30); labor issues (Nos. 2, 9, 11, 13, 17, 20, 23, 26 (most strongly interested in this field), 28, and 29); and children's rights, juvenile law, and school rules (Nos. 2, 10, 12, 19 (including child abuse), 21, 23, and 26). Next most frequently mentioned areas were 'karoshi' (death from overwork) and worker's compensation (Nos. 5, 21, 22 (pneumoconiosis of mine workers), 23, and 28); medical malpractice (Nos. 10, 14, 16, 18 (vaccination), 19, and 23); consumer issues, including side effects of pharmaceutical products, the enactment of a PL law, and the protection of investors in securities and futures markets as well as multiple debtors of loan sharks (Nos. 3, 6, 8, 27, and 29); and foreigner's rights (Nos. 3, 17 (including the case of sex slaves of the Japanese army), 18, and 24). It is apparent that most attorneys are committed to more than one cause.

Probably the most salient and unexpected finding is that, except for labor issues and criminal defence work, these causes do not include movements which clearly seek a radical transformation of the Japanese society to a more egalitarian one. Most causes may be characterized as expressions of a rather diffuse sense of injustice. There are even arguably middle-class issues such as the protection of investors in securities and futures markets or multiple debtors of loan sharks. Clients in these cases are typically older people who invested their modest assets or borrowed heavily without clearly knowing the legal implications of their act, so that attorneys have taken these cases as examples of fraud by business corporations. Nevertheless, one cannot say that such cases represent an effort to create a radical, egalitarian transformation of the Japanese society as a whole. This finding is puzzling particularly because my interviewees include those closely related to the Communist Party or New Left. Indeed, I never heard any class-based analysis of Japanese society from them.

If an egalitarian transformation of Japanese society as a whole is too remote of a purpose for progressive attorneys in Japan, they may pursue the less remote purpose of equal access to the law. The data indicate, however, that my interviewees are not pursuing such a purpose either. It is true that many of them participate in duty solicitor programs, accept criminal cases as court-appointed defence counsel, or take legal-aid civil cases. However, these activities take place within formal programs of bar associations. While many of them participate in such programs considering their social and political significance, they may also participate in them from a more general sense of duty as attorneys and as members of their respective bar associations.

It is also true that when they work in environmental and other cases, they do so on a pro bono basis in most cases. If they win in civil damage suits, they may be compensated. But such occasions are rare, and compensations amounts are usually too small to cover their expenses and are provided only after working *pro bono* for many years. It must be noted, however, that my interviewees have participated in such cases not because their clients were indigent, but because of the social and political significance of such cases.

In this situation, probably the most anti-establishment cause lawyer among my interviewees was No. 17. He has worked not only on labor issues, for former sex slaves of the Japanese army, and for foreigners facing deportation, he has also participated in cases which directly or indirectly challenged the most deeply entrenched core of Japanese society, the Imperial system, including cases challenging the enthronement ritual of the present Emperor after the death of the Showa Emperor, 'Kimigayo', and 'Hinomaru'. The enthronement ritual included Shinto rituals and public funds were used, allegedly violating the separation of the state and religion. 'Kimigayo', which the government claims is the national anthem, was the national anthem of Imperial Japan, and it means a prayer for the long life of the Emperor. 'Hinomaru', which signifies the rising sun, and which the government claims is the national flag, was also the national flag of Imperial Japan. Environmental litigation, for instance, can be presented as a non-political, non-partisan cause when recruiting attorneys to form a lawyers' team for plaintiffs. These cases regarding the Imperial system cannot; these cases are definitely seen as both political and partisan by other attorneys. Only a small number of extremely political attorneys may be willing to participate in them.

However, No. 17 and, possibly, No. 9 (to the extent that he defends radical students) are exceptions. As I have already stated, the causes of most other attorneys can be characterized as expressions of a more diffuse sense of injustice and attempts to use law to correct it. In other words, liberal legalism can still be a progressive cause in the Japanese context.

How should this situation be explained? One plausible explanation may be that simply taking legal actions to challenge some unjust status quo is in itself a progressive action in Japan. In other words, the legalization of social ordering is still an unfinished project in Japan. It is in itself a radical action to use the human rights clauses in the Constitution to support one's claims, since mainstream judges in Japan have not yet fully recognized the clauses as part of the positive law enforceable in courts.[8] In such a situation, there is no so-called 'myth of rights', and the purposes of cause lawyering must inevitably be much more modest than American cause lawyering (Scheingold, 1974).

This explanation also applies to attorneys' sense of general purpose of their participation in cause lawyering. Social reform (including the reform of administrative processes, or the establishment of leading precedents) was the sole purpose for 10 attorneys (Nos. 1, 6, 7, 8, 17, 18, 20, 24, 26, and 27). Seven attorneys (Nos. 5, 6, 14, 19, 22, 25, and 29) simultaneously sought helping individual clients and social reform. Helping individual clients was the sole purpose for seven attorneys (Nos. 4, 10, 11, 13, 15, 16, and 21). Two attorneys (Nos. 2 and 27) mentioned the benefit to attorneys themselves in terms of morale or networking. Therefore, a majority of attorneys seem to seek to provide remedies to individual clients solely or in conjunction with their impact on social reform.

Indeed, given the difficulty of obtaining a legal victory in terms of a court decision and the likelihood of spending an extremely long period of time to reach a court decision, attorneys are often forced to choose between a less-than satisfactory settlement and a very unlikely legal victory. They are more likely to choose the former, except when they can sustain litigation as a forum to maintain social awareness of the existence of a social problem and to bind the government to the dialogue (Kidder and Miyazawa, 1993). This point leads us to an examination of the means of cause lawyering preferred by my interviewees and their sense of satisfaction.

The Means of Cause Lawyering and the Degree of Satisfaction

Progressive cause lawyers in the United States are often described as dispirited by the rapidly declining prospects of what they can achieve through litigation, yet reluctant to participate in more political, out-of-court activities. My interviewees appear to be generally more content and more willing to participate in out-of-court activities.

Probably the most dispirited one among my interviewees is No. 19. He lost his passion because internal conflicts erupted when his litigation on the side effects of vaccinations had been successfully concluded and monetary awards had been granted. He quit practising and became a judge in 1995. Since most judges are recruited immediately after graduation from the Judicial Research and Training Institute, he is one of the very small number of practicing attorneys who have been appointed as judges. It should be noted that in addition to his involvement in litigation, he clearly understood the importance of a variety of out-of-court activities in order to obtain major policy changes. Moreover, his move to the judiciary suggests that he is not yet totally disillusioned by the judicial system either. His move can be understood in terms of his desire to obtain a policy-making position. It is, of course, highly debatable to what extent the extremely bureaucratic structure of the Japanese judiciary will allow him to pursue such a desire. Yet, it seems that even No. 19 has not yet totally lost positive expectations of litigation and the judicial system.

On the other hand, if we want to find attorneys who prefer litigation over out-of-court activities and who wish to remain in a narrower role, Nos. 17 and 18 may be good examples. They are actually very similar to each other. They belong to the generation who carry the legacy of the campus riots in the late 1960s; they belong to New Left or Socialist-leaning attorneys; they pursue social reforms rather than helping individual clients; and they are more satisfied than other attorneys. Their morale and legalism seems to reflect the fact that they both became attorneys after they had probably been deeply disillusioned through their many years in a corporation or local government. It appears that their stake in their new occupation is high, so they seek satisfaction in the most typical role for attorneys.

Most other attorneys seem to combine litigation and out-of-court activities more naturally. Given the difficulty of winning in reform-seeking litigation, this result is understandable. By necessity, Japanese cause lawyers have become versatile in their tactics and strategies. By necessity, they have also become more realistic about what they can expect to achieve. Hence, they are less likely to get disillusioned. This observation leads us to the tentative conclusion of my data.

The Tentative Conclusion on Cause Lawyering

In Japan, Communist - or Socialist-oriented attorneys are the main forces of cause lawyering. In spite of their political positions, however, they engage in the form of cause lawyering which may be characterized as a kind of liberal legalism, rather than radical lawyering. This is because liberal legalism is an unfinished project in Japan, and pursuing it has a progressive meaning in this context. They understand that even with their form of cause lawyering, it is difficult to achieve tangible results through litigation, so they are not reluctant to engage in social movements outside the judicial system. Since they understand the difficulty of achieving tangible results either through litigation or social movements, they are less likely to become deeply disillusioned. Human rights protection committees and other activities organized by bar associations seem to provide a forum where they can interact with fellow cause lawyers, learn from others, and maintain their commitment. Even those who are most committed to cause lawyering can still maintain an acceptable level of income.

They identify two problems for their future. One is increasingly more conservative or complacent university students. The other is the irresistible social demand for the expansion of access to attorneys. These problems would require JFBA involvement in legal education on the one hand, and the exploration of salaried and other forms of cause lawyering on the other.

Although cause lawyering has been indispensable for progressive social movements in Japan, we must also note that it has an inherent limitation as a method of providing legal services to the indigent and other underrepresented people in general. That is because lawyers will provide their expertise only when the case fits their causes. Although simply claiming legal rights in the court can in itself have a social transformative meaning in Japanese society as I have already discussed, lawyers are inevitably more interested in larger or apparently more significant cases than in smaller or routine-looking cases. They need to find personal meaning in the case before deciding to devote their limited time and other resources. In other words, there is inevitably a large number of routine-looking cases which fail to attract the attention of cause lawyers. Although a small case can be critically important from the perspective of the client, lawyers may ignore it.

That is why Japan needs a broader system to provide the indigent and other underrepresented groups with legal services, one that does not rely on the individual initiative of lawyers. We are thus led to a discussion of legal aid in Japan.

Legal Aid

I will limit my discussion to the essential points of legal aid in Japan.

First of all, the Japanese Legal Aid Association was established in 1952 mainly by the initiative of the JFBA. There was no nation-wide legal aid system in pre-war Japan. The government had no interest in providing legal services for the indigent and other underrepresented people. The situation did not change after the war. The law which established the Justice Ministry became effective in 1948 and designated the Human Right Protection Bureau (Jinken Yogo Kyoku) of the Justice Ministry to handle assistance to the indigent in litigation. However, the Justice Ministry made no effort to create a legal aid system. On the other hand, the Practicing Attorneys Act of 1949 had a provision (Art. 33, Par. 2) that the bylaws of the JFBA and local bar associations should include provisions regarding legal aid for the indigent. Thus, the Japan Legal Aid Association was established by bar associations in 1952. This should in itself be considered a tangible result of the official commitment to public interest proclaimed in Art. 1 of the Practicing Attorneys Act. The government assumed no responsibility for legal aid in the first few years.

Considering this process of establishing the legal aid system in Japan, it is not surprising that the system relies heavily on attorneys, and attorneys virtually control the system (Horitsu Fujo Seido Kenkyukai, 1998). For instance, the Japan Legal Aid Association might have up to 100 board members. In 1998, only seven were from outside the bar. The rest of the board members, including the President and eight Vice Presidents, were all attorneys. Furthermore, only the headquarters of the Association and the Tokyo branch employ their own staff members. All other branches rely on staff members of local bar associations.

Secondly, the national government started to provide funding for the system in 1958. While only less than 50 cases received assistance each year until 1957, the number jumped to 256 in 1958. However, various constraints are attached by the national government. The funds from the government are limited to civil cases including both litigation and mediation. The purpose is to loan funds to indigent plaintiffs who are unable to hire attorneys by themselves. Plaintiffs are required to repay the funds in principle. The amount of the national governmental fund grew from 10 million yen in 1958 to 271 million yen in 1996, excluding separate funds for cases related to the Great Earthquake in 1995. The number of cases receiving assistance grew from 256 in 1958 to 7,265 in 1996. However, initial constraints still remain, except that the national governmental fund have also been used for legal counselling since 1993. Moreover, 7,265 assisted cases in 1996 means that on average, each of approximately 16,000 attorneys in Japan takes only one case every two years. This may be a result of the lack of commitment of a majority of attorneys, the difficulty in obtaining assistance under the fiscal constraint, or both.

Under such a funding system, the largest income source for the system is repayments by plaintiffs. In 1996, excluding those for the quake-related cases, the amount of repayments was 961 million yen, while the national governmental fund was only 271 million yen, and the total amount of loans was 1,310 million yen. In other words, activities of the system are largely determined by its ability to enforce repayments by assisted plaintiffs.

In spite of its fragile financial basis, the Association has expanded its activities to areas outside civil disputes. It now provides assistance in juvenile cases (since 1973), free legal counselling (since 1974), legal assistance for refugees (since 1983), legal assistance for obtaining Japanese citizenship for Japanese nationals left in China at the end of the war (since 1986), and criminal defence at the pre-indictment stage (since 1990). These activities rely totally on funds obtained from sources other than the national government. In 1996, local governments donated 109 million yen, the Nippon Foundation 58 million yen, the JFBA 172 million yen, and the local bar associations 195 million yen (Horitsu Fujo Kyokai, 1997). Furthermore, donations by criminal defendants, namely 'keiji shokuzai kifu' or repentance donations, totalled nearly 600 million yen. In other words, excluding national governmental funds earmarked for quake-related cases, civil plaintiffs were the largest financial sources for the system, criminal defendants the second, and attorneys the third. One may call this system almost immoral since it rips off indigent civil plaintiffs through the requirement of repayment and forces criminal defendants to make donations in anticipation of lenient treatment.

Naturally, the size of the system is extremely small compared to other countries (Horitsu Fujo Seido Kenkyukai, 1998). The annual budgets of legal aid systems in England and Wales (1994), France (1993), Germany (1990), Sweden (1993), the United States (1994), and Korea (1997) were respectively, 120 times, 14 times, 28 times, 3.6 times, 50 times, and 1.3 times the budget in Japan (1996). The amounts of funds from national governments in England and Wales, France, Germany (including Land governments), Sweden, the United States (including state governments), and Korea were, respectively, 420 times, 67 times, 134 times, 17 times, 170 times, and 5.3 times the amount in Japan. The number of court cases assisted by legal aid in England and Wales, France, Germany, Sweden, the United States, and Korea were, respectively, 50 times, 47 times, 50 times, 8.5 times, 26 times, and 6 times the number in Japan. 93 per cent of the Swedish population, 50 per cent of the English and Welsh, French, and Korean populations, and 40 per cent of the French population were eligible, while only 20 per cent of the Japanese population was eligible, according to the income eligibility thresholds of these countries. The income eligibility threshold was lower only in the United States (18 per cent).

It is fair to say that the Japanese legal aid system is the weakest among developed countries. It is even smaller than the system in Korea which was established only in 1986. Is there any hope for expansion and improvement of the legal aid system in Japan? This is the topic for the next and final section of this chapter.

The Movement to Strengthen Legal Aid in Japan

The Changing Political Environment in Japan

Before discussing the present situation of the movement to strengthen the legal aid system in Japan, one should look at the changing political environment.

The predominant theme of Japanese politics in recent years has been deregulation. Unlike neo-liberal political reforms in the United Kingdom and the United States, however, reduction of governmental interventions for the sake of increased efficiency has not been the only purpose of deregulation in Japan. Since governmental regulation in Japan has not only been extensive, but also lacking legal accountability and transparency, reform on the latter aspect has become an important issue in Japanese politics. This is the first time in modern Japanese history in which the national government has admitted that it is unable to intervene in every aspect of Japanese society, and has expressed doubt about its traditional style of regulation. The Administrative Reform Committee (Gyosei Kaikaku Iinkai) of the Cabinet presented its final report to the Prime Minister on December 12, 1997 (Gyosei Kaikaku Iinkai, 1998). In addition to deregulation, the report also recommended that public access to governmental information should be radically expanded, consumer protection systems should be strengthened, anti-monopoly laws should be more strongly enforced, and product liability and other appropriate methods should be utilized. The logic behind these proposals is that the legal protection of the people should be expanded if administrative regulation is to be reduced. Based on these final opinions, the Cabinet adopted a 3-year plan to promote deregulation (Kakugi Kettei, 1998).

This situation has created a window of opportunity for various law-reform movements to realize at least part of their long-standing goals. They include, among other things:

- Amendment of the *Commercial Code* in 1993 to strengthen shareholder's rights. For instance, a shareholder derivative suit is now defined as a suit seeking a non-monetary result because losing board members pay damages not to shareholder plaintiffs, but to the company, and its filing fee is fixed at 8,200 yen. Approximately 200 such suits are now pending.

- Implementation of the *Administrative Procedure Act* in 1994. Governmental agencies are required to provide reasons when they reject applications for licenses and permissions or make decisions unfavorable to private parties; governmental agencies are prohibited from providing administrative guidance in areas outside the jurisdiction of the given agency and from treating unfavorably private parties who refuse to comply with administrative guidance.

- Implementation of the *Product Liability Act* in 1995. Now negligence is not required; strict liability has been introduced.

- Implementation of the new *Code of Civil Procedure* in January 1998. Judicial power to require parties to produce documents has been strengthened.

- The first *Freedom of Information Act* has been passed in the Diet in May 1999.

These reforms are certainly less than what activists of reform movements had originally demanded. However, even these partial victories represent significant achievements of the reform movements which have existed through the entire postwar period.

Furthermore, governmental committees and even the Liberal Democratic Party have recently published reports on judicial and legal reform which include proposals to strengthen legal aid. For instance, the Research Committee on Business Law (Kigyo Hosei Kenkyukai) of the Ministry of International Trade and Industry (MITI), which has long been considered the champion of business interests, published a report on June 1, 1998 that advocated that private legal actions be allowed against unfair trade practices and that the legal aid system be strengthened.[9] The Special Research Committee on the Judicial System (Shiho Seido Tokubetu Chosakai) of the Liberal Democratic Party, the ruling conservative party, published a report on June 15, 1998 proposing a comprehensive reform of the judicial system and legal professions in Japan and recommending the strengthening of the legal aid system.[10] The Federation of Economic Organizations (Keidanren), which is usually considered the most powerful economic organization in Japan, also recommended similar reforms in early June, 1998.[11] Finally, the Deliberative Committee on Industrial Structure (Sangyo Kozo Shingikai) of MITI published a report on July 1, 1998, and proposed a comprehensive reform of the judicial system in order to secure compliance with the rules of market economies. Strengthening of legal aid was again included in recommendations.

Many attorneys and academics are suspicious about the motives behind these reform proposals from the conservative elite, in spite of the fact that these proposals include several liberal ideas they themselves have proposed. Some of them reject deregulation itself as an effort of the national government and conservative elite to abandon ordinary people without providing proper protection by the government. These attorneys and academics have a dilemma, however. If they totally oppose deregulation, what will remain is the present regulatory system, which lacks legal accountability of governmental agencies and allows collusive relationships between regulators and regulated businesses. Any window of opportunity for reform movements to increase the accountability and transparency of the regulatory system will be closed, and bureaucrats will be just delighted.

Other attorneys and academics reject these proposals because all of the proposals include plans to deregulate the legal profession. They are afraid of a large increase in the number of attorneys, the merger of spheres of activities of attorneys and other legal professionals, and the loss of control of the bar to business-oriented, more conservative attorneys. They still argue that a small bar is better for the public because such a bar will be more easy to maintain its commitment to public interest. These critics also have a dilemma. Their position can easily be criticized as a thinly veiled attempt to protect their vested interests based on a small and closed bar. As I have already mentioned in connection with the average number of legal aid cases taken by attorneys, only a small minority actually spend a sizable proportion of their time doing public interest activities. More than half of attorneys practice in Tokyo and Osaka, and there are nearly 50 branches of district courts (trial courts with general jurisdiction) that have no attorneys in their geographical jurisdictions. It is difficult to convince the public that the bar is already large enough.

After all, this is the first time in modern Japanese history that all the players of the so-called 'iron-triangle' of the ruling elite, the conservative ruling party, big business organizations, and national governmental agencies, have shown interest in the expansion of the judicial system and the strengthening of legal aid. Under the parliamentary cabinet system, the conservative elite can pass laws without consulting progressive reformers if they wish. Therefore, progressive reformers do not have the option of ignoring the reform proposals from conservatives. They must engage with conservatives.

Moreover, progressives' own reform proposals ultimately require participation in the political process. The challenge for progressive reformers is whether they can exploit this extremely rare opportunity to realize their ideals, while at the same time preventing the introduction of unacceptable changes.[12]

In any event, the Diet has passed the law to establish the Judicial System Reform Committee (Shiho Seido Kaikaku Iinkai) on June 2, 1999. The government will appoint 13 members, and they are expected to produce final recommendations in two years.

It is in this context of rapid and broad political change that the Research Committee on the Legal Aid System (Horitsu Fujo Seido Kenkyukai) of the Justice Ministry studied, deliberated, and finally published a report in March, 1998 (Kakugi Kettei, 1998).

It should be noted here that the bar has lost its noble position as the sole supporter of legal aid among major organizations in Japan. Moreover, while the bar has no direct access to the legislative process, the conservative elite does. Whether the actual reform is based on the proposal from the bar or from the conservatives, an expanded legal aid system will certainly require a larger number of attorneys to provide legal services. Unlike earlier times when the bar was the only major group proposing reform of legal aid, a reform can actually be made this time, and the bar must be ready to expand or otherwise adjust itself to an expanded legal aid system.[13]

The Final Report of the Research Committee on Legal Aid

The Justice Ministry and the Japan Legal Aid Association formed a joint study group on legal aid in 1988. The JFBA later joined it. This study group met 50 times through to June 1994. In the meantime, the Executive Committee of the Judiciary Committee of the House of Representatives (Shugiin), the more powerful lower house of the Diet, issued a statement in June 1993 that the Justice Ministry should engage in systematic research for the further development of legal aid in Japan. Thus, the Justice Ministry formed the Research Committee on the Legal Aid System in October 1994, including members from the Supreme Court, the JFBA, the Japan Legal Aid Association, and academia. The Justice Ministry immediately excluded criminal legal aid at the pre-indictment stage from the scope of this committee in spite of the JFBA's demand to include it.

Nevertheless, it is fair to say that the creation of this committee in itself was the culmination of efforts by the Legal Aid Association and the JFBA.

The Committee published its final report on March 23, 1998. Although the report did not go so far as to recognize the people's right to legal aid per se, it still said that legal aid would substantively guarantee the people's constitutional right to have access to the courts (Art. 32 of the Japanese Constitution, 'No person shall be denied the right of access to the courts'), and fit the spirit ('shushi' in Japanese) of their rights to wholesome and cultured life (Art. 25, 'All persons shall have the right to maintain the minimum standards of wholesome and cultured life'), respect as individuals and pursuit of happiness (Art. 13, 'All of the people shall be respected as individuals. Their right to life, liberty and the pursuit of happiness shall, to the extent it does not interfere with the public welfare, be the supreme consideration in legislation and in other governmental affairs'), and equality under the law (Art. 14, 'All of the people shall be equal under the law and there shall be no discrimination in political, economic or social relations because of race, creed, sex, social status or family origin'). The report said that a legal aid system could be based on both the ideal of the rule of law and the ideal of a welfare state, so that the state shall have the responsibility, among other things, to establish a system by legislation and to bear the financial burden appropriate for its responsibility. This is the first time in Japanese history for a governmental committee to recognize the state's responsibility for providing legal aid to indigent people.

On the other hand, the report also recognized the responsibility of attorneys to actively participate in legal aid in light of their required commitment to public interest (Art. 1, the Practicing Attorneys Act) and their monopoly of legal services (Art. 72, same). The report does not say explicitly either that the bar should continue to share financial burdens with the state in the future, or that the bar's financial responsibility will be reduced. Some attorneys have expressed concern about this ambiguity (Kodera and Kamei, 1997).

I limit my discussion here to the most fundamental point in the report: the report clearly stated that a law should be enacted on legal aid, and that a corporation should be established and designated to operate the legal aid system (shitei hojin). Since there is no law on the legal aid system per se right now, this simple proposal represents a significant step towards the eventual strengthening of the legal aid system. Details are left for further discussion among the Justice Ministry, the JFBA, and the Legal Aid Association. This report is still quite vague on many points. Much is left for further efforts by the JFBA and the Legal Aid Association in their continuing negotiations with the Ministry and the other players in the political process. Nevertheless, it seems safe to expect that legal aid in Japan will grow in the near future.

Finally, it should be noted that international comparison of legal aid systems has played a significant role in the deliberations of the Research Committee. This is a positive example of the impact of the globalization of legal ideals.

In anticipation of a fundamental change the legal aid system, the Japan Legal Aid Association radically changed its Board in April 1999. The number of Board members has been reduced to 25, and only 12 attorneys have been appointed to the Board, including President and two vice Presidents. The change has been introduced because the new legal aid corporation is likely to be required by the government to reduce the proportion of a single profession to less than half.

Conclusion

There have been two ways in which the Japanese bar has provided legal services for free or reduced fees to the indigent and other underrepresented people. One is cause lawyering based on the desire of individual attorneys for social reform. The other is legal aid which has been financially supported by recipients, criminal defendants, and attorneys.

Cause lawyering has been indispensable in Japan particularly because the legal aid system has been small. Cause lawyering has been available even to plaintiffs who do not seek apparently radical causes. Simply using law to claim one's rights has a progressive meaning in Japan. However, cause lawyering provides legal services only when attorneys find that a plaintiff's claim has some political significance. It does not cover totally ordinary cases. Contrary to cause lawyering, legal aid can provide legal services in ordinary cases. However, the financial basis of the Japanese legal aid system is so weak that the number of cases supported by the system is still minuscule. These features of legal services to the indigent and other underrepresented people in Japan are the results of several factors. On the one hand, the official ideology of the bar has provided morally higher positions to attorneys engaging in cause lawyering, and has made the bar as a whole committed to support the legal aid system. On the other hand, the lack of law, meagre financial support from the state, and constraints attached to governmental assistance, have all prevented the growth of legal aid in Japan. Moreover, the small size of the bar and the lack of commitment to public interest by many members has made the bar unable to actually provide legal assistance to large numbers of people.

However, we are now seeing the possibility to change these conditions. Conservative elites in politics, bureaucracy, and business are now proposing to strengthen the legal aid system as part of their broader policy of deregulation. The bar has just started to expand. The Justice Ministry seems to be preparing to draft a law on legal aid. Since this abrupt change is part of a larger modification of Japanese politics under the globalization of a market economy, it is likely to produce a tangible result. The problem is whether the result will actually help the indigent and other underrepresented people.

Details are unknown about the new legal aid system. For instance:

1 Will the system still require repayment by recipients?

2 Will the income eligibility ceiling be raised?

3 Will organizations with staff attorneys working full-time on legal aid cases appear?

4 Will attorneys be required to take legal aid cases?

5 Will pre-indictment criminal legal aid be introduced?

6 Will legal professions other than attorneys be allowed to participate in legal aid?

7 Will professional legal education be introduced in Japanese universitics so that law students will become resources of legal aid?

8 Will the bar continue to provide free legal services outside the areas covered by funds from the central government?

It will certainly be exciting to see how these issues will be solved in the near future. It will be even more exciting to participate in the process of creating a new and a stronger legal aid system. Many issues may be the same or similar in other countries. It is time for mutual learning and mutual support for legal aid reformers in Eastern and South-Eastern Asian countries.

Notes

1 This paper is a slightly revised version as of June 1999, of a paper presented at the Conference on 'Providing Legal Services for Underrepresented Groups in East and Southeast Asia: Creating A Forum for Dialogue', on July 21-23, 1998, at Thammasat University, Bangkok, Thailand. The author gratefully acknowledges the editorial assistance provided by Louise G. Trubek and her staff.

2 See Oda, 1992: 14-34, for a brief description of Japanese legal history.

3 For a general discussion of the situation of practicing attorneys in Japan, see Rokumoto, 1988.

4 For a general discussion on the status of lawyers in different political structures, see Halliday, 1989, although Japan is not included in his analysis.

5 On the concept and forms of cause lawyering, see Sarat and Scheingold, 1998.

6 On legal education in Japan, see Taniguchi, 1994.

7 For a general discussion of the recent situation of Japanese practicing attorneys, see Ota and Rokumoto, 1993; for non-academic, but interesting description of different styles of Japanese practicing attorneys, see Foote, 1995.

8 See Okudaira, 1993, on the situation of judicial review in Japan.

9 *Shukan Horitsu Shimbun* (Weekly Legal News), June 5, 1998.

10 *Shukan Horitsu Shimbun* (Weekly Legal News), June 19, 1998.

11 *Shukan Horitsu Shimbun* (Weekly Legal News), June 12, 1998.

12 For an example of documents presenting competing views within the bar, see Nichibenren, 1998.

13 See Kodera and Kamei, 1997, for an article written by attorneys on this point.

References

Foote, D. (1995) 'Four Views of Japanese Attorneys', *Law in Japan*, Vol. 25, 102.

Gyosei Kaikaku Iinkai (Administrative Reform Committee) (1998), 'Gyosei Kaikaku Iinkai Saishu Iken' (Final Opinions of the Administrative Reform Committee), *Jiyu to Seigi* (Liberty and Justice), Vol. 49, (2), 170.

Haley, J. (1991), *Authority Without Power: Law and the Japanese Paradox*, Oxford University Press, Oxford.

Halliday, T. (1989), 'Legal Professions and the State: Noecorporatist Variations on the Pluralist Theme of Liberal Democracies', in Richard Abel and Philip S.C. Lewis (eds.), *Lawyers in Society, Vol. 3, Comparative Theories*, University of California Press, Berkeley, 375.

Horitsu Fujo Kyokai (Japan Legal Aid Association) (1997), *Horitsu Fujo Dayori* (Legal Aid Journal), No. 57.

Horitsu Fujo Seido Kenkyukai (Research Committee on Legal Aid System) (1998), 'Hokokusho (Report)', *Jiyu to Seigi* (Liberty and Justice), Vol. 49, (5), 183.

Kakugi Kettei (Cabinet Decision) (1998), 'Kisei Kanwa Suishin Sankanen Keikaku' (3-Year Plan for Promoting Deregulation), *Jiyu to Seigi* (Liberty and Justice), Vol. 49, (5), 178.

Kidder, R. and Miyazawa, S. (1993), 'Long-term Strategies in Japanese Environmental Litigation', *Law and Social Inquiry*, Vol. 18, (4), 605.

Kodera, K. and Kamei, T. (1997), 'Horitsu Enjo Rippo to Bengoshi Bengoshikai no Aratana Kadai', (Legal Aid Legislation and New Tasks for Attorneys and Bar Associations), *Jiyu to Seigi* (Liberty and Justice), Vol. 48, (9), 52.

Miyazawa, S. (1994), 'Administrative Control of Judges', in Philip S.C. Lewis (ed.), Law and Technology in the Pacific Community, Westview Press, Boulder: 45.

Miyazawa, S. (1996), 'Cause Lawyering by a Cartelized Legal Profession: Profiles of Cause Lawyering in Japan', a paper presented at the joint annual meeting of the Law and Society Association and the International Sociological Association's Research Committee on Sociology of Law, July 10-13, 1996, Glasgow, Scotland.

Miyazawa, S. (1997), 'Legal Education and the Reproduction of the Elite in Japan', a paper presented at the Conference on 'New Challenge for the Rule of Law: Lawyers, Internationalization, and the Social Construction of Legal Rules', November 7-9, 1997, University of California, Santa Barbara.

Nichibenren (Japan Federation of Bar Associations) (1998), '2010 Nen eno Shiho Kaikaku' (Judicial Reform for 2010), *Jiyu to Seigi* (Liberty and Justice), Vol. 49, (4), 155.

Oda, H. (1992), *Japanese Law*, Butterworths, London.

Okudaira, Y. (1993), 'Forty Years of the Constitution and Its Various Influences', in Percy R. Luney, Jr. and Kazuyuki Takahashi (eds.), *Japanese Constitutional Law*, University of Tokyo Press, Tokyo, 1.

Ota, S. and Rokumoto, K. (1993), 'Issues of the Lawyer Population in Japan', *Case*

Western Reserve Journal of International Law, Vol. 25, (2), 315.
Rokumoto, K. (1988), 'The Present State of Japanese Practicing Attorneys: On the Way to Full Professionalization?' in Richard Abel and Philip S.C. Lewis (eds.), *Lawyers in Society, Vol. 2, The Civil Law World*, University of California Press, Berkeley.
Sarat, A. and Scheingold, S. (1998), *Cause Lawyering: Political Commitment and Professional Responsibilities*, New York: Oxford University Press.
Scheingold, S. (1974), *The Politics of Rights: Lawyers, Public Policy, and Political Change*, Yale University Press, New Haven.
Taniguchi, Y. (1994), 'Legal Education in Japan', in Philip S.C. Lewis (ed.), *Law and Technology in the Pacific Community*, Westview Press, Boulder, 295.
Tokushu (Special Feature) (1998), 'Higisha Kokusen Bengo Seido no Jitsugen wo' (For the Realization of State-Appointed Attorneys for Pre-Indictment Suspects), *Jiyu to Seigi* (Liberty and Justice), Vol. 49, (2), 24.
Upham, F. (1987), *Law and Social Change in Postwar Japan*, Harvard University Press, Cambridge, MA.

3 Current Issues for Legal Aid in Japan - Reform Perspective

GOTARO ICHIKI AND TETSUO OHISHI

Introduction

Currently Japan is experiencing large-scale changes, which extend from the restructuring of social systems, political party reforms, the financial sectors' 'big bang' and changes in the employment system to company structure reforms. These changes substantially affect people's present daily life as well as the futures of Japanese people.

In our society, the role of the judiciary has been relatively small and weak, while the bureaucratic administration's functions, both in the central government and local governments, are enormous and tend to cover all areas of people's lives, which are, in part, controlled through unclear guidance and unwritten regulations. However, as society becomes more and more complex and people's values diversify, various types of conflicts and controversies have been increasing. Together with the advancement of deregulation and the shrinking of preventive functions by administration sectors, and the expectation of problem-solving through open discussions, the roles and functions of the judiciary are expected to greatly increase in order to maintain the fairness and smoothness of social and economic activities.

Political and administration reform have been discussed and some reform plans have been commenced. In connection with these reforms, the importance of the 'rule of law' has become emphasized to promote deregulation and abolish unclear interventions by administrations. In this context, some reforms to strengthen judicial functions have been introduced or are expected to be introduced, which include an increase in the number of lawyers, the reform of the training system for legal apprentices, revision of the civil procedural code, and improvements in court procedures. The reform of the legal aid system is considered in line with this overall judicial reform.

In this short memorandum, we would like to introduce some issues which were raised at meetings of the Legal Aid System Study Group. Also, we would like to point out some problems to be overcome and solved before the contemplated reform in legal aid in Japan will be realized.

The Legal Aid System Study Group (the 'Study Group') was organized in November 1994 by the Minister of Justice, upon recommendation by the Legal Affairs Committee of the House of Representatives. The members of the Study Group consisted of university professors, representatives of the Supreme Court, the Ministry of Justice, the Japan Federation of Bar Associations ('JFBA') and the Japan Legal Aid Association ('JLAA'). Having 32 meetings during a period of more than three years, the Study Group issued its Report in March 1998. Reflecting differences of opinion, mainly between the Ministry of Justice, on one part, and the JFBA and the JLAA on the other, several issues were not in agreement and remained unsolved. They are expected to be further discussed among the relevant parties before the new legal aid system will be actually organized.

Features of Legal Aid in Japan

Before discussing the proposed reforms, we should explain the history and current situation of legal aid in Japan for the better understanding of readers. Also, we recommend reading the *Business Report for Fiscal 1997* prepared by the JLAA for detailed information as to businesses being conducted by the JLAA.

The JLAA was founded in 1952, mainly sponsored by the JFBA. The JLAA had been managed with poor financial resources, mainly relying on donations. From 1958, a small amount of an annual subsidy has been given by the Ministry of Justice to the JLAA, which could be used only for civil legal aid services (as opposed to criminal cases).

With such poor financial resources and little support from the government, the JLAA has long relied on the JFBA in its management, in terms of personnel and financial resources. It has its headquarters in Tokyo, and branch offices in each local court jurisdiction, most of which are located in the bar associations' buildings. Most directors of the Headquarters and branch offices are lawyers, and most employees of branch offices are seconded from or concurrent with the bar associations.

The JLAA, among others, rendered the following services in Fiscal 1997:

1) Legal Aid in Civil Affairs
   a) litigation aid 7,828 cases

b) pre-litigation aid negotiation for out-of-court settlement 344
c) aid in connection with the Great Earthquake
i) litigation and mediation 310
ii) negotiation for out-of-court settlement 19
2) Free legal consultations 49,327
3) Aid in defense of suspects in criminal cases 2,836
4) Aid in attendance on juveniles in criminal cases 973
5) Activities for Japanese who were left in China after World War II 33
6) Refugee Aid 8

It should be noted that the subsidies from the Ministry of Finance can be used only for Item (1) above, and legal aid for services listed in Items (2)-(6) must be funded from other sources, such as contributions from the bar associations, donations from lawyers and other entities, atonement funds, and other governmental agencies.

The overall expenditures of the JLAA in Fiscal 1997 were approximately Yen 3,195,000,000 (or US$ 22,820,000 at $1= Yen 140), out of which Yen 539,000,000 was for the general administration and Yen 2,358,000,000 for legal aid activities.

Sources of income are (i) contributions from the bar associations Yen 408,973,000, (ii) atonement funds Yen 403,462,000, (iii) subsidy from the Ministry of Justice Yen 443,144,000 and (iv) refund from clients Yen 1,130,197,000.

Also, it should be noted that criminal legal aid is administered by courts, through state-appointed lawyers. However, such aid is offered only after suspects are charged (or indicted). Thus, at the stage of detention before the charge is laid (or indictment) which may extend up to 23 days at police stations or detention centers, such criminal legal aid is not covered by the state-appointed lawyer system. To render legal aid to suspects who are detained at such facilities, the JLAA, in cooperation with the JFBA, offers legal aid services listed in Item (3) above, using non-governmental funds, mainly contributed by the bar associations.

Report Issued by Legal Aid System Study Group

After a lengthy and serious discussion, the Report was issued in March 1998. However, as mentioned, there were several issues which were not in agreement, reflecting the different positions taken by the Ministry of Justice, the JFBA and

JLAA. Generally speaking, the JFBA and the JLAA had asserted much more drastic changes and expansion, while the Ministry of Justice showed a relatively conservative attitude. Many compromises among the members representing each institution were reached to finalize the Report and different opinions were reflected in the Report, which will be subject to further discussion and negotiation among the relevant institutions, because unless these issues are solved, the new system cannot be organized and started with the cooperation of all parties concerned.

The following describes the summary of the Report and gives some explanations of issues, on which different opinions were expressed.

Significance of Legal Aid

Significance of legal aid In general, the significance or meaning of legal aid is generally and globally considered from the viewpoint of access to justice and, in some countries, means to improve and reform the social system, mainly to overcome poverty. However, the Report emphasizes the need for legal aid in Japan in relation to the right of indigent people to realize their rights through the use of civil court procedures. The Report stated that 'the legal aid system, which covers civil affairs in particular, is designed to substantially enable a person of limited means to realize his or her own legitimate rights in a civil litigation with the support and assistance of a lawyer'. The Report also recognized the necessity of legal consultation and pre-litigation aid services which work for problem-solving before formal procedures are utilized.

The JFBA and the JLAA asserted that the contemplated legal aid services shall include services not only to those people of limited means but also people who have difficulties to access legal services, such as mentally or physically handicapped or socially depressed people. Also they stressed the necessity of services to provide legal information and legal education in order to avoid the occurrence of legal problems and to solve them at an early stage. Also they emphasized the necessity to organize the overall legal aid system, integrating legal aid for civil matters and criminal matters.

Grounds in the Constitution of Japan There is a controversy whether the Japanese Constitution guarantees Japanese nationals the right for legal aid in civil matters. The position expressed in the Report is that as the Constitution contains no express provision concerning the right to receive legal aid, it is left to legislative policy to decide the particulars, including rights under the legal aid system.

In this connection, although it did not characterize legal aid as one of the Constitutional rights, the Report stated to the effect that 'the purpose of the legal aid system is to guarantee the right of access to the courts under Article 32 of the Constitution; the provision of legal aid services and the improvement and expansion of this system conform to the purport of Article 25 (the right to maintain minimum standards of cultured living), Article 13 (the right to be respected as individuals; the right to pursue happiness), and Article 14 (equal treatment under the law)'.

Duties of the Government, Lawyers and Bar Associations

Duties of the government The most significant point in the Report is a request to the government (virtually this is an acceptance of its own responsibility by the Ministry of Justice) to organize and operate appropriate legal aid entities with adequate funding.

The Report stated that 'the government is responsible for formulating and consolidating the legal aid system that constitutes an important part of the judicial system as well as for maintaining the proper management of the system. In Japan, legislation is required so as to establish a system that enables the government to take the initiative. An integrated management structure should also be created to provide equal and efficient services throughout the country. The government should be required to assume due financial responsibility and to properly supervise the legal aid body, taking on a nationwide point of view, so that legal aid services might be further improved and developed'.

Responsibility of lawyers and bar associations The JFBA and local bar associations as well as individual lawyers have been major players in and supporters of legal aid services with a small amount of government subsidy, which can be used only for the expenditures of rendering services, as opposed to operation costs. They contributed funds for the operation of JLAA. Many lawyers have been taking up legal aid cases at a low legal fee and have worked as a member of the operational and reviewing committee of the JLAA and its local branches at no charge.

The JFBA's position has been that the funds for both the cost for services and operational costs must be borne by the government, although the JFBA and lawyers are willing to render high quality services to legal aid clients at a reasonable level of fees. The Ministry of Justice strongly requested the cooperation and assistance by the JFBA and lawyers by providing personnel resources and facilities (such as office space) and funding (continuation of the contribution of funds by the JFBA and lawyers). The Report concluded that 'it goes without saying that the improvement of the legal aid system is the task of the government; however lawyers and bar associations are also expected to play an active role in the future as in the past, through participating in the operation of the legal aid system as their own duties, as well as providing legal services equally to Japanese people'.

Need for Legal Aid

Use of the judiciary system is relatively limited. People tend to use court procedures only in circumstances where there is no choice other than the judiciary system. This is reflected in the high percentage of cases handled by the JLAA in divorce and family matters (31 per cent) and consumer bankruptcy cases (43 per cent), where there seems to be no other choice to rescue them from a distressed situation.

The survey conducted by the Study Group revealed that it is estimated that in the past decades persons (who are among the approximately 17,140,000 people of legal age entitled to receive legal aid under the current system) involved in approximately 420,000 cases in total (42,000 cases per annum) were unable to receive legal aid services from lawyers although they needed it.

As the legal aid cases in *Fiscal 1997* amounted only to about 8,000, it is estimated that there are more than five times that number of cases needing but unable to receive legal aid in Japan.

The legal consultation service provides an important initial point of contact for people of limited means. Consultation services are being provided all over Japan by many local governments as free services to local residents (in some cases in cooperation with local bar associations) and by other institutions. Also local bar associations give free or low-cost consultation services together with lawyer referral services. However, for the purpose of appropriately referring needy people to legal aid services, consultation services operated by the JLAA are very important.

Problems in the Present Legal Aid System

The JLAA and the JFBA consider that the most serious obstacle for needy people to use legal aid is the reimbursement system, where all recipients, even people on welfare support, must repay all assisted costs in installments. They have long criticized such a system as simply a loan together with a referral service to inexpensive lawyers and such a system cannot be considered as true legal aid. In spite of such assertion, the Ministry of Justice, as it hopes to maintain the reimbursement system, refused to point out the reimbursement system as a problem under the present system. On this point the Report simply noted that some members pointed out a problem in the present reimbursement system where all recipients are required to repay all aided costs.

Lack of legislation Since no act concerning legal aid has yet been enacted, it is not clear what responsibility the government should take in the legal aid system. Also it is not laid out by law how lawyers and bar associations should perform their duties under the system.

Financial problems Although the amount of the government subsidy has recently been increasing, the scope of the services has not yet met the needs of the Japanese people. The management and operation costs entirely depend on funds from the JFBA, local bar associations, municipalities and non-governmental circles. Of the funds necessary for legal aid, the ratio of the government subsidy is smaller than that provided in overseas countries. Also the financial support from non-governmental circles is insufficient and unstable as a financial basis. These factors greatly limit the financial scale of the organization.

Organizational problem The system, operation and management of branches of the JLAA are not individually well-organized enough to respond to the people's needs. Its weak financial foundation makes it difficult to station a sufficient number of full-time staff members. The difference in the organization and/or financial ability of each bar association in which each branch is set up causes regional disparities in the system, the procedures used and the number of cases handled. Consequently aid services are not provided uniformly throughout the country.

Operational problems Legal aid services, such as legal consultation or negotiations for private settlement, serve to speed up the settlement of disputes as well as reduce the costs of the entire proceedings. However, these services are under-provided because only aid in litigation is emphasized under the current legal aid system.

Legal Services

There are many differences in the views of the Ministry of Justice, and of the JFBA and the JLAA as to legal services to be provided, in particular the kind of services to be provided, who can be recipients, costs to be borne by the recipients, the lawyers' fees, and the legal aid service body.

Kind of services to be provided The JFBA and the JLAA have been asserting that the new legal aid system consist of services for civil matters and criminal matters (for suspects before charge). However, the Ministry of Justice has been reluctant to discuss issues relating to criminal matters, because the criminal matters are out of the scope of business of a department which is historically in charge of civil legal aid, and the criminal matters have to be studied further by other departments in the Ministry of Justice to reach an agreement as to such need. Therefore, the Report only covered civil matters. The Report stated that any civil litigation in a broad sense shall be covered by legal aid. Included in civil litigation are provisional measures (such as provisional attachments and injunctions), enforcement, bankruptcy, domestic mediations and decision procedures, and administrative litigation as well as ordinary civil litigation.

The Report also emphasized the need for advice and instructions in litigation rather than representation in court, such as the provision of advice and assistance in and/or preparation of necessary documents to be submitted to the court. Also the Report recommended the use of such advice and instructions for small claims litigation. In small claims procedures, cost-effective legal aid services ought to be provided, such as advisory and instruction services, aid by staff lawyers, and service through contract bases where a particular lawyer intensively takes charge of cases under a contract with the legal aid body.

Pre-litigation aid promotes settlement before litigation and reduces total costs. Thus, the preparation of letters, negotiation representation and involvement in arbitration procedures are included in such pre-litigation aid. However, the Ministry of Justice refused the aid in administration procedures such as applications for labor accident compensation or immigration. Therefore the Report only noted that there are opinions which asserted the necessity to provide legal aid services in administration procedures where conflicts exist between applicants and the administration offices or in other cases where a lawyer's involvement is needed.

Coverage of recipients The coverage of recipients is one of the most seriously discussed points between the Ministry of Justice, and the JFBA and the JLAA. Present coverage is limited to people in the lowest 20 per cent income bracket. The income level of possible recipients is 1.3~1.7 times the level of income of those supported by welfare. The JFBA and the JLAA strongly demanded that coverage be expanded to encompass the lowest 40 per cent, which would include a part of middle income people. However, the Ministry of Justice's position is that access by middle income people can be realised by other means such as legal cost insurance (which however presently does not exist in Japan). Thus, the Report concluded that, although the current legal aid system covers those in the lowest 20 per cent income bracket, it does not sufficiently meet their needs. Therefore the system shall be organized and funding shall be improved in order to enhance the level of legal aid to these people. It is necessary to examine how coverage can be expanded in view of such factors as the understanding and desire of the public as well as the financial conditions of the government.

As to legal aid to non-Japanese people, the Report stated that services be rendered at least to non-Japanese who legally reside in Japan. To this limited position some objections were raised in the Report to the effect that legal aid should be given to non- Japanese people who legally entered Japan (but whose visas expired) and who were involved in workers' accidents or traffic accidents.

Requirements for entitlement to aid There are two tests applicable for qualification for legal aid. One is the means test which is discussed above in the section of coverage. The other is the merit test.

Presently the criterion is the possibility of winning the case. However, the Report states that the criterion be that 'it cannot be said that there is no possibility of winning the case'. Such a possibility of winning includes a possibility of settlement through compromise or mediation. The Report also requires suitability to legal aid. This includes various situations and such suitability is not satisfied where (1) the defendants are so poor that there is clearly no chance to recover through enforcement of the judgment, (2) the litigation would be an abuse of rights, or (3) a lawyer's involvement is not needed.

Financial burden of aid recipients On this point, there was a severe controversy between the Ministry of Justice and the JFBA and the JLAA. As mentioned above, the JFBA and the JLAA have long criticized the present reimbursement system, where all recipients, even people on welfare support, must repay all assisted costs, even in the case where their litigation or procedures result in no payments or damages payable to the recipients. They characterize the reimbursement system simply as a legal costs loan and without changing this reimbursement system to a non-reimbursement system, it is impossible to achieve an accessible legal aid system.

The Report concluded that the periods of grace for reimbursement and/or release from reimbursement under the current system are not being administered effectively. Thus, procedures must be improved so that these systems work properly and promptly.

The Report mentioned that the following two views have been expressed as to how much of the cost a recipient should bear: (a) basically free funds should be granted to the applicant with two conditions, namely that a recipient is required to bear some amount according to his or her means and that a recipient is required to reimburse the costs up to a certain amount when he or she has acquired any proprietary interest as a result of litigation; and (b) the current reimbursement system should be maintained as it is. Opinions were thus split as to the basic form of the system. However they all agreed that, in principle, an exception should be made for a person who is on welfare, namely that the person is not required to make reimbursement.

Methods of providing legal services Currently, legal services are provided by practicing lawyers only. The JLAA has employed no lawyers to render legal services, although some lawyers give services to legal aid clients referred by a branch of the JLAA on a monthly fixed remuneration basis paid by the JLAA.

The Report concluded that under the current legal aid system, practicing lawyers take up legal aid cases. On the basis of the same system, a system that allows as many lawyers as possible to be involved by utilizing the 'Lawyers Enrolment System', where the JLAA selects lawyers in charge for individual cases from the list of enrolled lawyers, and the 'Bring in' method, where practicing lawyers bring in a case to the JLAA for legal aid, shall continue to be used. It further concludes that the following methods can be considered to provide legal services: (a) Lawyers specializing in legal aid become staff lawyers of the legal aid body and assume aid cases (Staff System); and (b) Particular lawyers intensively take up legal aid cases on a contract basis with the legal aid body.

Attorneys' fees No specific standard was agreed by the Study Group and the Report concluded that the standard of attorneys' fees must reflect the opinions of three groups of people; people in need of aid, taxpayers, and lawyers and bar associations. Moreover, the standard should be clear and objective according to the types and content of services so as to assure the smooth operation of the legal aid system. While attorneys' fees should be appropriate for the public service nature of the lawyers' duties as well as be in line with the purport of legal aid, these fees should be maintained at the level that enables lawyers to provide sufficient and appropriate legal services, in order to further consolidate and develop the legal aid system. Details of the specific standard of attorneys' fees for legal aid, including the issues of whether to basically conform to the standard regulations of the Japan Federation of Bar Associations and whether to adopt a fixed fee system or a time charge system depending on the type of case, are subjects for future discussion.

Legal consultation The most significant and drastic proposal made by the Study Group is the Lawyer Enrollment System in connection with legal consultation and the acceptance of applications for legal aid services. Presently, legal consultation is rendered only at the branch offices of the JLAA, which in principle are only found in no more than one large city per prefecture, so that it is very difficult to access legal consultation as well as apply for legal aid. Under the proposed Lawyer Enrolment System, lawyers who have registered as an enrolled lawyer are required to render legal consultation services at their offices and upon the request of applicants, to take up their cases, or if they are not willing, to refer to the branch offices of the JLAA after completing the application form for legal aid. This means a drastic increase in access points to enrolled lawyers, from about one hundred to an expected several thousand.

The Report concluded that legal consultation should be conducted without charge. To ensure easier access to legal consultation, it is necessary not only to make it available at each branch of the legal aid body but also to set up a system to have lawyers enrolled at the management body ('Lawyer Enrolment System') to conduct legal consultation whenever necessary; these enrolled lawyers are obliged to make the system widely known by putting up a designation notice at their offices; an application for legal consultation is received at each branch as well as at each office of an enrolled lawyer; the lawyer conducts consultation for a person judged to meet the means requirement; and each branch examines the case after consultation upon receipt of an invoice for consultation fees from the lawyer.

Management Organization

Management body After a lengthy discussion, the proposed new legal aid body was a non-governmental corporation, such as the JLAA, which will be designated as the legal aid body by the government. As to such new body, the Report stated as follows:

> It is desirable to have a management body in the future that allows the government to take the initiative, in which lawyers and bar associations can actively participate and that is vitalized by non-governmental circles. The JLAA has historically conducted various aid services other than those related to civil affairs. From the viewpoint of management efficiency and finances, it is preferable that the management body have unified control over all legal aid businesses and legal aid services. For this purpose, a suitable form of management body may be a 'non-government corporation designated by the Ministry of Justice for the purpose of rendering legal aid services'.

The Report pointed out as follows:

> 'The organization is required to conduct business nationwide in an efficient and unified manner; it must properly and promptly respond to arising needs for legal aid; in order to provide legal aid services uniformly throughout the country, the businesses of each branch need to be conducted under the proper direction and supervision of the headquarters under uniform nationwide standards and procedures; also in order to respond exactly to the needs of each local area and realities of individual situations, each branch ought to be allowed a certain degree of independence and discretion; and it is necessary to have a practical number of full-time staff members stationed at each branch according to the amount of business the branch processes.

It is generally considered that the JLAA will be designated by the Ministry of Justice as the new legal aid body after making necessary reforms.

Finance Finally, the most important issue is how legal aid will be funded. The JFBA and the JLAA's original call for reform started as a demand to the government to greatly increase the government subsidy. The Report did not specifically mention the required size of the government subsidy for the new legal aid system. It simply pointed out that the government ought to assume a financial burden commensurate with its share of responsibility; it must financially support the business not only by increasing the amount of subsidy to the operation but also by bearing the administrative and operational costs of the organization; and lawyers and bar associations should take part in the management body by offering human and physical resources and also by bearing the administrative and operational costs within the limit of their financial ability.

Conclusion

There are many issues to be agreed among the relevant parties before the new legal aid body will be organized and the new services will be commenced. The Ministry of Justice and the JFBA and the JLAA are continuing discussions to solve the pending issues mentioned above and the new system is expected to be introduced at the latest by 2000 with cooperation by the Ministry of Justice, the JFBA and the JLAA and practicing lawyers.

4 Current Reform Efforts in Legal Education and the Delivery of Legal Service in Korea[1]

DAE-KYU YOON

From Sanctuary to Scrutiny

Kim Young-sam's inauguration in 1993, the first civilian government since the military coup of 1961, had a great impact on Korean society.[2] This paper will describe the events that transformed the Korean judicial system, focusing on the changes in the production of lawyers during the reform movement of Kim's government.

The judiciary in Korea has been very successful in remaining aloof and relatively insulated from the rapid changes taking place in other areas of society during the last few decades. It remains one of the most impenetrable domains, resisting change, let alone reform, in Korea. Although this results, in part, from the very conservative nature of judicial institutions anywhere in the world, there is a unique condition to explain the Korean peculiarities involved.[3]

As late as 1995, there was a series of 'meaningful' debates providing a driving force towards judicial reform. For the first time in Korea's half a century judicial history, the debates were successful in commanding broad public attention beyond the limited interest of the legal profession and related groups, and finally brought about significant change. Why had such debates not been successful before?

Korea has attracted a good deal of foreign attention, largely due to the country's rapid economic development and political democratization, and recently its financial crisis and subsequent IMF bail out. Until the 1980s, Korea's economic success was achieved with the assistance of past authoritarian regimes. Under the authoritarian rule, proposals which *could possibly* undermine political stability were discouraged. The judicial system was one area that was closely intertwined with political mechanism and had a direct bearing on political stability, so active discussion on its improvement was prevented in the authoritarian atmosphere. Even though there was a demand for changes in judicial institutions, for reasons such as the expansion of economic volume and activities, the government was reluctant to initiate such changes for fear of damaging the political *status quo*.[4] That is why a serious discussion on judicial reform could not take place before political democratization, despite the large number of previous discussions.

The new civilian government, launched in 1993, provided fertile ground for public debates concerning the reform of the old system which had been established, more or less, to expedite the exercise of public power. However, the judiciary did not respond to the changing atmosphere prevailing throughout society and made only minor procedural adjustments by its own initiative. It seemed to be very successful in ignoring public demands until the second round of reform movements initiated under the globalization policy in 1995 with the conclusion of the Uruguay Round and the subsequent WTO system.

After a series of changes were concluded under the previous government of Kim Young-sam, Korea reached another turning-point when political power was transferred to the opposition party, led by life-long dissident Kim Dae-jung. However, the IMF situation proved to be a much greater force than the change of political power in transforming Korean society. Even Kim Dae-jung's campaign platform was shadowed and modified by the urgency and magnitude of the IMF situation. Judicial reform could not be a high priority under these circumstances, nor could it command the attention of the public or political powers as did the economic crisis. On the contrary, such indifference allowed interest groups within the legal profession to implement reactionary measures while the general public remained obsessed with the economic turmoil.[5]

Peculiarities of the Korean Judicial System

The Unusually Small Size of the Legal Profession

The number of legal professionals in Korea is extremely small in proportion to the country's population, economic volume and number of legal disputes. In addition to practising lawyers, judges and prosecutors are also in short supply. As we will see in this chapter this is the main source of the many problems the

Korean judicial system suffers. The small size of the profession is as a result of the stringent quota applied to successful candidates in the bar examination which designates who shall receive licenses to practice law. Hence, judicial reform or a meaningful change in the judicial system cannot be discussed apart from the bar examination.

As of March 1995, the total number of legal professionals - that is, judges, prosecutors and practising lawyers - was only 6,256. That is, 1.27 per 10,000 people. This figure is very small in comparison with other major countries (See Table 4.1 and Table 4.2).

Table 4.1 Statistics of Legal Professionals by Countries

	Korea	Japan	U.S.A.	Germany	France
Total (year)	6,256 (1995)	18,500 (1992)	769,000 (1992)	84,000 (1992)	31,890 (1992)
Lawyers	1.27	1.52	31.3	11.5	4.28
Judges (year)	1,262 (1995)	2,823 (1990)	Federal 802 State 28,958 (1990)	17,627 (1989)	4,486 (1990)
Prosecutors (year)	989 (1995)	2,092 (1990)	Federal 4,294 State 20,826 (1990)	3,759 (1989)	1,529 (1990)
Practicing Attorneys	3,571* (1995)	14,173 (1990)	690,994 (1990)	54,107 (1989)	17,775 (1987)

*Those who currently do not practise are included (See Table 4.2).

Source: Kwon (1996).

Table 4.2 Statistics of Legal Professionals by Year

Year	Population	Those who Passed Bar Exam	Judge	Pros.	Atty[a]	Total	Pop. Per Legal Pro.
1971	32,139,000	81	387	350	748	1,485	21,642
1972	33,505,000	80	415	360	745	1,520	22,043
1973	34,103,000	60	438	372	785	1,595	21,400
1974	34,692,000	60	460	378	812	1,650	21,025
1975	35,281,000	59	477	398	809	1,684	20,950
1976	25,860,000	60	482	396	819	1,697	21,131
1977	36,436,000	80	496	424	811	1,731	21,049
1978	37,019,000	100	546	436	832	1,814	20,407
1979	37,354,000	120	502	446	890	1,838	20,323
1980	37,448,000	141	536	437	940	1,913	19,575
1981	38,693,000	289	571	409	1,013	1,933	19,414
1986	41,568,000	300	837	557	1,483	2,877	14,448
1991	43,268,000	287	1,187	827	2,258	4,272	10,221
1992	43,663,000	288	1,066	867	2,450	4,383	9,962
1993	44,056,000	288	1,103	907	2,634	4,644	9,487
1994	44,500,000	290	1,130	947	2,852	4,929	9,028
1995	45,093,000	308	1,374	947	3,078	5,399	8,352
1996	45,545,000	502	1,434	997	3,188	5,619	8,106
1997	45,991,000	604	1,494	1,047	3,364	5,905	7,788
1998	46,430,000	700	1,370[b]	1,097	3,521	5,988	7,754

a Those not practicing are excluded.
b This decrease was made due to the associate judge system.

The small size of the legal profession not only gives judges and prosecutors excessive work-loads, but also contributes to the provision of a very poor legal service to the public. For example, a district judge disposes of almost 5,000 cases a year, while a Justice of the Supreme Court disposes of more than 1,200 cases a year (See Table 4.3).[6] A prosecutor also handles more than 2,000 cases a year, which is an incredible burden (See Table 4.4).[7]

Table 4.3. Yearly Work-load (Number of Cases) per Judge

Year	Supreme Court		High Court		District Court	
	No. of Judges	Work-load	No. of Judges	Work-load	No. of Judges	Work-load
1963	8	315.5	50	133.7	242	4,806.4
1973	15	633.8	60	201.6	365	5,648.0
1983	13	769.0	101	332.3	500	4,773.5
1993	13	1,264.2	163	399.4	840	4,576.8
1996	14	1,123.3	162	218.1	874	5,001.1

Source: Judicial Yearbook, 1997.

Table 4.4 Work-load of Prosecutors in 1996

Total No. of Prosecutors	997
Total No. of Cases Handled By All Prosecutors	2,017,354
Monthly No. of Cases Handled By a Prosecutor	169

Source: Prosecution Yearbook, 1997.

The shortage of practicing lawyers has a direct impact on the citizens. According to the principle of supply and demand, legal fees are too expensive. Although the maximum limit for fees in criminal cases are set by the bar association, such limits are not binding. Thus, high limits often breach the allowed rate without sanction.[8]

As statistics show, high fees result in the low rate of retaining lawyers. As of 1993, lawyers were hired in 37.6 per cent of total civil cases, while the remaining 62.4 per cent of cases were represented by the concerned parties themselves. In particular, in small-sum civil suits of 10 million won or less (about US$7,000), 97.4 per cent proceeded without lawyers. In civil suits of 30 million won or less, which are handled by a single judge, 34.5 per cent did not have lawyers (Kwon, 1996; Table 4.1). In criminal processes, almost 44 per cent of the indicted cases of 1995 were handled without representation by lawyers.[9]

What makes access to legal services worse is the disparity in locality. More than 60 per cent of Korean lawyers practise in Seoul. Furthermore, almost 80 per cent are concentrated in Korea's five major cities (see Table 4.5). Lawyers are still few in number and geographically concentrated in a few areas, making it difficult for ordinary citizens to retain them in general legal matters.[10]

Table 4.5 Attorneys versus Population by Locality

(December 31, 1997)

Locality	Atty	(%)	Pop. (Thou.)	Pop. per Atty
Seoul[a]	2,044	(60.8)	10,389	5,083
Pusan[a]	217	(6.5)	3,865	17,811
Taegu[a]	166	(4.9)	2,502	15,072
Inch^n[a]	107	(3.2)	2,461	23,000
Kwangju[a]	98	(2.9)	1,326	13,530
Taej^n[a]	90	(2.7)	1,323	14,700
Ulsan[a]	36	(1.1)	1,013	28,139
Ky^nggi[b]	169	(5.0)	8,515	50,385
Kwangwon[b]	55	(1.6)	1,540	28,000
Chungbuk[b]	52	(1.6)	1,475	28,365
Chungnam[b]	50	(1.5)	1,903	38,060
Ch^npuk	71	(2.1)	2,007	28,268
Ch^nnam[b]	38	(1.1)	2,166	57,000
Ky^ngbuk	57	(1.7)	2,812	49,333
Ky^ngnam[b]	90	(2.7)	3,058	33,978
Cheju[b]	24	(0.7)	528	22,000
Total	3,364		46,885	13,937

[a] Major Cities [b] Provinces

The shortage of lawyers, by default, elevates their scarcity value and secures professional oligopoly. Because the oligopolistic structure is deep-rooted and vested interests have been fortified, lawyers' opposition to any increase in the number of professionals has naturally been intense. The profession, comfortable within this oligopolistic market structure, is not too concerned about the clients' position. In this regard, lawyers are inclined to exert more energy on developing human relationships rather than providing better services at a better price, through improving their expertise and specialties. It is quite natural that there is little differentiation in legal services according to specialties. The vast majority of lawyers practice as generalists, representing their clients in the courts as litigation (trial) lawyers, while only a few can be referred to as specialists in a particular field, such as the environment, taxation, labor, consumer protection, mergers and acquisitions, intellectual property, securities, maritime and international transactions. Generalist practices are a common phenomenon, occurring in oligopolistic markets that strictly restrain entry and hamper competition. The basic assumption of the market economy is that competition contributes to the public interest. The size of the Korean bar is too small and its entry barrier is too formidable to guarantee meaningful competition.

This small size of the legal profession is a direct consequence of the nature of the Korean bar examination. Before 1981, the bar examination was only conducted to recruit new judges and prosecutors, not to produce practicing attorneys directly. Attorneys joined private practices later in life, usually after retiring from public service.[11] Hence a substantial number of private attorneys are former judges and prosecutors. This pattern is precisely the reverse of what prevails in Britain and the United States. Thus, in Korea, the quota of the bar examination was determined according to the demand from the courts and prosecutors' office. In this sense, it is quite right that the 'bar' examination was called the 'judicial' examination in Korea. Under this system, it was quite natural that the size of the bar was small until the quota exceeded the number of vacancies for new judges and prosecutors to be filled.

Another aspect to be noticed was that this system inevitably produced old attorneys with conservative values. It was difficult to expect lawyers' *pro bono* involvement in public issues or their initiatives for social change. To see reform-minded young lawyers actively participate in public issues, we had to wait until the bar examination could systematically produce young private attorneys by increasing the quota of the examination. As a result of the 1981 increase in the examination quota, we have a substantial number of young attorneys with liberal perspectives who do not have experience and are not accustomed to the indulgences within the bureaucratic environment following a long period of public service in the courts or prosecutors' office.[12]

Judicial Cronyism

One distinction of the Korean legal profession is its unusual cohesiveness. Although judges, prosecutors and attorneys carry out respective roles in separate domains, they interact as one integrated group. As a result of the importance of human relationships in Korean society and the broad entertainment of a common background of their profession, they share a very strong sense of *esprit de corps*. To practice law, one is required to pass the bar examination and then finish a two-year course at the Judicial Research and Training Institute. This is the only way to become a lawyer. Most practicing lawyers, let alone judges and prosecutors, are alumni of this institute.[13] In addition, the vast majority of individuals in the profession are graduates of a small number of major law colleges such as Seoul National University or Korea University. Once assigned to respective branches upon graduation from the institute, they will find many opportunities to work together within the same office or branch, or to meet one another while conducting their business. Once a person is allowed to practice law, they will serve as a judge, prosecutor, or private attorney throughout their life. It is rare for a lawyer to quit the profession and engage in non-legal business in Korea. It is very likely that members of the profession will know one another in person or become acquainted through various associations. Korean culture places strong emphasis on human relationships and its relatively small geographic size contributes to expediting such acquaintances. Under these circumstances, it was quite natural for the profession to maintain a strong cohesiveness among members. Such cohesiveness developed *camaraderie* with a guild mentality. Their privileged position of being able to monopolize legal practices was utilized to promote and maintain their vested interests, instead of serving the public interest. Furthermore, as we will see, it went so far as to distort justice to the detriment of the public interest.

The situation is aggravated by the small size of the legal profession and its oligopolistic structure. The more there is at stake, the more cohesive their solidarity. They tend to defy any changes which undermine their vested interests. One typical example is their intense opposition to increases in the quota of the bar examination. The extraordinary cohesion among judges, prosecutors and practicing attorneys appears to be a major cause of judicial irregularities.[14]

The most collusive practice deriving from this unusual guild mentality is the so-called 'preferential treatment in favor of recently retired judges or prosecutors'. That is, after a judge or prosecutor quits office and practices law as a private attorney, they receive more favorable treatment from the court or prosecution in the judicial procedure or the verdict than other attorneys. Obtaining decisions in favor of their clients enables them to charge higher fees and earn more money within a short period.[15] This egregious practice is frequently seen in criminal procedures.[16] It has been accepted by legal professionals for a long time and justified on the grounds that pecuniary disadvantages during office should be compensated for a while when they practice law as a private attorney. This is obviously a flat denial of the just administration of the judicial system by the legal profession themselves. Although the Supreme Court devised some measure to abolish this practice, it remains and continues to cause public grievances.

This 'preferential treatment' practice has been alleviated to some degree in recent years. It is not because of the effort by judicial institutions to prevent it, but because of the increase in the bar examination quota, or rather structural changes. Until 1980, the bar examination was conducted to recruit new judges and prosecutors to fill vacancies that would occur through attrition. Successful candidates, with few exceptions, were appointed as judges or prosecutors after two year's internship at the Judicial Research and Training Institute. They would then start their careers as private attorneys after they quit these offices. Until the mid-1980s, it was quite natural for private attorneys to be much older than judges or prosecutors, since they would leave office only after a significant period in service. In 1981, the authorized number for successful candidates was increased to 300 a year. This was a substantial increase and sufficient to fill all vacancies. In reality, almost two-thirds of them had to practice law without having the opportunity to serve as a judge or prosecutor (Yoon, 1990, 228; Table 4.2). Before this increase in the quota, most attorneys were ex-judges or prosecutors. Under the increased quota, however, as the majority of the candidates in the bar examination were forced to practice law without experience in the court or prosecution and could not entertain such preferential treatment, they challenged this unfair practice that had been taken for granted in the profession for a long time. Before the increase in the quota, the *camaraderie* of the profession was more cohesive. The increased quota has undermined professional solidarity as a result of the ensuing competition. A typical example of cohesion between judges/prosecutors in office and practicing attorneys that undermines the fair administration of justice was recently made public through the disclosure of an irregular practice at a district court. It was found that many of the judges in this court regularly received money from attorneys under the guise of seasonal, vacational or farewell gifts. Some of these gifts amounted to several hundred dollars each time. In some cases, on-line bank accounts were used for the transfer of money. It proved that such cash gifts had been made on a regular basis. Some of them received up to one hundred thousand dollars, which the parties concerned contended were no more than loans. If we consider other possible pay-offs, for example, entertainment or golf sponsorship, the amount involved would be much higher. Among all 17 judges in this particular court, nine received disciplinary punishment that ranged from a warning to suspension from office. These nine judges resigned from the bench thereafter and will possibly start new careers as private attorneys.[17] For the remaining eight judges, the Supreme Court stated that appropriate measures would be taken, after further investigation. All 17 judges of the court were transferred to other courts. Never before, in Korean judicial history, have all the judges of a court been simultaneously transferred *in toto*.

Although issues of bribery were involved, none of the judges concerned faced criminal indictment by the prosecution. Other bureaucrats would certainly have been indicted or dismissed in similar cases.[18] This episode proved once again that judges and prosecutors cannot be prosecuted or penalized. The prosecution professed from the beginning that it would not initiate an investigation until the Supreme Court, the highest authority of the courts' administration, requested it to do so.[19] Predictably, the Supreme Court carried out a self-examination of the episode and found no serious legal violations. The authorities concerned, including the Supreme Court, agreed that receiving money was no more than a practice, not a bribe, though it did describe it as deplorable. The prosecution concluded the scandal by indicting one attorney on account of hiring brokers in retaining clients. The attorney concerned complained at the trial that it was unfair for him to be punished since the practice had been broadly accepted as routine among the profession throughout the country and pleaded that he was an unlucky scapegoat.[20] The Supreme Court denied that such practices can be found in other courts.[21]

The situation for prosecutors is worse than for judges. Korean prosecutors have great authority - well out of proportion to such positions in other societies (Yoon, 1990, 120). The duties of the prosecutorial office cover not only criminal investigation and indictment, but the execution of a sentence giving them comprehensive power over criminal justice. The prosecution exercises such authority with virtually full discretion, in particular, in investigation and indictment. Yet, there is no effective mechanism to restrain the arbitrary exercise of prosecutorial authority, though the parties concerned can file a petition to the ordinary court or the Constitutional Court under provided legal conditions.[22] These petitions have not proved effective and are easily ignored by the prosecution. On the other hand, all these circumstances contribute to the prosecution's vulnerability to political powers. The lawyer's role in this criminal process is therefore very important for the suspect or accused. It is critical for a lawyer to have a good relationship with the prosecutors. Cash gifts, entertainment or golf sponsorship may provide an effective means to maintain amicable relations. If a lawyer shares some ties with prosecutors based on a common school, region of origin, or the like, the relationship will work far more smoothly as mutual trust is reinforced. Lawyers take treating judges or prosecutors for granted whenever they have a chance to do so, while the latter regard it a matter of course to be treated by the former.

These practices and episodes symbolically display intimate relationships and collusion among the legal profession. These circumstances signify irregularities in the administration of justice. No judges or prosecutors have been indicted while holding office on account of bribery. Disciplinary punishment is all they receive. If they quit the office in disgrace, they can start new careers as practicing attorneys.

The automatic reaction to this kind of episode by the profession, including the Supreme Court, is to reduce the quota of the bar examination. They believe that increased competition among attorneys is responsible for such behavior. Public opinion, including legal scholars, on the contrary, supports an increased number of lawyers on the assumption that greater competition will contribute to a fairer administration and broader access to justice. The issue involved here is how to balance the interest of lawyers motivated by selfish individuals or commercialism, and the public interest for fair and quality legal service. Which system better serves the public's interest should be determined from the citizen's perspective. In this regard, excessively high entry barriers to the profession, which have protected their vested interest, need to be lowered.

The Lack of a Link between the Bar Examination and Legal Education

The 'legal profession' in Korea is set within narrow parameters. It signifies the triumvirate of judges, prosecutors and attorneys. That is, the legal professionals include only those who are allowed to practice law as judges, prosecutors or attorneys after success in the bar examination and the fulfilment of two years at the Judicial Research and Training Institute. Even if individuals engage in full-time law positions as law teachers, judicial scriveners, bureaucrats, or employees in the legal department of a company, they are not regarded as legal professionals if they have not passed the bar examination, and thus are not licensed to practice law.[23] The bar examination is virtually the only way to become a lawyer, since only successful candidates are allowed to attend the Judicial Research and Training Institute. The bar examination is, in effect, the entrance examination to the Institute.

Although the bar examination is the exclusive means to become a lawyer, no minimum qualification is required to apply for the examination. Candidates do not have to be law school graduates, college graduates or have any educational experience to apply for the examination. Therefore, the subjects candidates pursue in college, along with their grades, are totally irrelevant. Of course, the vast majority of successful candidates in the examination come from major law schools; however a significant number of non-law college students also apply for it.

The lack of a link between the bar examination and legal education has naturally paralyzed the formal legal education system. Since students preparing for the bar examination choose courses out of consideration for the bar examination, the subjects not covered in the examination hardly attract attention. Only basic subjects such as constitutional law, civil law, criminal law, commercial law and administrative law are tested in the main part of the examination. Other important subjects or new fields of law such as tax, labor, intellectual property, environment and international transactions are easily ignored and find problems in attracting students.[24] The bar examination largely tests ability to memorize legal doctrines or exegeses rather than analytic thinking or critical analysis on the ground of general legal rules or doctrines. As a result, institutional legal education is slighted.[25]

This absence of a linkage between the bar examination and institutional legal education has deprived legal education in universities of its precise goal. Legal education in universities has not been successful in training the legal profession nor in cultivating a liberal education with basic legal knowledge. This situation is much worse if we consider that legal education in Korea is conducted at an undergraduate level.

This system has a redeeming feature in the sense that the bar examination provides an equal opportunity to individuals, regardless of their formal educational background. However, due to the unusual prestige of the legal profession, an extraordinary number of students are preparing for the examination with little chance of passing due to the severe competition.

Many able young people often spend years preparing for the examination, losing the opportunity to explore other areas. While the bar examination quota was 300, it represented less than 4 per cent of total law college graduates per year. In 1994, almost 1.5 per cent of the total applicants passed the examination. The following tables eloquently display the competitiveness and difficulty involved in the Korean bar examination. Table 6 shows how small the quota was before 1981. In 32 years, the accumulated total number of people who passed the examination was no more than 1,902.[26]

Training for the legal profession is performed by the Judicial Research and Training Institute for successful candidates of the bar examination. The Institute is under the direct control of the Supreme Court and provides practical training for judges and prosecutors by senior judges and prosecutors.[27] All the attendants receive a stipend from the state for the two year training period. This training and treatment was justified before 1981 on the assumption that the bar examination was conducted to recruit judges and prosecutors. A successful trainee found no problem in being appointed a judge or prosecutor upon completion of their two year training. Judges or prosecutors would become private attorneys later in their careers, after retiring from public office.

The increase in the bar examination quota in 1981 transformed the nature of the examination: from an examination for recruiting judges or prosecutors to one that produces lawyers, that is, from a judicial examination to a *de facto* bar examination. Among the 300 successful candidates, two-thirds practice law as private attorneys upon completion of the Judicial Research and Training Institute training, while the remaining one-third are appointed judges or prosecutors. It is extremely rare for them to engage in other offices, in public agencies or business. In general, judges and prosecutors are preferred due to their incomparable prestige and power. However, liberal and independent young candidates prefer to work in private practices rather than in the hierarchical bureaucracy of judiciary or prosecution.

In spite of the transformation in the nature of the examination, the Judicial Research and Training Institute continues simply to provide training for judges and prosecutors, without emphasis on training for private practice. When compared to other professions, it is hard to justify the fact that the expense for training private attorneys and their stipend is financed by the state treasury.

Another problem is that the lack of linkage contributes to the separation of the legal profession from legal academics. There is no systematic mechanism to bridge the two professions and to activate their cooperation. As a result, educational institutes remain impractical ivory towers while the bar examination churns out legal technicians lacking a broad perspective or responsible ethics. Under these circumstances, it is quite natural to search for change.

Table 4.6. Bar Examination Statistics until 1980

Year	Applicants	Those Who Passed	Rate of Success(%)
1949	625	16	2.5
51	457	39	8.1
52	258	21	8.5
53	711	16	2.3
53	842	12	1.4
54	1,141	17	1.4
55	1,999	30	1.5
56	2,855	108	3.7
57	3,414	51	1.4
58	3,047	50	1.6
59	3,416	24	0.7
60	5,557	31	0.5
61	4,450	110	2.4
62	3,036	50	1.6
62	3,825	56	1.4
63	3,194	56	1.1
63	3,450	41	1.2
63	2,318	45	1.9
64	3,770	10	0.3
64	3,251	22	0.7
65	2,141	16	0.7
66	1,858	19	1.0
67	2,304	5	0.2
67	1,837	83	4.5
68	2,070	37	1.8
69	2,363	34	1.4
70	2,326	33	1.4
70	2,531	49	1.9
71	2,629	81	3.1
72	3,215	80	2.5
73	3,614	60	1.7
74	3,311	60	1.8
75	3,344	59	1.7

76	3,625	60	1.7
77	4,011	80	2.0
78	4,153	100	2.4
79	4,506	120	2.7
80	-	141	-
Total		1,902	

Table 4.7. Bar Examination Statistics Since 1981

Year	Applicants	Those Who Passed	Rate of Success(%)
1981	6,085	289	4.7
1983	8,450	300	3.5
1986	11,708	300	2.6
1990	14,365	298(12)[a]	2.07
1994	19.006	290(31)	1.52
1995	19,934	308(27)	1.54
1996	22,771	[b]502(36)	2.20
1997	20,442	604(49)	2.95
1998	20,739	700(App.)	3.38

a The numbers in parenthesis signify the number out of the total who were women.

b This increase was decided in 1995.

Process to Initiate Reform

There have been many discussions addressing the above-mentioned problems, but they have all failed to produce a successful outcome. It proved almost impossible to find concrete measures to overcome the legal profession's cohesive solidarity and the political influence of the upper echelons of Korean society. Public demands based on abstract interests were no more than echoless monologues, especially before the new civilian government was launched.

When the first civilian government was inaugurated in 1993, vigorous discussions on major sector reform were held and the authorities concerned were eager to adapt to the new environment. However, the judiciary was very reluctant to transform itself and did not take reform seriously until a few dozen young lawyers submitted a recommendation to the Supreme Court calling for judicial reform. The Chief Justice, who had been criticized for his reluctance to change and his actions under the previous regime, and for alleged speculation on real estate, finally resigned. The new Chief Justice, appointed by President Kim Young-sam, promised to launch a series of reform proposals and to improve the public's trust in the judiciary. In spite of several changes initiated by the Court, they amounted to no more than minor adjustments. These changes, limited to procedural matters, fell far short of the public's expectations. Once again, it demonstrated that self-reforms that undermine an institution's own interests are impossible until enforced by outsiders. In the beginning, the new political power seemed willing to take charge of this responsibility, but its willingness and commitment soon petered out. The political power found other sources in the international environment to recharge the drive for reform.

Subsequent reforms were implemented as a result of Korea's economic involvement in the globalized market system with the conclusion of the Uruguay Round (UR) talks and the start of the World Trade Organization (WTO) system at the end of 1994.

Upon the conclusion of the UR talks and the inauguration of the WTO system at the end of 1994, the government initiated a so-called 'globalization' policy. This was aimed at upgrading the standard of public administration to that of an international and developed society. For this purpose, the Globalization Promotion Committee was created under the Presidential Office. The committee selected strategic projects that needed reform. It was broadly accepted that the judicial system was ineffective in facilitating business activities as well as in enhancing citizens' rights, in keeping with the rapidly changing international environment. Thus, the government concluded that the unreasonable judicial system, including the bar examination, contributed to the degradation of the state's competitiveness in international competition by failing to provide a relevant and professional service to government and business, let alone a decent legal service to ordinary citizens. The committee listed the globalization of legal services and legal education among the 46 subjects which required reform to improve efficiency or to meet international standards. This momentum brought about an unprecedented debate on the judicial system. However, this debate was later stalled. Although the change did not live up to the citizens' expectations, the lively debates were successful in making the public aware of the seriousness of the problems residing in the country's legal system (Yoon, 1996, 171).

The committee started to prepare a plan for 'the globalization of legal services and legal education', the focus of the judicial reform. The Supreme

Court reacted by asserting that judicial reform should be carried out by the Supreme Court itself, since many of the reform proposals were concerned with its business. It also argued that the performance of the committee was against the principle of the separation of powers since the committee under the president, the head of the executive, would handle the judicial matters of the court.

The initiative for judicial reform came from the presidential office through the committee, because judicial reform by the judiciary itself was impossible due to the conflict of interests as seen in the past. In the beginning, the committee wanted to pursue the reform unilaterally on its own initiative with the support of the public, from the perspective of citizens and national interests. The committee could achieve most of its intended goals unilaterally without the cooperation of the courts and the legislature.[28]

For example, the legal basis for the bar examination is provided by presidential order, not legislative act. The authority in charge of the bar examination was the Minister of Government Affairs that belonged to the executive.[29] Theoretically, no problem arose in carrying out judicial reform by the executive. However, the committee accepted the demand of the Supreme Court and decided to proceed with the reform in tandem, believing that the cooperation and understanding of the judiciary is necessary for success, since the courts are directly involved with the delivery of legal services and are representing the interests of the legal profession.

The joint operation soon proved dysfunctional due to opposing views on various issues. Though both parties could reach agreement comparatively easily on matters that did not seriously conflict with the interests of lawyers, such as the improvement of irregular practices, there was serious confrontation over how to produce lawyers and on what number of lawyers is the optimum number per year, an issue that significantly affects the status of existing lawyers.

The next section describes the outcome of their joint operation.[30]

Major Points of Change

Aborted Trial to Transform the Legal Education System

The key point of the ideas concerning judicial reform by the Globalization Promotion Committee was to transform the legal education system and thus produce lawyers through 'education and training', not through 'selection by the examination'. Thus it wanted to improve the chronic lack of a linkage between legal education and the bar examination, and normalize institutional legal education.

What the committee had in mind was to adopt the so-called professional law school, similar to the American style of law schools, at a graduate level. The committee suggested that the requirements to enter the graduate law school not be limited to graduates of the law department but open to those of all four-year educational institutes. The new school would provide professional training for two or three years. After this, more than half of the graduates would be permitted to pass the bar examination. The size and number of the school would be determined in consideration of the demand for legal services. To create new law schools or to transform existing law colleges into the new model schools was a possible option. The total number of schools, it was thought, would be five to ten. Of course, the current law colleges or departments could coexist with the schools, and graduates of the former could apply for the latter, the same as graduates of other departments.

The significant change resides in the fact that the professional legal graduate school system would systematically produce a large number of lawyers. This was the concern most abhorred by the legal profession. They were totally unable to accept the idea. The Judicial Research and Training Institute of the Supreme Court, which now produces lawyers, would also have to be abolished or drastically changed. This would deny one of the important roles that the Supreme Court currently entertains. Opposition to the professional law school was not limited to the legal profession. The vast majority of law colleges or law departments which did not have good records for producing successful candidates in the bar examination, and would therefore have very little chance of obtaining the privilege of transforming themselves into professional schools, also disliked the committee's idea. Under the proposed system they would remain second level institutes for legal education or be degraded to institutes for liberal education under the dual system of professional law schools and ordinary law colleges.

Along with the American style of professional law schools, an extension of the education period of existing law colleges was also examined, but the committee and the Supreme Court failed to reach an agreement.[31] Although both parties agreed on the necessity of change in the legal education system, they failed to arrive at a concrete solution. Thereby, they created the so-called 'legal education committee', consisting of six members - three from both parties - for further study and discussion.

The new sub-committee carried out a series of discussions and debates to redress the problems of the current legal education system, but apart from confirming basic principles, they again failed to reach agreement on specific measures. Finally, it concluded that the issue of the legal education system should be excluded from the ongoing judicial reform agenda, and delegated the matter to the education reform committee, which was under the minister of education.

As a result, legal education reform, initiated in the beginning as a part of 'judicial' reform, was shifted to the area of 'educational' reform which will be discussed over time. Thus, the original plan of the Globalization Promotion Committee, to establish a systematic link between the legal education system and production of lawyers, was aborted. This means that the fundamental problems of the current system remain.[32]

The basic principles agreed upon by the legal education committee were as follows:

1) The diversity of the legal profession should be extended by providing those who have different academic backgrounds with the opportunity to become lawyers.
2) Expert lawyers who are capable of delivering legal services in specialized areas such as international transactions, patents, environmental issues and so on, should be increased to a significant size.
3) The selection of a legal profession system should be improved to normalize legal education in universities.
4) Basic liberal and legal education should be reinforced to produce a quality legal profession.
5) Practical training should be improved and diversified to produce capable legal professionals.

Nobody denies the necessity of the above principles. The committee worked hard to agree on these principles, but failed to form a link between legal education and production of lawyers. However, it was a great achievement that the reform drive successfully forced the legal profession to accept, though very reluctantly, the necessity of increasing the number of lawyers.

Increase of the Quota in the Bar Examination

Both the Globalization Promotion Committee and the Supreme Court were in agreement on the necessity of increasing the number of lawyers, that is, the quota of the bar examination. However, there was a significant difference in the size of increase that the two considered appropriate. The committee insisted that about 2,000 lawyers be produced each year, considering social demands on the legal service, while the Supreme Court maintained that an increase of more than 1,000 a year would be impossible, considering the capacity of the legal profession to accommodate such a number and the ability of the legal education institute to supply so many lawyers. In spite of many complications, they finally reached a compromise in April 1995.

What they agreed upon was as follows: While the framework of the current bar examination was to be maintained until 1996, the bar examination quota would be increased to 500 in 1996 and to 800 in 1999, that is, increased by 100 each year until 1999. After the year 2000, between 1,000 to 2,000 candidates would be selected through a new education system for lawyers. The concrete number of the quota would be decided by the so-called 'lawyers' production committee' consisting of officials and citizens.[33]

By this agreement, the bar examination selected 500 candidates in 1996 and 600 the following year.[34] Although the total quota is not so impressive, the rate of the increase is very significant. This increase in the bar examination quota represents the core of the changes conducted by the previous civilian government under the name of judicial reform and will contribute to the easing of chronic problems in the Korean legal system by encouraging fair competition among lawyers and the diversification of specialization.[35]

Changes in the Bar Examination

Though the structural reform failed, the aforementioned 'legal education committee' decided to improve the current bar examination within the existing framework in order to contribute to the normalization of legal education in universities. The subjects tested in the bar examination were adjusted to the curriculum of law departments in universities so the more serious students would be more successful in the examination. Unnecessary subjects were cut down to reduce the burden of applicants, while new specialized subjects such as tax, patent, international transactions and foreign languages were added in preliminary examination.[36] The questions tested would be improved to effectively measure the abilities of candidates in problem solving, comprehensive thinking and their general understanding of the issues at hand.

In addition, a limit on the number of times an individual may apply for the bar examination was imposed to prevent people from wasting too many years preparing for the examination. From 1997, an applicant could not take the examination more than four times.[37] The committee would examine, though it was not adopted at this time, whether to impose academic requirements on applicants in consideration of the improvement in legal education in universities.

Changes in the Judicial Research and Training Institute

The Judicial Research and Training Institute is the only official institute to produce lawyers. The role of the institute remains the training of judges and prosecutors, even though many lawyers have not had an opportunity to work in courts or prosecutorial offices since the 1981 increase in the bar examination quota, as explained in the previous section. As another significant increase in the bar examination quota was permitted in 1996, the vast majority of the candidates will practice law as private attorneys upon finishing at the institute. It was inevitable that the institute transform its role according to the new environment, from training judges and prosecutors to cultivating capable and flexible legal professionals in line with social needs.

The Supreme Court, the supervising authority of the institute, decided to reinforce its teaching on specialized areas by inviting specialists - including professors - to teach in addition to senior judges and prosecutors. The trainees at the institute will have expanded choices in exploring their fields of interest and can develop their specialties at an earlier stage. If necessary, trainees can receive education outside the institute, such as in universities or even abroad. This kind of open and flexible system will contribute to producing more open-minded and liberal lawyers than those trained within the bureaucratic atmosphere.

The appointment of judges and prosecutors that has been based exclusively on grades in the bar examination and in the institute, will also take into consideration extra-curricular activities, voluntary service and ethical standards.

The institute will eventually be transformed into a professional school with the adoption of a semester system, a grading system and the provision of a professional degree to trainees. This will, hopefully, contribute to bridging the gap between legal practitioners and academics while combining legal theory and practice.

Improvements in Courts Administration

The Supreme Court, the most conservative and passive institution concerning reform since the new civilian government was launched, carried out a series of improvements in its administration, in response to internal and external demand.

The direction of the change was to accommodate citizens' needs by providing broader access to the judicial system and improving irregular and inefficient practices. Public demand for the change was reinforced by the transfer of political power from the authoritarian regime to a civilian democratic government.

At first, the Supreme Court's changes were restricted to procedural matters, leaving aside structural changes that might undermine the judges' authorities and other vested interests. Eventually, it was unable to avoid adopting measures at the expense of the judges' vested interests. As we have seen above, the increase in the bar examination quota or the increase of judges would have been impossible without the concession of the Supreme Court.

The first round of changes was restricted to improving the performance of the courts' work-load by creating special courts and upgrading the judges' qualifications.

For example, in order to reduce the work-load of the Supreme Court, the Court was given the discretion to decide whether to review.[38] This is the adoption of a kind of *certiorari* system practiced by the American Supreme Court. The Patent Court and the Administrative Court was created in 1998.[39] The qualifications for a judge have been reinforced since 1997 by appointment, after the completion of two years, as an *associate-judge*. In order to be appointed as a judge to a single-judge court, more than seven years of professional experience are now required.[40] More branch courts will be created in local areas to make access to the courts easier and faster. All of these measures were concluded by revising relevant statutes such as the Court Organization Act (Yoon, 1996, 181).

The Supreme Court has also announced a second reform alongside the enactment of the Charter for Judges' Ethics. Its key points are to increase the number of judges by 50 per cent over the next ten years, to appoint some judges from among practicing attorneys and to improve the frequent transfer system in order to secure the stable performance of the judges without interference from outside influences.

Again, the Supreme Court has produced some measures to improve lingering problems. Special scrutiny will be given to prevent preferential treatment accorded to newly practicing ex-judges or ex-prosecutors.[41] Attorneys' legal fees are to be determined with the participation of citizens and the unrestrained contingency fee will be prohibited in criminal cases.

A great number of minor changes in judicial administration have taken place since the civilian government was inaugurated.

The Meaning of Changes

The key point of the changes taking place under the last civilian government has been the increase in the number of lawyers through the increased quota for the bar examination. This increase will contribute to coping effectively with the demand from public agencies and business, as well as ordinary citizens. Reinforced competition among practicing attorneys will help reduce legal fees and promote transparency in legal services, and also encourage the diversification and specialization of the profession. Many young lawyers want to develop their own specialties in order to overcome increased competition by engaging in specialized experience or going abroad to pursue advanced study in a specific field. Another desirable outcome is the significant increase in lawyers interested in *pro bono* activities.[42] Furthermore, the increased quota in the bar examination will help the courts and prosecution fill shortages, enhancing fair investigations and trials.

These phenomena will upgrade the quality of legal services and contribute to the strengthening of meeting citizens' interests and the state's capacity in international competitiveness.

In spite of these benefits, the increase in the quota has resulted in the further paralysis of institutional education by failing to link it with legal education in universities. Since the license to practice law as a judge, prosecutor or lawyer is one of the most preferred positions for the young, the increase in the quota in the bar examination has contributed to an increased number of youngsters preparing for the examination. The majors of those preparing for the examination are not limited to law or related areas, but extend to liberal arts and even natural sciences. The bar examination, that used to retard education in law departments, now retards the education of the entire university since the sharp increase in the quota in 1995. The toll that society has to pay for producing lawyers has increased significantly due to the lack of a linkage between the bar examination and the legal education system.

All attempts to redress judicial problems still fall far short of meeting the public's expectations. Continuous changes or adjustments are required to overcome them and keep abreast of social changes. New solutions or compromises will be achieved by striking a balance between public interests at large and the vested interests of the legal profession. How to reflect the unqualified public interest by mitigating the keen interest of such a cohesive group depends on the capability of society in general and politics in particular.

It should be noted that the judicial reform undertaken under the last civilian government, though far short of the intended plan and the public's expectations, was the first trial to bring about a fundamental change in the Korean judicial structure. All the changes brought on by the reform movement were initiated or accelerated as a direct result of the inauguration of the civilian government, reflecting and enhancing the citizens' perspective.

In this regard, the Korean experience once again has proved that a vested interest group will not change unless forced to do so and that the judicial system is a direct reflection of the political system.

Notes

1 An earlier version of this chapter was prepared for the conference held in Bangkok between June 21-23, 1998, under the title of 'Providing Legal Service for Under effectively Represented Groups in East and Southeast Asia - Creating a Forum for Dialogue'.

2 However, this first civilian government did not represent a change in political power but the transfer of political power from the ex-military president to a civilian president in the same political party. On the grounds of this civilian rule, political power was finally transferred from the ruling party to the opposition party in the December 1997 presidential elections won by Kim Dae-jung.

3 It should be noted that, in comparison to other areas, the Japanese influence on the Korean judicial system cannot be overemphasized since the Korean judicial system imposed by Japanese colonial authorities has remained strongly influenced by the Japanese system even after liberation in 1945. The Japanese influence on the Korean judicial system is firmly entrenched and any departure from the Japanese version has been strongly resisted. The Japanese judicial system has been, in reality, the reference point for the Korean judicial system. To find an alternative to the Japanese system has thus been another burden for Korea to overcome. See Yoon, 1996, 175.

4 For example, the active involvement of young lawyers in political issues in the late 1980s was a direct outcome of the increased quota of the bar examinations, exceeding the number to fill the vacancies for new judges and prosecutors. Almost two-thirds of the successful candidates in the bar examination had to practice law as private lawyers without serving in bureaucratic agencies as judges or prosecutors. Thus these young lawyers were independent and liberal working in an environment that produced quite a few reform-minded lawyers. See Yoon, 1990.

5 Contrary to its platform during the campaign, the new government of Kim Dae-jung announced the possibility of decreasing the quota of the bar examination to mitigate competition among practicing attorneys. In tune with this announcement, the bar association suggested that the quota of four to five hundred a year be appropriate. *The Hankyoreh* (Newspaper), January 20, 1998. These comments were to abolish the agreement already made under the Kim Young-sam government as described in this paper, for the sake of the legal profession at the expense of the citizens.

6 The heavy work-load of Korean judges also results partly from the monopolistic performance of judges on the dispute resolution process, without allowing for the participation of alternative personnel such as in the magistrate system or other alternative devices. It is still a natural law and a constitutional principle in Korea that a judge should decide a case regardless of its nature or weight. See the Korean Constitution (1987), art. 27 (1).

7 The burden on prosecutors is greatly exacerbated in consideration of their broad authority in the investigation process supervising police. See Yoon, 1990, 123.

8 The basis for a criminal case set by the bar association is no more than 10 million won in total, respectively no more than 5 million won for the initiation fee and no more than 5 million won for the success fee (US $1.00 = 1,400 won, May 1998).

9 The Hankyoreh, May 31, 1996.

10 Quasi-legal professionals such as judicial scriveners, to some extent, contribute to alleviating the scarcity of lawyers in Korea. See Yoon, 1990, 131.

11 For example, in 1980 the average age of private attorneys was 58.3.

12 As matter of fact, before the increase in lawyers, with the 1981 change in the bar examination, voluntary legal aid by the bar or publicly-funded legal aid was very limited due to the lack of lawyers interested in *pro bono* work, though the Korean Legal Aid Corporation, the only government funded official legal aid agency, created in 1987, still has a serious problem in recruiting lawyers. Legal representation provided by the Criminal Procedure Code (art. 33) was almost all that was available to citizens in need. See also Yoon, 1990, 112 and 126.

13 Separate from the bar examination, the military bar examination which produces military advocates is conducted regularly. If a successful candidate serves as a military advocate for a minimum of ten years, he will be allowed to practice law. Thus ex-military advocates can practice law without proceeding through the institute. See *ibid*, 117.

14 Concerning the question of what should be the top priority for the judicial reform, 34.4 per cent of those questioned answered that it should be to abolish adhesive relationships among judges, prosecutors and private attorneys, while 31.8 per cent said that their irregularities should be strictly dealt with. *The Hankyoreh*, Feb. 27, 1998.

15 This preferential treatment usually continues for about two years.

16 *The Chosun Ilbo* (Daily Newspaper) *March* 5, 1995; *The Dong-A Ilbo* (Daily Newspaper), February 27, 1995.

17 *The Hankyoreh*, February 20, 1998. As matter of fact, it was the first time in Korean judicial history for a judge in office to receive disciplinary punishment. In this regard, we can understand how plain and systematic the irregularities involved were. In many similar cases, the heaviest punishment incurred by judges or prosecutors was a request for their resignation.

18 There is a strong tendency to apply more lenient punishment to officials in Korea. Bureaucrats have always enjoyed many privileges and perks beyond the law. In reality, however, the law provides that an extra penalty be added to an offender who is an official. This is ignored on the grounds that their devotion to society and the state should be considered. This anachronistic notion of discriminatory treatment between officials and common people still remains. See Yoon, 1990, 61-63.

19 In the same district, prosecutors were also proved to have received money from attorneys. Two prosecutors in the same district prosecution office received disciplinary punishment.

20 Contrary to public expectation and prosecutors' efforts, as recently as June 16 this year, the court in charge of this case adopted a narrow interpretation of the relevant statute (the Lawyers Act, art. 27) and found the individual concerned not guilty of employing brokers. This decision will shrink efforts to clean up irregularities in the legal profession. This is additional evidence confirming the existence of collusive relations within the profession. See *The Kukmin Daily*, June 17, 1998.

21 As this incident broke out, the bar association conducted a self-examination and recognized more than a dozen lawyers who had hired brokers so extensively as to retain 2-300 criminal cases a year. Most of them were ex-judges and ex-prosecutors. However, the association did not request an investigation of the prosecution but concluded its self-investigation by imposing disciplinary punishment by the association. Nor did the prosecution go further on account that there was no request from the association, even though it could initiate, *ex officio*, investigation and indictment. Along with so-called 'preferential treatment', hiring brokers is also a serious irregularity in judicial practice in Korea. In fact, both practices are closely intertwined. Most judicial brokers are current or former policemen, or clerks of courts or prosecutors. When brokers introduce clients to lawyers, they are paid almost 30 per cent of the legal fees by lawyers. It is known that a substantial number of criminal cases are retained through brokers in Korea. More than half of all lawyers are presumed to hire brokers on a regular basis. See *The Hankyoreh*, December 6, 1997. Surprisingly big law firms with international reputations are known to pay discreet rebates to appropriate corporate executives in order to retain corporate clients or large cases like mergers and acquisitions. *Maeil Business Newspaper*, October 29, 1998.

22 See Criminal Procedure Code, arts. 260-265; Constitutional Court Act, art. 68 (1).

23 The bar examination is generally considered the most difficult examination in Korea due to the severity of the competition. This contributes to enhancing the *esprit de corps* of the profession and their elitism.

24 As a result, scholars who major in these peripheral subjects have much more difficulty in finding a tenured position in a law department.

25 For the details of legal education in Korea, see West, 1991.

26 The total number of private attorneys in 1980 was a meagre 1,000 for a population of more than 38 million.

27 However, prosecutors belong to the Ministry of Justice, an executive department. See Yoon, 1990, 122.

28 When legislative cooperation is required for new laws or revision, the legislature has often proved to be a major obstacle when the bill concerned affects lawyers' interests. The Judicial Committee of National Congress,

which has the authority of initial review, consists of congressmen most of whom have a license to practice law.

29 The latest administrative reform of early 1998 under Kim Dae-jung's government abolished this ministry and reverted its authority to the newly created Ministry of Government Administration and Home Affairs.

30 Before the Globalization Promotion Committee was inaugurated, the Supreme Court announced several measures to improve judicial administration.

31 Another reason for the failure to create a professional law school lay in the conflicting position between the Supreme Court and the Ministry of Justice on the supervisory authority of the school. The Ministry of Justice insisted on its jurisdiction over the school, since legal education is the responsibility of the executive. It is not surprising for the ministry to have sought control of the production of lawyers, even amid future-oriented reform processes, considering that the keenest interest of bureaucracy is always the expansion of its organization. *The Hankyoreh*, September 12, 1995.

32 Very recently, the Ministry of Education of the current Kim Dae-jung government expressed its plan to pursue again this aborted legal education reform. *The Hankook Ilbo* (Daily Newspaper), November 5, 1998.

33 The increase in the quota contributed to the advance of women lawyers. Since 1981, almost 10 per cent of successful candidates have been female. See Table 4.7.

34 See Table 4.2 and Table 4.7.

35 The bar association decided to allow attorneys to advertise their services as of July 1, 1998. This is also a result of the increased number of attorneys.

36 The bar examination consists of two tiers of examinations. The first level examination is tested by multiple choice in many legal and non-legal subjects including languages. Among these, the applicants can select various subjects depending on their interests. The second level or main examination is tested in an essay style and consists of major legal subjects: constitutional law, administrative law, commercial law, civil law, civil procedural law, criminal law and criminal procedural law. Ethics was dropped from the subjects of the main examination as of 1997.

37 All the changes were made through revision to the Presidential Order on the Judicial Examination in August 31, 1997 by Presidential Order No. 15144.

38 For the work-load of Korean judges, see Table 4.3.

39 According to this proposal, the two courts were inaugurated in March 1998.

40 The law at the time did not require single judges to have experience before being appointed.

41 The incident introduced in the second section took place after this measure. Preferential treatment is hard to eradicate. One device to overcome the preferential treatment is to place restrictions on lawyers from practicing law where they have previously served as judges or prosecutors. Though this device is now under consideration, it was decided unconstitutional by the Constitutional Court on November 20, 1991.

42 The Korean Legal Aid Corporation has been mandated to employ a total of 115 lawyers. As of October 1998, it employed only 23 practicing lawyers representing a severe shortfall of 92 lawyers. The Corporation could secure public advocates from graduates of the Judicial Research and Training Institute who would otherwise have to serve their compulsory military service. Though not voluntary, this would make up for the lack of applicants.

References

Kwon, O. (1996), *Judicial Work is Also a Service: On Judicial Reform,* Mirae-Media, Seoul, 31.

West, J. (1991), *Education of the Legal Profession in Korea,* International Legal Studies, Korea University, Seoul.

Yoon, Dae-Kyu. (1996), 'Recent Judicial Reform on Access to Justice in South Korea', *Yearbook: Law and Legal Practice in East Asia,* vol. 2, 175.

Yoon, Dae-Kyu. (1990), *Law and Political Authority in South Korea,* Westview Press, Boulder.

5 Legal Aid in the People's Republic of China: Past, present and future

WEIDONG JI

Introduction

Since the 14th National Courts Working Conference in 1988, trial procedure reforms in the Chinese courts have been aimed at shifting the burden of proof to the parties, and requiring the parties to prove the authenticity and legality of their allegations. In 1992, the legal services market surfaced and the Ministry of Justice began to consider law firms as part of the third industry.[1] Because of the comparatively small size of the Chinese bar, demand now exceeds supply, and privatized attorneys are occupied with remunerative work. These emerging changes have created a competitive market, causing lawyers to charge high hourly rates.

At the same time, the poor-rich polarization has appeared in Chinese society. Incomes are becoming increasingly unequal and regional disparities are quite evident.[2] Some people can well afford expensive legal services, but other people cannot. According to rough statistics, there are about 18,500,000 urban poor and 70,000,000 poor peasants currently residing in China.[3] Therefore, a serious task is presented to judicial organs and lawyers, who must prevent legal disparity by providing indigent members of society access to the justice system. Although private prosecution and *pro domo sua* have eased the need for representation by lawyers, it is already clear that the current system cannot supply sufficient legal services, especially to the poor. The legal aid system, one of the methods for providing necessary legal service, has been highlighted as the major objective of the justice administrative authority in the period of 1996-2010.[4]

This paper will sketch the history and the current situation of legal aid in China, and will analyze some basic features of the system, as well as different programs and relevant regulations. Finally, new trends of the reform will be discussed.

Two Different Approaches of Legal Aid in Modern China

The Private-Bar-Centered Approach

Modern legal practitioners and bar associations began appearing in the Republic of China in 1912. The first rules governing lawyers, 'Provisional Regulations on Lawyers',[5] were promulgated in the same year. Twelve years later, the first legal aid organization, 'Shanghai Lawyers' Society for Legal Assistance', was set up by dozens of practitioners in Shanghai on 20 April, 1924. This gave an impetus to other local bar associations.[6] In 1928, the Shanghai Bar Association organized a special agency which provided legal services without compensation to labor unions and workers. In 1934, private attorneys heeded the suggestion of influential members of a National Bar Association committee and set up a national system to provide legal aid to the poor. Many local bar associations established similar organizations.[7]

Based on the legal aid practice of the private bar, the Ministry of Justice of the Republic of China promulgated 'Measures for the Implementation of the Legal Aid for the Populace Provided by the Bar Association' on 20 September, 1940. This decree provided that clients can get free legal aid if they cannot afford the lawyer's fee. In some cases, the client is required to submit a certificate given to him by more than two neighbors or the head of his *baojia* (a network of social control, self policing and mutual aid based on neighboring households). The on-duty member of the bar association board of directors consults other lawyers and immediately assigns the case to lawyers who take turns at providing legal aid. When dealing with civil cases without compensation, the lawyer may try mediation. The entire cost for the legal representation is borne by the bar association. Lawyers must report the content of legal aid to their bar associations monthly. In turn, bar associations must submit a summary to the Ministry of Justice.

Because of the functional disorder in the private bar legal aid system, a government-financed program of assigning public counsel for legal aid in the High Courts has been required since 1935. However, this requirement was not accepted until June of 1945 when the Ministry of Justice promulgated the 'Service Rules of Public Counsels'.[8]

The Ultra-Governmental Approach

In 1949, the Communist Party of China seized state power and began to build a new legal order. The Ministry of Justice of the Central People's Government ran a pilot scheme of 'People's Lawyers' in some cities from July 1954 to July 1957. Under the authority of Article 7 of 'The Organic Law of the People's Courts of the People's Republic of China' adopted in 1954, courts began appointing defenders for defendants requiring counsel. New methods of reducing or remitting the cost of legal services for those who could not afford it were provided by the 'Interim Measures for Lawyers' Charge' in 1956, although attorney's fees in the People's Republic of China were very low then and remained low for a long period.[9] See Table 5.1.

Table 5.1 The Criteria for Lawyers' Charges (for each task)

Items	1981 Criteria	1990 Criteria
Giving Legal Advice:		
(1) non-property problems	RMB¥ 0.5-3	RMB¥ 1-5
(2) property problems	RMB¥ 2-5	RMB¥ 2-10
(3) business problem	RMB¥ 3-10	RMB¥ 10-30
Drafting Documents:		
(1) common legal matters	RMB¥ 0.5-3	RMB¥ 2-10
(2) plaints	RMB¥ 2-5	RMB¥ 10-30
(3) property legal documents	RMB¥ 5-10	RMB¥ 10-30
(4) contracts	RMB¥ 5-30	RMB¥ 10-50
Criminal Trial:		
(1) first instance only	RMB¥ 10-30	RMB¥ 30-150
(2) second instance only	RMB¥ 10-30	RMB¥ 30-150
(3) first and second instances	RMB¥ 10-20	RMB¥ 30-50
Civil Trial:		
(1) non-property cases	RMB¥ 10-30	RMB¥ 70-15
(2) service charge for property	RMB¥ 10-30	RMB¥100-200
(3) amount of property in controversy		
less than RMB¥ 5,000	free of charge	free of charge
RMB¥ 5,000-10,000	free of charge	+3%
RMB¥ 10,001-100,000	+2-3%	+1.5%

RMB¥ 100,001-1,000,000	+1-0.5%	+1%
RMB¥ 1,000,001-10,000,000	+0.5-0.2%	+0.5%
RMB¥ 10,000,000 and up	+0.2-0.1%	+0.5%
Others	nonentity	omitted here

In fact, except for a token filing fee and possible attorney's fees, the expenses of litigation, including the cost of investigation and testimony, were covered by the state. Therefore, the personal monetary burden was not an obstacle to access to the courts.[10]

We may even say that the whole system of justice, including the role of 'state legal workers',[11] is just a government-financed legal aid program. It means that the government buys all of the legal services and then provides them to the people for free or at a minimal price. In the socialist legal discourse, the typical exposition concerning the basis for compensation for lawyers providing legal service to the common people is as follows:

> In capitalist countries, with the exception of some lawyers with progressive ideas in the minority, most legal practitioners supply their service independent of pay. Their principle is to do work for those who can afford it. It is very difficult for laboring people to get help from attorneys . . . The lawyers in our country are state legal workers . . . the relationship between a lawyer and his client is not wage labor.[12]

The logic here is that once the state monopoly for the marketing of legal services is set up, lawyers become free from business pressures and justice can be accessed equally. As a result of state-financed legal services, the principle of partisanship to the clients must be transformed into the opposite principle of loyalty to the state and to the legal system. However, the remaining problems are whether attorneys will do their best for their clients in any given case, and how a lawyer can keep his independence from the state and those who have political power. In fact, there have been some severe criticisms from the government authorities in the 1950s,[13] of lawyers who 'depart[ed] from the correct stand to defend evildoers' and, from the common people in the 1980s,[14] of those who 'yield[ed] to pressure from the state power'. The development of events has shown that if lawyers lose their partisanship, they will naturally lose their professional position in society. Additionally, the proportion of judicial spending in the government budget and financial burdens will inevitably impose some restrictions on the development of legal service.

In spite of the above-mentioned problems, we can still find the interesting phenomenon of an invisible legal aid system and some functional legal aid programs. For example, the 'Civil Procedure Law of the People's Republic of China' adopted in 1991, stipulates that '[O]rgans, social organizations, enterprises and institutions may support the injured units or individuals to file a suit with the People's Court against acts that have damaged the civil rights or interests of the state, collectives or individuals' (Article 15). This principle of public intervention in civil disputes may provide legal aid to weak parties in varying degrees. There are also three dispute resolution networks which have played an important role as the functional substitutes of a structured legal aid system.

The network of people's mediation committees (PMCs) This is widely known as the most popular alternative and as an informal means to resolve disputes in modern China.[15] During the period of 1978-88, PMCs mediated approximately eight times as many civil disputes as were accepted for hearing by the formal courts. The proportion of disputes resolved by PMCs has decreased relatively each year in the 1990s because of the concurrent increase in cases filed in the first instance with the civil division of courts. Nonetheless, PMCs still mediate an average of seven million disputes per year. This number is two to three times the number of civil cases in the first instance every year. See Table 5.2.

Table 5.2 The Structure of Civil Dispute Resolution Alternatives (1986-1996)

Items Year	Disputes by PMCs	Civil Cases in 1st Instance	Different Settlements of Civil Cases in 1st Instance Judicial Mediation	Judgment	Ruling	Removal	Dismissal
1986	7,307,049	978,990					
1987	6,966,053	1,196,494					
1988	7,255,199	1,419,056(100%)	1,017,829(71.7%)	213,664(15.1%)	10,725	17,173	151,025
1989	7,341,030	1,808,538(100%)	1,253,895(69.3%)	297,999(16.5%)			
1990	7,409,222	1,849,728(100%)	1,194,350(64.6%)	353,940(19.1%)			
1991	7,125,524	1,910,013(100%)	1,128,465(59.1%)	456,000(23.9%)			
1992	6,173,209	1,948,949(100%)	1,136,970(58.3%)	460,932(23.7%)			
1993	6,222,958	2,091,651(100%)	1,224,060(58.5%)	487,005(23.3%)	367,222	13,364	

1994	6,123,729	2,382,174(100%)	1,392,114(58.4%)	547,878(23.0%)	429,895	12,287
1995	6,028,481	2,714,665(100%)	1,544,258(56.9%)	658,187(24.2%)	498,636	13,584
1996	5,802,230	3,093,995(100%)	1,672,892(54.1%)	815,741(26.4%)	579,320	16,511

Note: The blank space is unknown.
The number of rulings is included.
Source: *Zhongguo Falu Nianjian* (Yearbook of Chinese Law) 1987-97.

PMCs are forbidden from charging parties for dispute resolution. The remuneration or subsidies for people's mediators are paid from rural local funds or by local governments.[16] Considering the scale of disputes resolved by PMCs, we can say that government-financed or society-shouldered people's mediation has indeed played an important role in access to justice for the common people in contemporary China.

The network of letters and visits reception offices (LVROs) Because the Chinese government prefers an informal style in response to social needs at almost every level, the LVROs have been performing problem solving and providing legal services to a certain degree since 1951.[17] In the 1980s, China began to reconsider the relative merits of LVROs.[18] However, the Central Commission for Inspecting Discipline has emphasized the importance of LVROs.[19] In the judicial system, LVROs have played a very important role in dealing with criminal cases and reversing unjust or wrong verdicts. LVROs are progressively being channelled into the appellate courts to handle claims against legally effective judgments or orders and into the procedure for trial supervision.[20] According to judicial statistics provided in the *Yearbook of Chinese Law*, the people's courts at all levels are currently handling about 2,000,000 letters and 4,500,000 visits every year, besides filing 70,000 appeals cases through the procedure for trial supervision. LVROs and the procedure for trial supervision are so easy to access that people even overstate the cheapness of this legal service, saying that it is possible to get help with an ordinary postage stamp. Paradoxically, however, it is the inexpensiveness of mobilizing LVROs that leads to the new problem of too much access, not enough effect.

The network of township-level legal service offices (TLSOs) Arising in 1981 as experiments, TLSOs have developed into an important legal institution since 1987 when the Ministry of Justice issued 'Interim Provisions Concerning Legal

Service Office at Township Level'. There are now more than 35,000 offices and the number of practitioners who are quasi-attorneys with the title of 'Township Legal Worker' in TLSOs has amounted to more than 110,000 (Figure 5.1). Table 5.3 examines the legal services provided by TLSOs. Although the services provided by TLSOs are not free, the standard charge must be lower than attorneys' fees would be.[21] It is possible to demand the reduction or reimbursement of legal expenses for the indigent or litigants who are incapable of litigant action.[22]

Figure 5.1 The Development of TLSOs

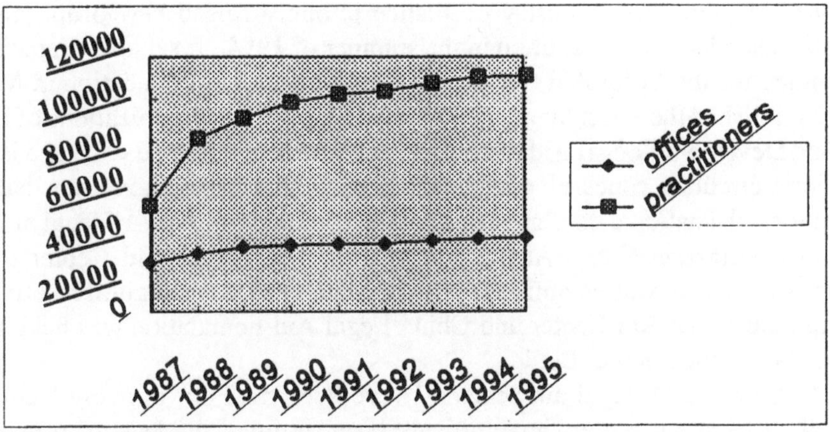

Source: *Zhongguo Falu Nianjian* (Yearbook of Chinese Law) 1987-96.

Table 5.3 The Changes in Legal Services of TLSOs by Type of Job

Items Year	Mediating Disputes	Notarization Assistance	Counsel of Civil Lawsuits	Civil Agency	Legal Advice	Drafting Documents
1987	905,793	855,429	31,759	56,836	4,592,208	248,403
1988	1,224,600	1,366,200	70,500	129,400	23,619,300	481,300
1989	1,419,200	1,769,200	120,500	243,100	4,092,300	614,000
1990	1,300,700	2,554,900	163,500	334,200	4,335,000	710,200
1991	1,295,200	5,450,200	202,300	613,500	4,834,200	861,400
1992	1,144,500	3,828,300	236,600	906,700	5,142,500	865,700

1993	1,167,300	2,834,000	263,800	735,200	5,046,700	1,320,700
1994	1,169,300	2,309,800	322,600	926,300	5,143,200	1,355,100
1995	1,144,200	2,261,600	385,500	998,900	5,256,000	1,044,700
1996	1,252,500	2,609,500	491,700	1, 154,400	6,092,900	1,198,900

Source: *Zhongguo Falu Nianjian* (Yearbook of Chinese Law) 1988-97.

The Reconstruction of the Legal Aid System in 1990s

The Whole Story of Legal Aid in China Today

For the first time, the Ministry of Justice publicly raised new proposals for establishing a legal aid institution in the summer of 1994. It set up a preparatory committee for the Legal Aid Center and China Legal Aid Foundation in March 1996, published the 'Circular on the Rapidly Establishing Organizations of Legal Aid and Developing Legal Aid Activities' on 15 May in the same year, and issued four joint circulars concerning legal aid in particular cases soon after that. In November, the national conference about theories and practices of legal aid was held in Guangzhou City. At the end of 1996, the Legal Aid Center of the Ministry of Justice was established. On 26 May, 1997, an inaugural meeting for the national Legal Aid Center and China Legal Aid Foundation was held in the Great Hall of the People, Beijing.

Since 1994, legal aid schemes have been tried out in many localities. Dozens of legal aid centers have already been set up at the level of provinces, municipalities and cities. In November of 1995, for example, Guangzhou City Legal Aid Center had provided legal representation for parties in 494 criminal or civil cases and supplied free advice to about 1803 people in just one year. In Dalian City, Liaoning Province, some law firms began to give free legal consulting on street corners every Sunday morning, to sign contracts to supply free legal aid to welfare facilities, schools for deaf-mutes, psychiatric hospitals and kindergartens. One law firm even invested RMB¥ 200,000 per year to institute a legal aid telephone hotline. In Beijing, the Justice Bureau and Lawyers Association made joint efforts to establish a legal aid foundation, and demanded that every law firm supply free services two days each month and institute the duty lawyer scheme after 1994.[23]

According to the provisions of 'Measures for Trial implementation of Legal Aid' issued by Guangzhou Justice Bureau, whether a person is eligible for legal aid depends very much on his financial circumstances, judged by the standard for social relief and minimum life security in Guangzhou. In the following cases, a person would not be entitled to legal aid: (1) an action considered unreasonable; (2) an action considered unwinnable; (3) an action that is difficult for the lawyer; (4) a small claim in which the amount in controversy of property is less than RMB¥ 3,000; (5) an action in damages for defamation, etc.[24]

The Official Conception of Legal Aid

The Ministry of Justice issued 'Circular on Launching the Legal Aid Work' (SFT, 1997, No.56) on 20 May, 1997, by which the basic framework of legal aid was defined. Looking at the text of this circular, we are able to grasp the essence of the Chinese conception of legal aid.

Legal aid in China is defined as a legal institution that requires legal service personnel such as attorneys, public notaries and basic legal workers to provide free or fee-reduced legal assistance to parties with economic difficulties. Sometimes these services are supervised by the legal aid organizations set up by the state. The Ministry of Justice is establishing a Legal Aid Center that will guide and coordinate legal aid work throughout the whole country. All law firms, notary public offices and basic level legal staff will provide legal aid under the unified coordination of their local legal aid center. The legal assistance provided by other organizations, associations and schools is also a part of the Chinese legal aid scheme (Cf. SFT, 1997, No. 56, Article 1).

Legal aid is intended for Chinese citizens who meet at least one of the following requirements: (1) to have enough reasons confirming the necessity for legal assistance; (2) to be incapable or partly incapable of paying for legal services because of true indigence, determined by the standards promulgated by the local government; (3) to be blind, deaf-mute, or a minor who is a defendant or suspect in a criminal action and has no counsel (necessary legal aid); (4) to a disabled or elderly defendant or suspect in a criminal action, who cannot afford counsel (discretionary legal aid); (5) to be a defendant who may be sentenced to death but has no counsel (necessary legal aid). The foreign defendant who has no counsel in a criminal action can get legal help if the people's court appoint counsel for him (Cf. SFT, 1997, No. 56, Article 2 (1)–(3)).

The aided person, whether he is an applicant granted free legal representation in a civil case or a defendant or suspect who has a government-financed counsel in a criminal case, has a right to know what services are provided by the legal aid scheme, and to be able to ask to replace his duty lawyer if the duty lawyer is neglecting the duties of representation. When a duty lawyer refuses to do his duty or is negligent in his duties and this behavior results in heavy losses to the aided person, the legal aid organization can propose that the organs of judicial administration concerned take appropriate disciplinary measures against him. However, when the aided person does not abide by the legal provisions, or does not give necessary cooperation according to the agreements of the legal aid scheme, his duty lawyer can break off or turn down the legal aid, with the approval of the legal aid organization (Cf. Article 2 (4), Article 5 (3),(4)).

Following is the range of legal aid in China: (1) criminal actions; (2) claims for maintenance, alimony and support payments; (3) claims for compensation of work-caused injury and disability except liability accidents; (4) claims for compensation of tort liability by the blind, the deaf-mute, the otherwise disabled person, minors and the elderly; (5) actions for state compensation; (6) claims for pension and relief payment; (7) other legal matters genuinely requiring legal aid (Article 3 (1)). At present, the focal point of the legal aid system is to put Article 34 of the new Criminal Procedure Law and Article 41 of Lawyers' Law, i.e. (1), (3), (5) into effect.[25]

The Legal Aid Fund

According to Article 6 of the *Circular on Launching Legal Aid Work* issued by the Ministry of Justice on 20 May, 1997, the major sources of legal aid funds include state financial allocation, revenue percentage deductions from the professional charges of law firms, notary public offices and basic legal service offices, as well as social donations. Before the unified stipulations concerning state financial allocation of legal aid are made by the Chinese government, the program is encouraged to win over the support of local financial administrations. At present, the range of social donation is limited within the boundaries of China itself and any donations from foreign countries or other areas are prohibited. All local legal aid foundations are operated in conjunction with the China Legal Aid Foundation. The China Legal Aid Foundation is geared to meet the needs of the whole nation, but its emphasis is on supporting legal aid work in impoverished areas.

The Forms and Procedures for Legal Aid Provision

In China today, the major forms of legal aid are as follows: (1) legal consultation and scrivener's services for drafting legal documents; (2) criminal agency and defense; (3) representation in civil lawsuits and administrative proceedings; (4) representation in non-contentious legal matters; (5) public notary certification; and (6) other legal services.

Any legal aid program must be practiced according to an agreement between the duty lawyer, the legal aid organization and the aided person. This agreement is signed after an investigation and approval of the application by the legal aid organization. If a person is refused legal aid, there is a procedure for rehearing the decision of the legal aid organization.

Legal Aid for Criminal and Civil Cases

Although the number of attorneys has been growing rapidly since 1980, especially in the 1990s, the supply is still not enough to meet the demand. The percentage of both criminal and civil cases represented by lawyers in the first instance is comparatively very low (Cf. Figure 5.2).[26]

Figure 5.2 The Structure and Change of Criminal and Civil Cases Presented by Attorneys

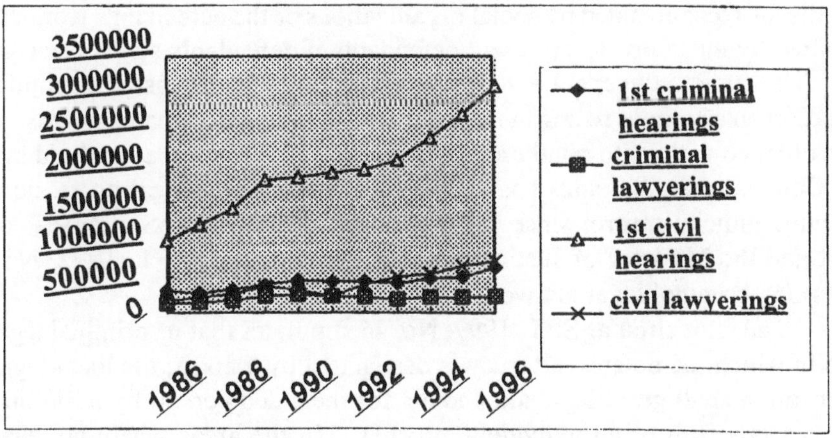

Source: *Zhongguo Falu Nianjian* (Yearbook of Chinese Law) 1987-97.

The lawyers' participation in the first instance of criminal cases has even declined since 1991, when the number of civil cases in which the parties are represented by an attorney began to rise remarkably, although the rate of lawyers' participation in civil cases was only 24 per cent in 1995 due to an increased civil caseload. The number of criminal cases in which the defendant was represented by an attorney was 252,344 in 1990, 230,967 in 1991, 219,739 in 1992, 191,657 in 1993, 208,806 in 1994, 204,382 in 1995, and the proportion of criminal lawyering in criminal cases filed and put into hearing in the first instance has declined from about 55 per cent to 41 per cent.

There has been a tendency for many attorneys to avoid criminal cases because of the low pay. According to the criteria for lawyers' charges issued in 1990, a counsel who works for the defendant in both the first and second instances of a criminal case, can only charge RMB¥ 30-50 for each task (Cf. Table 5.1). This price is lower than the cost of a taxi in Beijing to drive to Tiananmen Square from Peking University! When an attorney is appointed defense counsel, the payment has been less than even one-third or one-fourth of the retainer.[27] Therefore, some attorneys prefer civil representation to criminal defense, and some defendants must pay more than the official charge criteria for access to counsel. As a result of the informal price for representation in criminal cases, a public opinion poll on criminal problems revealed that 29.38 per cent believed that 'lawyers' charge[s] [are] too expensive'. Moreover, it becomes more and more difficult for poor people to get legal service.[28]

It is because of this background that the newly revised Criminal Procedure Law permits non-lawyers such as close relatives, friends, guardians, and citizens recommended by social organizations or the defendant's work unit or permitted by the court, to represent defendants if defendants so choose (Article 32). The new Lawyer's Law promulgated in 1996 imposes a mandatory obligation on attorneys to engage in legal aid, including designated defense work in accordance with state regulations (Article 42).[29] Creating a legal aid system with Chinese characteristics has been a focal point of the legal profession and continued judicial reform since 1994 (Cooper, 1999). The Supreme People's Court and the Ministry of Justice issued a joint circular (SFT, 1997, No. 46) concerning criminal legal aid work on 9 April, 1997.

The joint circular SFT, 1997, No. 46 stipulates that in criminal legal aid cases in which the defense attorney is designated by a court, the local legal aid organization shall grant legal aid and act for the aided person by assigning the case to a law firm or an individual attorney. In the areas where no legal aid organization has been established, the local justice bureaus are responsible for granting and organizing legal aid to defendants (Article 1). Legal aid for designated defending shall be provided within three days after the service date of court notice. Any legal aid case for designated defending must meet one of the following six criteria:

1) the defendant actually lacks a source of income and the court is unable to determine the economic situation of the defendant's family;

2) the defendant actually lacks a source of income and the defendant's family is still refusing to pay for a counsel in spite of repeated persuading;

3) the defendant who has not retained a counsel is a joint defendant and the other defendants have already retained counsels;

4) the defendant is a foreigner and has not retained counsel;

5) the case has major social importance;

6) the court considers that the reasons in indictment for bringing an action or the evidence in the case are questionable, and may influence the court in reaching a correct verdict (Article 4).

In the cases in which it is necessary to assess the economic hardship of the applicant for criminal legal aid, the test criteria are different and determined by local governments (Article 3). However, legal aid is available without preconditions to those who are blind, deaf-mute, of minor age, or those who may be sentenced to death and have no counsel (Article 2).

Compared with criminal cases, the number of civil cases without the representation of an attorney is astonishing, and there is a notable disparity in the distribution of the source of legal services between the two kind of cases (Cf. Figure 5.2). In a sense, this means that there exists a market of civil legal service with great potentialities. Therefore, it is difficult to define the proper targets and standards of free legal aid in civil cases. The Ministry of Justice recommends the following areas in need of immediate assistance in the development of legal aid work: (1) claims for maintenance, alimony and support payments; (2) claims for compensation of work-caused injury and disability except liability accident; and (3) claims for compensation of tort liability by the blind, the deaf-mute, the other disabled person, the minor and the aged. Actually, these types of cases can also be considered as the present limits to legal aid for civil cases.[30] However, it is estimated that China will extend the range of legal aid for civil cases in pace with economic development and legal reform.[31] Moreover, in some regions, legal aid is available for most civil proceedings.[32]

Three Basic Types of Legal Aid Schemes in Practice

Although there are many pilot projects and institutional designs for legal aid in different areas now, three basic categories can be summarized through trial and error.

The standard scheme of legal aid center network The national and local legal aid centers which are set up by organs of judicial administration and financed by governments, bar associations and social donations decidedly play a key role in the Chinese legal aid system. So far, the legal aid centers are characterized by three main forms:

Mandatory assignment of legal aid cases to attorneys When defense counsel is designated by a court or a person is accepted to receive legal aid, the legal aid center assigns the case to a law firm or to an individual attorney in a for-profit practice. For example, the 'Measures for Trial Implementation of Legal Aid' issued by the Guangzhou City Justice Bureau stipulates that all lawyers who register to practice law in Guanzhou are duty-bound to provide legal aid (Article 18) and to cooperate harmoniously with the legal aid center (Article 21). The legal aid center establishes a registry of lawyers on duty, in which an attorney clearly states the type and number of cases that he wishes to undertake and his available office time. The director of the legal aid center must approve any changes in an attorney's registration (Article 19). According to SFT, 1997, No. 46, the joint circular of the Supreme People's Court and the Ministry of Justice, this form of assigning legal aid work to lawyers is the official form to provide legal aid in criminal cases. In Guangzhou City, all the criminal cases in which legal aid is applied must be accepted by the legal aid center.[33]

Independently providing services and reimbursement by legal aid centers Many law firms accept and handle legal aid cases by themselves, reporting to the legal aid center for record-keeping and to receive reimbursement. This is known as the Beijing Model. The municipal justice bureau and municipal lawyers association of Beijing jointly established a legal aid fund in 1994 for reimbursing lawyers who have provided free legal aid. They requested that each attorney registered in Beijing Municipality should do legal aid in at least one case every year. This course of action was institutionalized in the form of the Beijing Legal Aid Foundation and Beijing Legal Aid Center in 1997. According to the Rules of the Beijing Legal Aid Foundation, the organization will be an independent aggregate non-profit corporation (Article 3), the Council and its Standing Committee of Beijing Legal Aid Foundation will decide and supervise the provision of legal aid funds and services provided by the organization (Article 4).

Duty to provide free services in the legal aid centers Many legal aid centers have duty or full-time lawyers to provide services for those who cannot afford it. The legal aid scheme of the Pudong District in Shanghai Municipality is the most typical case. This legal aid organization is composed of the Pudong Legal Aid Center and the law firms located in this district. It has established a duty-lawyer system that allows the lawyers who are on duty to receive the aided person and to provide services in the office of the Center. However, the Center may also assign legal aid cases to law firms in the district, and law firms may also accept legal aid cases directly, while going through the formalities of application and approval retroactively.[34] Where a legal aid center has its office and its full-time lawyers, the services may be considered more similar to the following categories.

The auxiliary scheme of public lawyer offices for legal aid Because legal aid centers are not law firms,[35] the Lawyers Law does not allow full-time lawyers in legal aid centers to get the required license for practicing the law and handling cases directly. In some areas such as Qingdao, the full-time lawyers in the centers have actually been accepting and handling the cases in which legal aid is applied. In other areas such as Chongqing, however, specialized legal aid public lawyer offices that are state-financed have been organized.[36] Some people maintain that the existing state-run law offices should be transformed into public attorney offices for legal aid.[37]

The voluntary scheme of society-based legal aid In Wuhan City, legal aid is basically provided by law firms and bar associations. According to 'Legal Aid Measures of Wuhan City's Lawyers', adopted by the Standing Council of Wuhan City Lawyers Association on 5 May, 1995, every law firm should establish their own legal aid measures for encouraging free work to help the poor (Article 2). The Wuhan City Legal Aid Fund stems from: (1) the allocation in proportion of 10 per cent of membership dues *per annum* of the City Lawyers' Association; (2)

social donations and other income; (3) the legal aid funds set up in each law firm (Article 6). The Wuhan Model is actually not very popular in China because of its inadequacy and ineffectiveness.

Chinese legal authorities understand the concepts of legal aid and legal aid providers within a broad view of the objective conditions. Many legal aid organizations have been set up by law students in universities or colleges such as Peking University, Fudan University, Wuhan University and the Middle South College of Political Science and Law. Some of these organizations have been supported by foreign foundations.[38] However, it must be noted that the legal aid organizations on campuses are still informal and peripheral in terms of the whole legal aid system.

Prospects for Legal Services for the People

In 5-15 years from now, legal aid development will be the central goal for the legal profession, judicial reform and the construction of the legal system in China. Bt the end of 1997, the number of legal aid centers established in provinces and municipalities reached 19, and the number of legal aid organizations at the level of prefectures, cities and counties reached 112. All provinces and municipalities were scheduled to set up legal aid centers by the end of 1998.[39] As a more long-term plan, China will establish the National Committee of Legal Aid in addition to the existing National Legal Aid Center and China Legal Aid Foundation. The National Committee of Legal Aid will set up legal aid centers in all areas at the county level and above.[40] The National Legal Aid Center of the Ministry of Justice has started a training course for specialized legal aid providers. The draft of 'Measures of Legal Aid Work for Trial Implementation' as a decree of the Ministry of Justice was discussed by officials of the judicial administration in November 1996, and was scheduled to be announced in 1997 but has been postponed.[41] At the same time, legal scholars proposed to draw up a Legal Aid Law as soon as possible.[42]

According to the predicted data of the authorities concerned, assuming the rate of application for legal aid among the poor of approximately 85 million people to be 1 per cent, the number of cases in which legal aid is provided *per annum* may be in the range between 80,000 and 90,000. There are 400 million minors in China today, supposing the rate of legal aid needs to be 0.1 per cent, the number of application cases *per annum* may reach 40,000. There are also 60 million disabled people with many legal problems; supposing the rate of legal aid cases to be 3 per cent, the number of cases for legal aid *per annum* may be 180,000. In addition, the elderly over the age of 65 made up 65 per cent of the whole population at the end of 1994, and there are about 80 million elders at present. Supposing the rate of elder legal assistance to be 1 per cent, the number of cases for handling *per annum* may be 80,000. The above data add up to approximately 385,000 legal aid cases *per annum*. Of course, there are some overlapping parts in the estimation of that number. However, if the underestimated parts are included, the number of possible cases is substantial. If the minimum standards for legal aid are: (1) that two full-time legal aid providers are disposed in every ten thousand of indigent people; (2) that each lawyer provides free legal aid in one or two cases *per annum*; and (3) that the average available legal aid fund is RMB¥ 1,200 for each case, then at least 17,000 full-time lawyers specialized in legal aid for the poor and annual budgetary receipts of three hundred million yuan are necessary for the scheme to operate.[43]

In view of the tension between needs and resources in the legal aid system, China must bring more lawyers' subjective initiatives into full play. It must utilize social resources more thoroughly and more effectively, and set up an informal legal service network for the common people by a diversified approach. In 1998, the ranks of voluntary legal aid providers was composed mainly of law students and academic lawyers. The role of NPOs, and NGOs is beginning to be emphasized, especially in legal aid and class actions.[44] As for legal aid development in rural areas, People's Mediation Committees and Legal Service Offices at the grass-roots level are considered as the basic model. As for legal aid development in big or middle-sized cities, the Guangzhou Model is considered as the orientation which the Ministry of Justice is expecting.

Although many problems in legal aid practice have been pointed out and criticized, the legal aid movement is checking and correcting unhealthy tendencies towards legal commercialism, and changing the image of lawyers from serving the political power or seeking private profits to serving the poor people, in accordance with the *pro bono publico* ideal of modern legal professionalism.

In fact, Chinese lawyers are enjoying a rapid growth. Between 1986 and 1996, the number of lawyers increased by about 500 per cent (See Figure 5.3). Lawyers are no longer disadvantaged, but are now considered a profession having a strong appeal to the younger generation. In this respect, the key point is to provide legal services for enterprises. Through legal services to business, Chinese lawyers have proven their usefulness and exhibited benefits to the society in which private legal practitioners had traditionally been considered useless.[45]

Against this background, however, it becomes more important for Chinese lawyers to reconcile the tension between their pursuit of economic success and their legal ideal of guaranteeing human rights or social justice in order to establish true professional identity. Otherwise the prestige of the legal profession will certainly be injured. Now the legal aid movement in China is fine-tuning the unbalanced relations between the profit motive and the *pro bono publico* spirit in lawyers. If we can say that legal services for business has been a lever to introduce legal professionalism into China, we must also consider legal aid for the indigent as the lever to spread and popularize legal professionalism in Chinese society.

Figure 5.3 The Growth of the Legal Profession

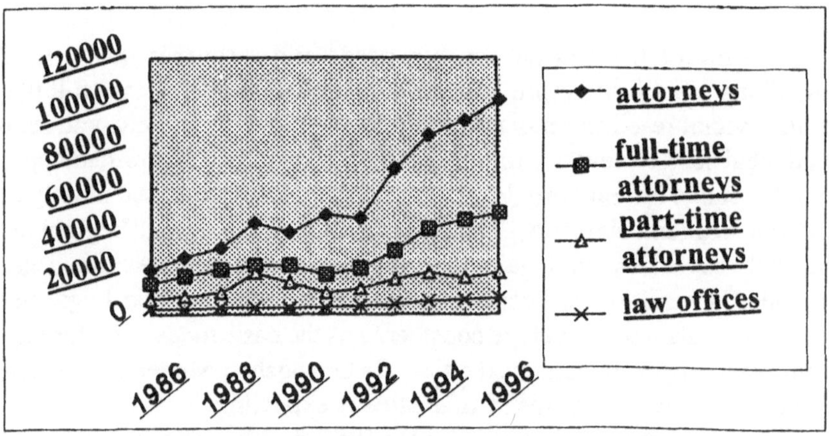

Source: *Zhongguo Falu Nianjian* (Yearbook of Chinese Law) 1987-97.

Notes

1 *Zhongguo Lüshi* (Chinese Lawyer), No. 5 (1992), 4-9, and the front-paged news report about opening the market of legal service in *Fazhi Ribao* (See the Ministry of Justice 'Opinions on Deepening Reform of Lawyer Work', Daily of Legal System) 27 June, 1993.

2 Cf. Peilin, 1995, Qiang *et al*, 1995, 61-64, Angang *et al*, 1995.

3 According to Li Peilin, *op. cit*, 382, 415.

4 See the Ministry of Justice 'Circular on Rapid Establishment of Legal Aid Organizations and Rapid Development of Legal Aid Work' (issued on 3 June, 1996).

5 Many amendments to it have been introduced from time to time in the period from 1913-1938. Cf. Chang, 1938, 146-184, and an English translation of the lawyers' laws 'Revised Regulations Governing Legal Practitioners', 'Regulations for the Discipline of Legal Practitioners' and 'Regulations of the Commissions for the Discipline of Legal Practitioners' in *The Chinese Social and Political Science Review* Vol. No. 3 (1938), 309-330.

6 Cf. *Falü Pinglun* (Law Review) No. 46 (1924), 9, cited in Shen, 1994, 114. Concerning the bar associations, see Chang, 1938, 235-281.

7 Shen, 1994, 115.

8 Shen, 1994, 118-120.

9 The 'Interim Measures for the Lawyers' Charge' enacted in 1956 was not really applied because the institution of legal attorneys was negated in 1957 and was suspended for twenty years after 1959. At the end of 1981, 'Trial Measures for the Lawyers' Charge' was issued. The decree currently in effect is 'Measures for the Control of Lawyers' Professional Charge and the Criteria for Charge' issued on 15 February 1990. Table 5.1 reports data according to the latter two decrees.

10 Cf. Li, 1978, 376.

11 'Interim Regulations of the People's Republic of China on Lawyers' (adopted in 1980 and abrogated in 1997) stipulates that '[L]awyers are state legal workers whose task is to give legal assistance to state organs, enterprises and institutions, public organizations, people's communes and citizens in order to ensure the correct implementation of the law and protect the interests of the state and collectives as well as the lawful rights and interests of citizens' (Article 1).

12 Sifabu gongzheng-lüshisi (the Notarization and Lawyers Department of the Ministry of Justice), 'Zhonghua renmin gongheguo lüshi zanxing tiaoli xuanchuan tigang (the Propaganda Outline of Interim Regulations of the

People's Republic of China on Lawyers)', *Lüshi Gongzuo Ziliao Xuanji* (The Collected Working Materials of Lawyers) No. 3 (1980), 25f.

13 For example, Yi, 1958, Xingqiao, 1958, Yixiang, 1958, Cf. Pengnian and Bida (eds) 1992, 40.

14 Eg. The Joint Fact-finding Group of Intermediate People's Court of Yueyang City and Basic-level People's Court of Pingjiang County, 'Nongcun 'Tulüshi' Wenti Tantao (Probing into Problems of the Self-taught Local - Legal Practitioners)', *Faxue Zazhi* (Journal of Legal Studies), No. 1 (1987). Cf. Lubman, Cohen, 1970, Cities, *Studies in Chinese Law* No. 13 (Harvard Law School), Palmer, 1987, Clarke, 1991.

15 *Infra* fn. 16.

16 See the Ministry of Justice, 'Guanyu Renmin Tiaojie Weiyuanhui Buying Xiang Dangshiren Shoufei Wenti de Fuhan (Official Reply Concerning the Problems of Forbidding PMCs to Charge Parties for Mediating Disputes)', (issued on 6 December, 1983), the *Joint Circular of the Ministry of Justice and the Ministry of Finance Concerning the Funds for People's Mediation and the Budget of Remuneration for Mediators* (issued in September, 1985 as SFJZ, 85, No.384).

17 The Government Administration Council of the Central People's Government (replaced in 1954 by the State Council), 'Decisions Concerning the Work of Handling People's Letters and People's Visits' (issued on 7 June, 1951). The State Council, 'Directive on Strengthening the Work of Handling Letters and Visits from the People' (issued in November of 1957).

18 Cf. The State Council, 'Some Stipulations on Keeping Order of the Work for Handling Letters and Visits' (issued in August of 1980).

19 Cf. Wanzhong (ed.), 1993, 794.

20 Wanzhong (ed), 1993 .2 93f. See also the Supreme People's Court, 'Interim Provisions Concerning the Handling of Criminal Appeal by the People's Courts at All Levels' (issued on 10 October, 1987).

21 According to the Ministry of Justice and the Ministry of Finance, 'Measures for Financial Management of Township-level Legal Service Offices' (issued on 1 September, 1990), Article 3.

22 See Measures for the Control of Lawyers' Professional Charge and the Criteria for Charge (1990), Article 12. Civil Procedure Law in effect stipulates that 'Where the litigant is incapable of litigant action, he may be represented by his legal representative; where he has no legal representatives, the people's court shall appoint a representative for him. Where the legal representatives shirk the representation responsibilities among themselves, the people's court shall appoint one of them to represent the litigant in the action' (Article 57).

23 Cf. Yinchao, 1997, 7-8, Dezhu, 1997, 23.

24 See Article 8 (2) and Article 9. Cf. Xiaofei and Jingchun 1997, 9.

25 According to 'Circular on the Rapidly Establishing Organizations of Legal Aid and Developing Legal Aid Activities' (issued on 3 June, 1996) Article 2.

26 Cf. Pengnian and Bida (eds.) 1992, esp. pp. 28ff., 170ff, Alford, 1995, Ji, 1996, 311.

27 See Ji, 1996, 329.

28 Zexian, 1995, 493.

29 In fact, at the end of 1993, the Ministry of Justice issued 'Standards Concerning Professional Morality and Practicing Discipline of Lawyers' (MJ decree No. 30) and imposed the mandatory *pro bono publico* requirements on attorneys (Article 8, Article 12 (2), (3)). See also the Measures for the Control of Partnership Law Firms (issued by the Ministry of Justice on 25 October, 1996, Article 13 (4), Article 32), of Cooperative Law Firms (25 November, 1996, Article 23), of State-Financed Law Firms (25 November, 1996, Article 21).

30 See also Lawyers Law Article 41, Law on Guaranteeing Rights and Interests of the Aged (promulgated on 29 August, 1996) Article 39, the State Council 'Circular for Ratifying and Transmitting the National Program for the Disabled People's Cause of Ninth Five-year Plan'(GF, 1996, No.15, issued on 26 April, 1996) Section 8. Cf. Xiaobing and Zhen, 1997, Liebman, (unpublished), 3.

31 Cf. The former Minister of Justice Xiao Yang's speech at the inaugural meeting for the national Legal Aid Center and China Legal Aid Foundation held on 26 May, 1997. Gong Xiaobing, Chief of the preparatory team of the national Legal Aid Center of the Ministry of Justice, said that '[i]n light of

Chinese circumstances, not only natural persons, but legal persons such as State and collective enterprises may also receive legal aid, if they have financial difficulties and need legal services', and '[l]egal aid primarily covers the reduction or exemption from legal service fees the clients pay to lawyers and for notarization'. Cited from his article 'China's Legal Aid System Under Exploration' (trans. by Jiang Mingshan), *China Law* No. 3 (1996), p. 69. According to the plan of Chinese government, the legal aid institution will be established and perfected in the coming 5-15 years. See also Cooper, 1999, 82.

32 Eg. in Dalian City, there are cases in which legal aid was provided to legal persons, workers in labor disputes, consumers in claims for injury compensation. Cf. 'Shanghai Pudong District Legal Aid Scheme (temporary provisions)' Article 5, Guangzhou City Justice Bureau 'Measures for Trial Implementation of Legal Aid' Article 2 and Article 9, in addition, see also Chow, A. 1997, 155.

33 Xiaofei and Jingchun, 1997, 9.

34 Cf. Shanghai Pudong District Legal Aid Scheme (temporary provisions) Article 2, Article 6 (3),(4), Article 15.

35 Legal aid centers are generally considered as one of the inside functional organs of the institutions of judicial administration. See Zhen, 1998, 8-10.

36 Xiaobing and Zhen, 1997, 14. In fact, the institution of public lawyer began to be advocated in December, 1993, in 'Sifabu Guanyu Shenhua Lüshi Gongzuo Gaige de Fangan (The Plan of the Ministry of Justice About Deepening of Lawyers Work Reform)'. Cf. also the relevant news report in Zhongguo Lüshi Bao (Chinese Lawyers News), 19 July, 1994.

37 Zhonghong, 1997, 97. By the way, the State-run law offices or the State-financed law firms are still making up 70 per cent of the total sum of law firms in China now.

38 Cf. Yongjun, 1997, 10.

39 Xiaobing and Zhen, 1997, 8.

40 Xiaobing and Zhen, 1997, 14.

41 Xiaobing and Zhen, 1997, 10, 14.

42 Zhonghong, 1997, 62: Xianhuan, 1997, 58.

43 Xiaobing and Zhen, 1997, 13.

44 Eg, Yongjun, 1997, 10. About class actions and the role of lawyers in this kind of litigation, Liebman, 1998.

45 Cf. Ji, 1993, 99.

Bibliography

Angang, H. *et al* (1995), *Zhongguo Diqu Chaju Baogao* (Regional Disparity in China), Liaoning renmin chubanshe, Shenyang.

Alford, W. (1995) 'Tasselled Loafers for Barefoot Lawyers: Transformation and Tension in the World of Chinese Legal Workers', *The China Quarterly*, March, 1995.

Chang, Y. (1938), 'The Legal Practitioner in China', *The Chinese Social and Political Science Review*, Vol. No. 2, 146.

Chow, A. (1997), 'Legal Aid in Hong Kong', *China Law*,7, 155.

Clarke, D. (1991), 'Dispute Resolution in China', *Journal of Chinese Law* Vol. 5.

Cohen, J. (1970), 'Drafting Mediation Rules for Chinese Cities', *Studies in Chinese Law* No. 13 (Harvard Law School.

Cooper, J. (1999) 'Lawyers in China and the Rule of Law', *International Journal of the Legal Profession*, vol. 6, no. 1, 71.

Dezhu, P. (1997), 'Ai Sa Renjian Falü Yuanzhu zai Dalian (Giving Help to the Poor and Love to the People Legal Aid in Dalian', *Dangdai Sifa (Contemporary Judicature)*, 5, 23.

Ji, W. (1993), 'Professionalita e Dimensione Internationale Dell'avvocatura in Cina' (Traduzione dall'inglese di Maria Cristina Reale) *Sociologia del Diritto*, 2, 99.

Ji, W. (1996), 'Jinken Hosho to Bengoshi no Yakuwari (The Role of Lawyers in Guaranteeing Human Rights)', in Tsuchiya, H. (ed.) *Gendai Chugoku no Jineken (Human Rights in Modern China)*, Sinsansha, Tokyo, 311.

Li, V. (1978), 'Access to Justice: People's Republic of China', in Cappelletti, M. (ed.) *Access to Justice* Vol. 1 Book 1, Giuffre, Milan, 376.

Liebman, B. (unpublished), 'Legal Aid and Public Interest Law in China' (unpublished paper from Prof. Miyazawa and on file with author).

Lubman, S. (1967), 'Mao and Mediation: Politics and Dispute Resolution in Communist China', *California Law Review*, 55.

Palmer, M. (1987), 'The Revival of Mediation in the People's Republic of China: (1) Extra-Judicial Mediation', in *Yearbook on Socialist Legal Systems*, (ed.) Butler.

Peilin. L. (ed.) (1995), *Zhongguo Xinshiqi Jieji Jieceng Baogao* (Social Stratification in the Market Transition in China), Liaoning renmin chubanshe, Shenyang.

Pengnian, M. and Bida, L. (eds) (1992), *Zhongguo Lüshi Zhidu Yanjiu (The Studies in the Institutions on Lawyers in China)*, Falü chubanshe, Beijing.

Qiang, L. *et al (1995)*, 'Woguo Shehui Gejieceng Shouru Chaju Fenxi (Analysis on Income Gap or China's Social Groups)', *Keji Daobao , Introduction to Science and Technology*, 11, 61.

Shen, W. (1994), *Zhongguo Jindai Lüshizhidu yu Lüshi* (Modern Institution of Legal Profession and Lawyer in China), Shanghai shehuikexueyuan chubanshe, Shanghai.

Wanzhong, S. (ed.) (1993), *Zhonghua Renmin Gongheguo Falü Dashiji (Chronicle of Legal Events in People's Republic of China)*, Zhongguo zhengfa daxue chubanshe, Beijing.

Xiaobing, G. (1996), 'China's Legal Aid System Under Exploration' (trans. by Jiang Mingshan), *China Law* No. 3.

Xiaobing, G. and Zhen, G. (1997), 'Zhongguo Falüyuanzhu Zhidu de Shijian, Tansuo yu Qianjing, xia, (The Practice, Exploration, and Prospects of Legal Aid System in China, the second half)', *Dangdai Sifa (Contemporary Judicature)*,6,12.

Xiaofei. Z. and Jingchun, Z. (1997) 'Shui Neng Jieshou Falü Yuanzhu (Who Is Eligible for Legal Aid)', *Zhongguo Lüshi (Chinese Lawyer)*, 8, 9.

Xingqiao, L.(1958), 'Bianhuren Faxian Beigaoren Yinman de Fanzui Shishi Bixu Jielu (A Defender Must Expose the Criminal Facts Which the Defendant Want to Concea', *Faxue (The Science of Law)*, 3, 17.

Xinhuan, W. (1997), 'Xingshi Falüyuanzhu Zhidu de Jige Wenti (Several Problems Concerning the Institution of Criminal Legal Aid)', *Zhengfa Luntan (Forum of Politics and Law)*, 5, 58.

Yi, S. (1958), 'Bianhuren Yinggai Daji Fanzui Haishi Baohu Fanzui (A Defender Should Crack Down on Crime or Not)?', *Zhengfa Yanjiu* (Studies in Politics and Law), 2, 76.

Yinchao, W. (1997), 'Fangxingweiai de Zhongguo Falüyuanzhu (Legal Aid is Now in the Ascendant in China)', *Zhongguo Lüshi (Chinese Lawyer)*, 8, 7.

Yixiang, H. (1958), 'Yingdang Pipan Bianhuren de "Youli Beigao Lun" (The Partisanship of Defenders to their Defendants Must be Criticized)', *Faxue* (*The Science of Law)*, 3, 19.

Yongjun, X. (1997), 'Shui Lai Chengdan Falüyuanzhu (Who Are Legal Aid Providers?)', *Zhongguo Lüshi (Chinese Lawyer)*, 8.

Zexian, C. (1995), 'Xingshi Fazhi Fazhan yu Gongmin Quanli Baohu (The Development to the Criminal Legal System and the Protection to Civil Rights)', in Yong, X. (ed.) *Zouxiang Quanli de Shidai – Zhongguo Gongmin Quanli Fazhan Yanjiu (Toward a Time of Rights: A Perspective of the Civil Rights Development in China)*, Beijing: Zhongguo zhengfa daxue chubanshe. 493.

Zhen, G. (1998), 'Falüyuanzhu Jigou de Zhineng Jiqi Yunzuo (The Function and Operation of Legal Aid Organizations)', *Dangdai Sifa (Contemporary Judicature)*, 4, 8.

Zhonghong, L. (1997), 'Woguo Falüyuanzhu Zhidu de Jiben Gouxiang (The Basic Ideas for Legal Aid System in Our Country)', *Xiandai Faxue (Modern Legal Science)*, 4.

6 Thammasat Clinical Education and the Delivery of Legal Services: A historical and personal perspective

MALEE PRUEKPONGSAWALEE

Introduction

Legal education is a learning process of 'legal scientists' being expected to apply their knowledge, skills and inspirations to keep order and uphold justice for the peaceful well-being of human society. Legal education combines both theoretical and practical aspects. It is not a value-free but a judgment-science aimed at creating good society. In the author's view, legal science should be studied with a holistic approach by knowing how legal principles come into existence, how to apply these principles. Moreover, legal principles must be periodically appraised to see if they can effectively do justice to the parties involved.[1]

Clinical education is a practical dimension of the study and the application of legal science. It has to be discussed in the broader context of the socio-economic and political development which shapes the legal system and legal education of each country. Such development in Siam, the original and former name of Thailand, has evolved through two major periods, namely the Pre-1932 Revolution and the Post-1932 Revolution. The Post-1932 Revolution period can be divided into the Pre-1976 Military Bloody Coup and the Post-1976 Coup.

This paper provides a brief historical development of legal education in Thailand as background information on how clinical education and legal services at Thammasat University have developed. Being a participant in part of this development I share my personal experience, my analysis and my conception on the future outlook of these activities.

Legal Education in a Historical Perspective

The Pre-1932 Revolution and the Indigenous Legal System

Concept and sources of law Prior to the 1932 Revolution, Siam was an absolute monarchy state. It has been claimed that the kingship of Siam was strongly influenced by the Buddhist concept of Dharma Raja or the Righteous, Enlightened King.[2]

The pre-modern legal system of Siam was based on two major sources of law. The first unwritten source was the Siamese customary law and the second written source originated from the Code of Manu or Dharmasatr (or Thammasat), the ancient Indian law based on Hinduism. However, the version which the Siamese adopted was modified with the Buddhist concept by the Mon.

The main concept states that law is nature-given. It is not created by anyone not even the King. Law is identical to Dharma. It exists as a universal order. It renders good effects to those who comply with its principles while the non-compliants will be self-destructive. The most simple explanation of Dharma is that it is the Law of Nature or the Law of Causation. Traditional concepts hold that custom, law and justice are identical and are all encompassed in Dharma.

The Buddhist explanation of equality, fraternity and freedom deemed as the democratic foundation is profound and realistic. According to Buddhism, all human beings are equal under the Law of Nature which evolves from Birth-Decay-Death. No one, regardless of their socio-economic and political status, can escape from the Law of Nature. So all human beings are common friends of the same destiny. Therefore they should treat each other in the ways they would like to be treated. All human beings, men and women enjoy equal opportunity to escape from the Law of Nature and cease to evolve in the physical and psychological circle of Birth-Decay and Death by practicing the Buddhist teaching. Through the path of Dharma they can purify their mind and soul and become enlightened. All human conflicts and violence are caused by the three evils, hatred, greed and delusion. Buddhism praises the power of self-control from all evils. Self-restraint through the Buddhist process of self-internalization undoubtedly reduces the need for state control and punishment.

Impact of western imperialism on the legal system The concept of law in Siam started to change in the reign of King Rama IV. Despite a common accusation that the Thai women's movement was a product of westernization, the movement against unjust legal principles was sparked by two commoner women who petitioned the King on separate occasions. The first woman, Amdaeng Muan, was forced by her parents to marry a man whom she did not love and the second woman, Amdaeng Jun, was sold by her husband without her consent. These complaints led to royal orders to grant women more freedom as Rama IV openly criticized the ancient legal principles, on the grounds that they were unequally 'treating women like buffalo and men as human beings'.

Without the expansion of western imperialism, King Rama IV would have continued to revise the existing legal principles, on a case basis, to keep Siam in good order. He could have resorted to the Buddhist principles with which he was familiar as he himself was ordained for over 27 years before his coronation. However, Siam could not escape from the western 'gun-boat diplomacy' imposed by the Western powers, particularly the French and the British. The most significant factor during King Rama IV's reign which completely turned a new page of the Siamese legal system was western imperialism.

Although Siam was not an official colony of any Western powers it was forced by Britain to sign the Bowring Treaty of 1855, followed by trade agreements with several other Western countries. All Western powers and their subjects enjoyed the privilege of extraterritorial rights on the ground that the Siamese law and its justice administration were uncivilized. As a surviving strategy from a *de jure* colonial status, Siam undertook major administrative, legal and justice administration reform, to bring the country to an 'acceptable standard' of the Western powers.

The massive reform of 1892-1935 was under the close supervision of a Belgian, Gustave Rolin-Jaequemyns, a prominent International Law advocate, hired as the General Advisor to King Chulalongkorn (Rama V, the son of Rama IV). As part of this national reform, Prince Rapeepattanasak, son of King Rama V, was sent to study law at Oxford University. In 1897 he was appointed by his father to serve as a Minister of the modern Ministry of Justice. He started to teach high-ranking officials to serve in the new courts. After the enactment of the new codes, the Graduate Royal Law School attached to the Ministry of Justice was established to provide legal education to orient the students to the Civil Law System.

The need for the experts who could provide legal consultation for commoners unfamiliar with the complexity of the legal principles and procedures, was already identified by King Rama IV. There is a record that Prince Rapee also encouraged his students to provide advocacy service to the prisoners.[3] Prince Rapee was a living model of a bold and capable jurist. Rapee is well-known and highly respected by the legal profession up to the present for his professional dedication, expressed in his motto 'My Life is Service'.

The Post-1932 'Unfinished' Revolution

Thammasat University, Preedee Banomyong and the Inception of a Constitutional Democratic Nation

On June 24, 1932, a group of civilian and military high-ranking officials succeeded in seizing power in a bloodless revolution and transformed Siam into a constitutional monarchy state. On April 25, 1933, the Law School of the Ministry of Justice was transferred, to become the Law Department in the Faculty of Law and Political Science of Chulalongkorn University, the sole higher institution of the time.

The new Law Department of Chulalongkorn University was in operation for only a few months and finally was merged with the newly established institution, the University of Thammasat and Kan-Muang, founded in 1934. The English name of this new university is the University of Moral Science (Dharmasatr or Thammasat) and Politics (Kan-Muang).

The Thammasat and Kan-Muang University has a clear objective of orienting the Siamese to the democratic governance based on the Buddhist Principles. The founding father of Thammasat is Professor Dr Preedee Banomyong, a French law graduate and the civilian leader of the 1932 Revolution. After the revolution, Preedee played a major role in setting up all democratic infrastructures including the University of Moral Science and Politics. Apart from his academic and administrative function at the university, he served in several eminent positions, including the premiership and Minister of Interior, Foreign Affairs and Finance. Strongly influenced by the Buddhist teaching of respect for peace and non-violence and with a clear vision that a survival strategy for a small nation like Siam is neutrality, he started an underground Free Siam Movement among his colleagues, students and high-ranking officials to support the allies during World War II. The Free Siam Movement did indeed save the country from being a war loser and enabled her to renegotiate all unequal treaties and put Siam in a more equal position with the Western parties. Preedee Banomyong as the Prime Minister and Minister of Foreign Affairs, played a key role in the re-negotiation.

Thammasat and Kan-Muang University was the first open university which offered educational opportunity for the broader mass of people, with unlimited enrolment. Neither entrance examination nor class attendance were required. The applicants must, however, meet certain requirements. University officers were appointed in every province to smooth the path of the students. Upon passing six semesters of examination (three years of study) they received a Bachelor of Moral Science and Politics. Most of the subjects were law based on the new codes. In addition to general law courses there were other subjects, e.g. Economics Theories, Public Finance Law, Laws and Regulations of Public Law Organizations. There were both Siamese and Western law professors, particularly French and Belgian.

Most of the students enrolled in Thammasat and Kan-muang University were school teachers and junior or middle-level state officials. Upon graduation they filled up newly created public services positions in the bureaucracy and public organizations.

Legal Education Under Military Dictatorship (1947-1973)

Despite its modern appearance and image, democracy in Thailand is still in its infant stage as the right-wing faction led by the military has frequently intervened through bloody coups. The most recent military coup was in 1991 and the latest massacre of pro-democracy groups was the May Incident of 1992.

The first military coup was staged in 1947 after World War II as ideological conflicts between Preedee Banomyong, and General P. Piboonsongkram, the military leaders of the 1932 Revolution, had intensified. During his premiership after World War II, Preedee was accused by his political rivals as being behind the mysterious death of King Rama VIII, the older brother of the present King (Rama IX). After the coup, Preedee Banomyong took exile in China, and died in France in the early 1980s at the age of 82. Even in his exile, Preedee continued to assist Siam on many occasions in international affairs. He also won many court cases to prove that he was innocent of the royal assassination.

After the coup, the military gained full control of the kingdom which had changed to the new name of Thailand, which means 'Land of the Free People'. Ironically, during 1947-1973 (26 years), it was ruled by three successive Generals, P. Piboonsongkram (1947-1958), Sarit Tanarat (1958-1962) and Tanom Kittikachorn (1962-October 1973). The Martial Law, and the Communist Suppression Acts of 1952 were virtually the Supreme Laws of the country. The first phase of an endeavour to build up a new constitutional monarchy state by Preedee Banomyong and his Thammasat colleagues came to an end only 15 years after the 1932 Revolution.

Military dictatorship had a negative impact on Thammasat University for the main reason that it was accused of being Preedee's stronghold. Faculty members and students who collaborated with Preedee to struggle for democracy, peace and social justice were viewed as 'over politicized' and anti-military. As a means to depoliticize the Thammasat and Kan-muang community, General P. Piboonsongkram, the Prime Minister, became an Honorable President of the University in 1949. The original curriculum which offered a degree of 'Moral Science and Politics' was reorganized into four separate faculties namely Law, Political Science, Economics, Commerce and Accountancy. The phase 'Kan-muang' which means 'Politics' was excluded from the name of the university. Furthermore, it was transformed to a closed-university, with limited student enrolment and the requirement of attending class.

The new law curriculum concentrated on purely 'bread and butter' subjects. Courses on Economic Theories, Public Finance Law, and Laws and Regulations of Public Law Organizations, which were part of the original curriculum of Moral Science and Politics, were excluded.

An abortive coup led by the Navy in 1951 brought an even more severe impact to Thammasat University, as the government suspected that Preedee was behind it. All of Thammasat's properties were confiscated. The campus was under surveillance and later was completely occupied by the military for more than five months. Classroom instructions were relocated outside the campus. Finally the Cabinet led by General P. Piboonsongkram decided to sell the campus to the Ministry of Defense for 'military use'. Furthermore, all rights and privileges which Thammasat graduates used to enjoy on an equal status with Chulalongkorn students in the civil service were taken away. The students were concerned about their future as exam time was approaching. In order to put pressure on the government, the students appealed to the media, politicians and Thammasat alumni. They also organized public demonstrations and finally succeeded in forcing the government to return the campus.

The Present Legal Education in Thailand

A brief description of the present legal education in Thailand provides background information on clinical legal education.

Law school undergraduate curriculum At present there are six public universities and 16 private universities which offer study in Legal Science. They are under the supervision of the Ministry of University Affairs (MUA). It has been government policy to control enrolment in public universities on the one hand, and allow the private sector to set up Law Faculties on the other hand. A simple reason given was that the private sector can afford to set up Law Faculties and can depend on teaching-staff from public universities and from other governmental agencies. This indifferent attitude of the government to quality control of legal education and the legal profession, clearly reflects a lack of understanding of the social aspects of the subject matter.

According to the MUA's regulation, all public and private universities' curriculum must follow the 'standards' of Thammasat University which is the oldest university. Despite several curriculum reforms, Thammasat's law curriculum is much influenced by the curriculum of the Legal Education Institute of the Bar Association of Thailand which concentrates on traditional 'bread and butter' courses. Nevertheless a new trend in Thailand requires that all public universities will become an autonomous body financed by public funds. This trend should provide more leeway for adjusting law curricula to be more responsive to rapid internal and external socio-economic changes.

Each private Law Faculty has its own student recruitment process. The MUA put a limit of not more than 300 first-year students at every university. Law students of three public universities (Thammasat, Chulalongkorn and Chiengmai) are recruited through the national competitive examination after the completion of 12 years of primary and secondary schools. Ramkamhaeng and Sukothaitammatirat are the two public open universities with the largest law student enrolment.

Thammasat is the only university which conducts two teaching programs in law at the Bachelor Degree level. The Day-program Student course recruits about 300-400 high school students through the MUA national competitive examination. According to the MUA's system each high school graduate student can select four choices of faculties in any public universities and will be selected according to examination scores. Therefore the majority may not be students who are seriously interested in studying law. Accordingly Thammasat Law Faculty has just recently started to conduct a direct recruitment process to supplement its numbers and has a better turnout.

The day-program student must earn 146 credits to graduate with the Bachelor of Laws Degree. The subjects are classified as Liberal Arts fundamental course (30 credits), Compulsory Law Subjects (92 credits) and

Minor or free elective subjects (24 credits). The Night-program Student is similar to the J.D. program of the United States, as the students read for Bachelor of Law as the second degree. They study for three years on the same compulsory law subjects as the day student and are exempted from fundamental liberal arts and selective subjects. This program has existed since the early 1970s and has become quite popular. About 450 students are recruited through competitive examination each year.

There have been efforts to reduce the numbers of compulsory subjects in order to provide students with more leeway to plan their study. However, it has been difficult as the undergraduate curriculum of every Law School is designed, for the benefit of students, to meet the requirements of the Legal Education Institute of the Thai Bar Association.

The graduate levels Upon graduation, the law students usually enrol with the Legal Education Institution of the Bar Association of Thailand for at least two semesters. They have to pass the national Bar examination if they wish to become judges or public prosecutors. At the age of 25, with at least two years of practical training in private litigation work or serving in governmental organizations, they can apply to take the judicial or public prosecutorial examination. Many students enrol in the Master of Law programs which are offered in four leading universities. In addition, Thammasat offers diploma programs in Public Law and Business Law.

There is no requirement for the passing of the Bar examination if the law graduates wish to engage in private practice. However, as a requirement to acquire a lawyer's license they must engage in a one-year training program organized by the Law Society of Thailand. The Law Society is actually an association of practicing lawyers which used to be part of the Thai-Bar Association, originally composed of judges, public prosecutors and practicing lawyers. Prior to 1985 the Thai Bar Association was authorized to issue advocacy licences to all practicing lawyers. However, due to internal conflicts, the practicing lawyers lobbied to pass the Law Society Act to become a separate autonomous body. According to this new law the Law Society is authorized to issue and terminate the advocacy licence.

Clinical Education in a Historical Context

A systematic formal clinical legal education is a recent phenomenon in Thailand as compared with the situation in the United States. The development of clinical education at Thammasat can be classified into two major stages. They are closely tied up with the country's political development. The first stage of development prior to the 1976 Military Bloody Coup is characterized by its student-initiated, independent, voluntary nature. The second stage of the Post-1976 Military Bloody Coup is marked by the formalization of clinical subjects. This classification is, to a certain extent artificial, as in reality they should not be completely separated but should rather be integrated, reinforcing each other, to bring about a peaceful and just society.

Clinical Education Prior to the 1976 Military Bloody Coup

According to the original Moral Science and Politics curriculum, one practical training course named 'Advocacy Practice' was offered at the Master Degree level. It was prescribed that details of the course, in terms of duration, training site, etc. must be assigned by the University President.

There are several reasons why clinical education was only offered at the Master Degree level in the Thammasat and Kan-Muang University. First, it is not clear how many students studied the Master Degree, and with such a massive number of students in an open-university atmosphere, a systematic clinical education must be difficult to manage. Even after Thammasat was no longer an open-university, the student enrolment has always been massive (at present there are about 1,000 day and night students per year). During my student years (1968-1971) an informal clinical education was offered in the 'Summer Training Course on Advocacy Skills', co-organized by the Faculty of Law and the Lawyers' Association of Thailand. It was not a training in a practical sense because the trainers, who were senior and well-known practicing attorneys, only shared their working experiences through long lectures, without providing any practical skills training.

The second reason is that due to the lack of full-time staff, in the past Thammasat Law Faculty depended upon part-time lecturers from the judiciary and the public prosecutorial office. It was not until the deanship of Professor Sanya Dhammasakdi (1969-1971) that it started to recruit permanent and full-time faculty members. Apart from recent graduates recruited as junior-tutors, a few highly selective retired judges from the Supreme Court were hired to teach procedural law courses. It was around 1970 that one retired judge was assigned to supervise a moot court practice for the students. However, it was a non-credit course.

The third reason is that, in principle, there has been a clear concept of a division of task between the university and the Legal Education Institute of the Thai Bar Association that the university is responsible for the theoretical aspect while the latter is in charge of practical skill-training aspect. However, in reality the Legal Education Institute has failed to fulfil this role. Its instruction repeats the same subjects of the university but concentrates on the teaching on the decisions of the Supreme Court.

The fourth reason is that the law students have not been expected to acquire practical skills at their undergraduate level, so a legal infrastructure to accommodate this role has not been created. Although there is a Criminal Procedural Law provision, providing a court-appointed attorney, and a Labour Protection Law provision which provides advocacy assistance to the employees, the Faculty of Law and the law students are not connected with these activities. The opportunity arises only when clients come directly to seek legal assistance from the Law Center. In addition, the full-time faculty members of public universities are civil servants. They cannot engage in law practice so they spend all their lives in the academic world. Since clinical law subjects have been limited only, a few clinicians are hired.

Nevertheless, at Thammasat some activities comparable to informal non-credit clinical education were initiated by student volunteer groups in the late 1940s and the late 1960s.

The Thammasat and Kan-Muang Women Student Group

In 1949 female law students led by Supattra Singholaka started student-volunteer legal services. They provided legal consultation services under the supervision of the law professors. They also engaged in a legal literacy program and started a law reform campaign on sex equality issues. This group finally founded the Women Lawyers' Association of Thailand under Her Majesty the Queen's Patronage and has been active up to the present. It is an association of Thammasat women law alumni. Another organization, called the Women Advocates Group was founded by Jaruayporn Pattanangkoon, a female lawyer who has long been active on sex equality issues.

The Lawyers' Association of Thailand was also founded and dominated by male lawyers. This association played a vital role in liberating the practicing lawyers from the Thai Bar Association.

The Law Student Study Group (LSSG) or Klum-Nittisuksa

The formation of the LSSG The LSSG was founded by law students around 1970 with the aim of creating a forum to discuss contemporary legal issues related to the broader social context. It was part of the student progressive movement of Thammasat and a broader inter-university intellectual movement. The common objective of these study groups was to raise critical issues on the discrepancies in theoretical teaching and the reality of life under military regimes. They were deeply concerned with widespread corruption, abuses of power, and undue privileges enjoyed through family relations of the country's leaders. So the main thrust was to search for a better society through their respective disciplines.

The fact that all universities receive a certain amount of government subsidy has been used to inspire the students' dedication to serve the people who are the taxpayers. The progressive student groups viewed military dictatorship as a major obstacle to democratic development. These student groups were, nevertheless, the minority since most students under successive military regimes, and even up to the present time, are not aware and turn a blind eye to the fact that tax money has been the major source to support their education. The majority are occupied with studying, sports, dancing parties, etc.

All of the founding members of the LSSG were male students, who were the majority at that time. In addition to internal study circle and public discussions, the LSSG started legal aid services through correspondence. They also organized radio plays based on legal issues, produced analytical writing and engaged in an intellectual movement for democracy. Three successive Deans of the Faculty of Law, who were in office during 1969-1976, played a crucial collaborative role in the legal education reform of the Faculty which affected legal education reform in Thailand as a whole. These three eminent Deans of the Law Faculty were Professor Sanya Dhammasakdi (1969-1971), Professor Chitti Tingsabadh (1971-1974) and Professor Dr Preedee Kasamsup (1974-1976). All of them received legal education abroad and spent most of their life in the judiciary. With an academic and practical background, all of them see the need to combine the theoretical and practical aspects of legal study, so they provided their full support to the LSSG. Two crucial compulsory courses on Philosophy of Law and the Legal Profession were added and are still part of the present curriculum. These two subjects have broadened the students' perspective and have inculcated respect for the profession.

From 1969 onwards, Thammasat Law Faculty started to build up its own full-time faculty members rather than depending on external part-time lecturers.

Newly graduated law students were recruited as junior lecturers. Apart from teaching, they were assigned to supervise the legal aid service and other activities of the LSSG. This assignment started a tradition of student-faculty collaboration. At present, there are about 59 full-time Faculty members.

Reflecting on the historical development of Thammasat clinical education and its legal services is actually a reflection of my personal life. Although three decades have now passed, I can still vividly remember my impressions as a law school student and as a young Faculty member. The Thammasat community was highly inspired by Professor Sanya's motto which always stated, even during the military regime, that Thammasat was a land of freedom. The law students were inspired by the simple and honest ways of life of our law professors, despite their social prestige. Professor Sanya and Professor Chitti are highly respected and admired for the boldness of their judicial decisions under the military dictatorship.

I was a law student during the deanship of Professor Sanya and Professor Chitti and was recruited as a junior tutor during the latter's term. I was a secretary to Professor Dr Preedee Kasamsup who became the Dean after Professor Chitti's resignation. So I have witnessed part of this development. When the LSSG was founded I was a second-year law student. Although I was not a founding member I became an active member of the LSSG and was directly in charge of the legal aid service through correspondence activity throughout my student time. After recruitment as a junior tutorial Faculty member in 1973 I was appointed as one of the LSSG's advisors. I participated in LSSG activities until my departure to study at Yale Law School in 1975. At Yale I took a course on 'Prisoners' Legal Service' which gave me a personal experience of the legal aid service in the USA. After my return to Thailand in 1980, I was appointed as a committee member to supervise the Legal Literacy Group (LLG) which was the revival of the LSSG.

The October 14th, 1973 Uprising, an Intensification of the Student Activism and the Voluntary Legal Literacy Programs

The general atmosphere The anti-military intellectual movement, which the LSSG was part of, culminated in the People's Uprising of October 14, 1973 and brought an end to the 26-year military rule of three successive Generals, namely Piboonsonkram, Sarit and Thanom. King Rama IX intervened to terminate the military violent suppression of the democratic demonstrators. He appointed Professor Sanya Dhammasakdi, who was a member of the Privy Council and the Thammasat University President as the caretaker Prime Minister.

The common scene after the 1973 People's Uprising was the gathering and settling of farmers and workers in Thammasat campus with wholehearted support from the students and certain faculty members. In the morning, these under-privileged groups would gather at strategic sites to take grievances to the post-military dictatorial government. The people's movement did succeed in certain issues. For example the first Minimum Wage Law was passed, followed by the Labor Relations Act of 1975 which restored the right to organize to workers. The Farm Land Rent Control Act was also passed.

Apart from providing accommodation for the under-privileged groups, Thammasat University during 1973-1976 was turned into a people's learning center. The students organized evening classes for different disadvantaged groups. The main auditorium was open every day for public discussions and seminars on social, economic and political issues. Through the work of the Three-United Front of the farmers, the workers and the intellectuals, the progressive movement succeeded in driving out the United States Navy and Air Forces stationed in Thailand during the Indochina War.

In such an atmosphere, the LSSG and the Law Faculty members became more active during the period of three years from the October 14, 1973 uprising to the revival of military dictatorship in a bloody coup on October 6, 1976. During this period, Thammasat Law Faculty under the deanship of Professor Chitti Tingsabadh, followed by Professor Dr Preedee Kasamsup, became active in its legal aid service. It was also active in coordinating progressive law professors and students to provide legal solutions to the caretaker government to rectify illegal and unjust actions committed by the previous military regime.

The LSSG Voluntary Legal Literacy Program

One major activity after the People's Uprising of 1973 was a legal literacy campaign aimed 'to provide legal aid services to the farmers'. For 15 days from November 27 to December 11, 1974, about 70 students and Faculty members organized the Legal Literacy Campaign Project in various villages of Nakornsawan Province. The project was initiated by Montree Rupsuwan, a law student who appealed to the Law Faculty for legal assistance to the peasants in his hometown. The project received financial assistance from the Asia Foundation through Professor William J. Klausner, the Foundation representative who was a part-time lecturer of the Faculty. The students, as well as the Faculty members, including myself, went to this province with high hope that we could apply our legal knowledge to help farmers from losing their land. We divided into seven groups of seven to ten students. Each group was supervised by one Faculty member. The groups stayed in the Buddhist temples or in public schools. The daytime was spent in making a survey of legal problems and in the provision of legal consultations. The night-time was spent in informal legal literacy programs and simple entertainment activities like showing movies.

Although we could not solve the legal problems, this activity was indeed an eye-opener for us, as we were exposed to the reality of how the farmers were legally exploited. Upon our return to Bangkok, we proposed to the Faculty that a public legal service, including participation in a legal literacy project, should be mandatory for all students. The proposal was not approved as other Faculty members felt that a mandatory requirement would destroy the true value of the voluntary spirit. However, the Law Faculty continued its full support to the LSSG.

The Faculty members, in collaboration with the students, continued our public legal services, which included legal consultation for the indigent and legal literacy programs to disadvantaged groups, particularly workers and farmers. By this time, a few law activist students with outstanding academic performance were recruited as Faculty members and strengthened the LSSG's activities.

The political atmosphere after the People's Uprising had an effective impact on the Thammasat Faculty of Law. The student body succeeded in getting the Faculty to alternate one compulsory subject from Legal History to Labor Law with a rationale that it was more related to the life of the people. The Lawyers' Federation of Thailand was founded by Faculty members and the students in order to create a forum for broader participation of lawyers from other institutions. The Federation played a vital role in providing legal consultation to the progressive movement and in the drafting of recommended legislation to be submitted to the government. Many students who were inspired by the socialist ideology dropped study in order to work with the mass movement.

The post-1973 democratic movement led by the Thai intellectuals had apparently undermined the political and economic interests of the military and the national and foreign elites. So they collaborated in building up the right-wing para-military groups to counter the democratic movement. Political assassination of the pro-democratic movement leaders frequently occurred. Thammasat campus was again attacked and set on fire by these groups whilst the police turned a blind eye. On October 6, 1976 the military staged the bloodiest of coups and massacred hundreds of anti-military dictatorship demonstrators right on the Thammasat Campus. The Martial Law Act and the Communist Suppression Act were strictly exercised. All student activities, including the LSSG's, were banned.

The movement leaders were arrested under the Communist Suppression Act, with no rights to representation or appeal. During 1976-1978 thousands of social and political activists fled into the jungle to join the armed struggle led by the Communist Party of Thailand.

The Post-1976 Bloody Coup

The Legal Literacy Group (LLG) By 1978 when the political climate had become relaxed and students' activities were allowed, Thammasat Law students formed the Legal Literacy Group (LLG). A Faculty committee was set up to supervise its legal literacy program. It was around this period that I returned from my study in the United States and was appointed as a committee member. I worked closely with the students in their rural legal literacy programs. The main source of funding came from the Ministry of University Affairs (MUA) which usually provides financial assistance to support small community development projects undertaken by the students during the semester breaks. So the LLG combined the community development projects with a legal literacy program. Students also raised funds to support the projects. I found the students to be lively, talented and dedicated.

The activity started with a two to three day survey of targeted areas, to get a sense of local legal problems. After the survey the students organized a summer legal literacy camp of about seven to ten days. Information gathered from the survey was used to formulate an informal legal literacy program conducted by Faculty members and students during the nights. The provincial judges, public prosecutors or local land officers were usually invited as resource persons. The daytime was spent in the provision of legal consultation at the center site and home visits to the villagers. After a few months of the summer camp the team usually went back for a follow-up. Information gathered during the program would be analyzed and submitted for law revision and policy recommendations, or to a more complete research project. Presently, legal literacy programs are organized more often, with logistic support from government agencies or local organizations.

Apart from the revival of the student activities in 1978, hundreds of non-governmental organizations (NGOs) were founded. At present there are over 400 progressive NGOs. They form about 14 branches of a network with issues on women, children, workers, farmers, the disabled, health and environmental and consumer protection. All of these organizations need legal assistance. Some of them do provide legal assistance to their target groups. I myself was a founding member, and the Secretary General of, the Friends of Women Organization for a few years. The group has an internal unit called the Women's Rights Protection Center. This center provides legal assistance to girls and women who are survivors of sexual violence. I was commissioned by the government to review laws and regulations related to women. I also became the Director of the Women in Development Consortium in Thailand (WIDCIT). Through all these contacts I could contribute to the women's rights movement.

It is worth mentioning that during this period the American foundations like the Asia and the Ford Foundations started to provide support for legal service. International organizations such as the International Commission of Jurists (ICJ) were also active in providing funds to support the legal aid services activities. The activities included the provision of funds to support the student-faculty legal literacy program, study tour grants on legal aid services to the Philippines, and seminar grants to participate in regional workshops on human rights.

The Thammasat University Law Center With continuing efforts of young Faculty members, who were former members of the Law Student Study Group (LSSG) of the 1970s the 'Thammasat Law Center' was finally established as an official unit of the Faculty. The students' Legal Literacy Group became one component of the Center. University funds were allocated to support the Center's activities. From the late 1980s the Center has received an annual government budget.

The main objectives of the Center are:

- To disseminate legal knowledge to the general public.
- To provide legal assistance.
- To provide professional practical skills for the law students.
- To nurture professional ethics and responsibility among students and faculty members.

The Center undertakes the following activites:

- The provision of legal aid services which include free consultation for all cases and litigation services for the indigents.
- Legal literacy program.
- Conducting surveys and research for law and policy reform.

Organizing the summer training program for law students.

The Center is managed by the Director, who is a full-time Faculty member. The Director is the Chair of a committee consisting of full-time professors, retired lecturers and alumni. There are two full-time practicing lawyers, three full-time legal advisers and a few administrative staff. The students join the Law Center on a voluntary basis. The numbers of active student members range from 20 to 30 per year. They can choose to engage in the legal aid service activities, or form their own study groups and apply for financial support from the Law Center for their public activities. One major activity of the latter group is to organize a two-day orientation camp for the first-year law students. This camp's activities concentrate on promoting genuine relationships among students and Faculty members, and on inculcating professional consciousness in the students. Through participation in case meetings and by following the lawyers to the court trials, the students can acquire some knowledge and experiences of practical aspects.

The growth of the Law Center, and most related law student activities, were influenced by the standing and continuing dedication of the ex-Dean, Somyot Chuathai, who was in office during 1992-1997. He was a former active member of the LSSG and the President of the Lawyers' Federation of Thailand, founded after the People's Uprising.

Thammasat Formal Clinical Subjects

At present there are three elective clinical subjects in the Faculty curriculum: Advocacy and Moot Court, Legal Training I, Legal Training II. All of them are 3-credits courses taught for 16 weeks, or a total of 48 hours. Two other compulsory subjects which can influence the students' ideology, are Legal Profession and Philosophy of Law. Apart from these subjects there are compulsory courses on Procedural Law (Criminal, Ciyil and Bankruptcy) and the Law of Evidence. All procedural law and clinical courses are under the Department of Procedural Law. Due to the intensity of the teaching for the day and night programs with large numbers of students and heavy grading workloads, the Faculty still has to depend on external practitioners. Moreover, university funds to hire retired supreme court justices and senior attorneys for full time work at the Faculty have declined. A systematic collaboration between the Law Center and the Department of Procedural Law needs to be developed.

Among the clinical subjects, Advocacy and Moot Court is the oldest. At present, it is offered during both semesters. It is co-taught by two senior attorneys, one of whom is hired by the university to supervise the Thammasat Law Center.

About 40 students register in each semester. The main objective of the course is to provide practical skills for the students in their application of criminal and civil substantive and procedural laws. The course covers different stages of advocacy and representation. Throughout the course the students are trained in reading, writing and oral skills. One-third of the course is allocated for Moot Court which the students are assigned in role plays of particular law-suits. They are also trained in basic skills to arrange legal files and to manage the law office. The students are required to take an exam at the end of the semester. Part of their grade comes from their class-room exercises.

Legal Training I and Legal Training II are two new three-credits elective courses. One objective of offering these two clinical courses is to combine student voluntary activities, which have been a tradition of the Law Center, with academic work. So active student members of the Law Center as well as other student activist groups are encouraged to enroll in these courses. Enrollment in these two courses enables students to combine their study with their social commitments. The old tendency was an absolute separation of an academic and activist world.

Legal Training I is an ungraded three credit course. It is co-taught by several instructors (two full-time Faculty members, one senior attorney who teaches Advocacy and Moot Court, and a supervisor of the Law Center and one high-ranking public prosecutor). About 45 students are enrolled. The students are divided into three groups and study under these instructors on a rotation basis for 16 weeks with a total amount of 48 hours. The instructors concentrate on their fields which are civil/criminal procedures, basic skills for the provision of legal services and contract. Teaching/training topics include:

- Introduction to the legal professions, sharing of instructors' working methods and experiences.
- Techniques on fact finding/investigation, reading, writing and oral skills.
- Counselling techniques and actual training on provision of legal consultation at the Law Center under attorney's supervision.
- Practical training on the drafting of official letters, notice, and the law-suit.

- Application of the Law of Contract focuses on four different types of contracts - on the Establishment of Business Organizations, Secured Transactions, Hire of Service and Sale.
- Case analysis, role-play.
- Study-tour to observe court trials.

Legal Training II is a continuation course of Legal Training I. It aims at providing practical skills in special areas of law. After introductory training by the instructors, the students are assigned to work in specialized units in the public and private sector. They may work in the same offices with other Thammasat Law students who join the Center for the summer voluntary program. All these clinical courses are in the first stage of development and still need appropriate adjustment.

All these three clinical courses not only concentrate on practical learning skills but also emphasize professional ethics and responsibility, which is another component of these courses.

Conclusion

Clinical legal education at Thammasat Law Faculty has developed in two stages. The first was the student voluntary activity motivated by a desire to serve the public with their knowledge and skills. It was followed by a strong desire to struggle against the military dictatorship for a democratic society. The military violence of the bloody coup of October 6, 1976 completely destroyed the Thammasat student movement and the Law Student Study Group (LSSG). The Faculty regulations have been revised to enable the students to graduate within three and a half years. Although subsequently, formal clinical subjects existed side by side with the Law Center, most students overlooked these channels and were preoccupied with a single idea of rushing through their study as quickly as possible. It became a fashion for the students to finish the LLB program within this period, in order to be the first-comers in the economic boom competition and to prove their 'academic ability'. Such an educational system leads to individualism and lack of interest in social extra-curriculum activities.

There is also the bright side of the picture. Ironically, the slow-down of the national economy has pressured Thailand to rethink its future. Obviously, as part of the world community, Thailand is not free from the impact of globalization and powerful pressure for the liberalization of business and trade.

So there is a great need for the Thai legal profession to adjust itself to cope with this new change at an international level. On the other hand, there have been efforts by leading Siamese thinkers to search for alternative development models guided by Buddhism and local wisdom. Undoubtedly, law affects a social norm at both levels of jurisprudence.

The law school curriculum, therefore, must be reformed for our own survival. The new constitution of 1998 which the people have fought for in the hope that it will bring about progressive reform has broadened personal and collective rights and freedoms of the people. Article 242 stipulates the right to representation in both criminal and civil cases. Within the last two decades the Legal Aid Office of the Attorney-General and the Law Society are the two most influential agencies which can attract funding from the government. The future direction could be an enactment of major legislation to provide the legal services. In my view, clinical education courses provide a holistic learning opportunity. The students must cope with the positive legal principles of a case. In the formation of their arguments, the students trace the historical development of the law. An exposure to the surrounding socio-economic factors of a case, with appropriate professional guidance, assists the students to develop their critical thinking. Furthermore, the constitution has established various organizations aimed at a more effective check and balance system. New offices of these organizations will need legal human resources for provision of public service at different levels. The Thammasat Faculty of Law must take these facts into account and design clinical legal education programs which can combine professional excellence with a high voluntary spirit aimed at a better Thailand.

Notes

1 Preedee Kasemsup, Philosophy of Law [in Thai], printed by the Faculty of Law Textbook Project, 1996, 6.

2 Dr Tida Saraya, Dharma Raja During the Sukhothai Period, printed in 'The Ancient State in South East Asia: Origins and Evolution'.

3 Luang Saranaiyaprassasana (Tannya Na Songkha), Pattanakan Kansuksa Kodmai Nai Pratet Thai - the Development of Legal Study in Thailand, printed and published by Thammasat University, November 1956, 9.

7 Legal Education in Argentina and Chile

STEPHEN MEILI

Introduction

This chapter analyzes the history and more recent developments in the social justice mission of law schools in Argentina and Chile. Based on field work in the region since 1994, as well as archival research, it explores the varying ways in which law schools within the two countries have (or have not) attempted to promote progressive social change over time, and the many barriers that have impeded attempts to foster this kind of dynamic. It also focuses on more recent initiatives within certain law schools in the current post-authoritarian period which seek to create an intellectual and professional climate more consistent with progressive social objectives. As this chapter explains, there are numerous barriers - both traditional and modern - that have impeded these efforts, as well.

One of the more important themes of this chapter is the effect of the increased globalization of the legal marketplace over the past decade. In a variety of ways, this globalization has both advanced and hindered the social justice mission of law schools in Argentina and Chile. On the one hand, it has lead to the international exchange of ideas and strategies between legal scholars and administrators, which has promoted more progressive scholarship, curriculum, and other programs in many law schools of the region. On the other hand, however, the demands which the globalized legal market place on the scarce time and financial resources of these same law schools detracts from their fledgling social justice missions.

Historical Underpinnings

Law schools in Argentina and Chile, as in most other countries within Latin America, have traditionally had a very limited social justice mission. For reasons of politics, ideology, legal culture, lack of resources, and jurisprudence, law schools have rarely been at the forefront of any of the significant social movements that have mobilized various social sectors within the countries over the last century or so (Wilson, 1989, Junquiera, Chapter 8, Meili, 1998). According to Argentine attorney Alicia Curiel, who has worked with the Center for Legal and Social Studies (CELS), a non-governmental organization in Buenos Aires, Argentina, 'the legal education system here does not encourage public interest work' (Curiel, interview). And Professor Felipe Viveros of Diego Portales University in Santiago de Chile notes that public interest law is a new phenomenon in Chilean legal education (Viveros, interview). The major exception to this rule - at least until recently - is the array of clinical programs in which law students work for the poor in legal aid offices in low income communities. But this clinical component, described in more detail below, focuses on representation of individuals with particular problems rather than any kind of systemic reform.

The various impediments to social change lawyering in these two countries are described in more detail below.

The Traditional Social Justice Mission of Law Schools

The social justice mission of law schools in both Argentina and Chile has been traditionally confined to direct service clinical programs; i.e. programs in which law students spend at least part of their time representing low income clients.[1] Chile's legal aid clinical program is probably the most well-established and extensive in Latin America. Since 1928, Chile's public law schools have required their graduates to perform six months of free legal service at a legal aid center before taking the national bar exam (Samway, 1996). Most of the legal aid centers are run by the Chilean Bar Association, which has been more assertive in the representation of the poor than its Argentine counterpart.[2] Some critics of the Chilean clinical program note that it is not integrated into the law school curriculum and almost always involves the representation of a single client in a single case; rarely are law students involved in any kind of social change or social justice lawyering when they participate in this program. Nor is there any emphasis on developing creative ways of dealing with the underlying problems faced by the clients as a whole (Lowenstein, 1970).

In Argentina, several law schools include a mandatory one year course which involves representation of the poor in cases involving issues such as alimony, divorce, housing, inheritance, and adoptions. Representation in criminal and tort cases is excluded. According to Professor Christian Courtis of the University of Buenos Aires, which offers such a course, the major problems with this program are related to the sheer numbers of students who participate in it (approximately 25,000 students attend the law school). It is simply impossible to assure or ascertain the quality or effectiveness of the services students are rendering (Courtis, interview). And, as in Chile, the focus of these clinical programs has been on representation of individuals rather than assertion of rights on any group-wide or systemic basis.

Impediments to a Broader Social Justice Mission

The Traditional Law School Curriculum and Pedagogical Methodology

As Wilson notes, '[I]n South America, strict statutory regulation of the law school curriculum, with extensive control of the number and order of law school courses, leaves little room for curricular innovation by the faculty and can lead to rote presentation of required courses' (Wilson, 1989). Law schools in Argentina and Chile have certainly fitted this pattern. Most of their required curriculum focuses on the memorization of legal codes and other doctrine. There is a heavy emphasis on civil law, civil procedure, and legal positivism (Lowenstein, 1970; Viveros, interview; Meili, 1998). The faculty employs the *cátedra magistral* or formal lecture, approach, which allows for little class participation (Lowenstein, 1996, Wilson, 1989). Questioning of the social or political rationality of the laws is generally discouraged (Meili, 1998). While specifically about Chile, the following observation from Lowenstein summarizes the traditional pedagogical approach at law schools in both Chile and Argentina:

> ...[T]he cardinal objective of law teaching has been the transmission of information. The student's mind has been shaped by sitting through innumerable lectures, reading, if anything, expository class-note collections, manuals or treatises, and regurgitating ingested information on examinations. Professorial dogmatism and student memorization of secondary doctrinal sources has tended to produce relatively passive minds concerned primarily with recall of legal information. Even more troublesome, law has traditionally been viewed as a collection of ordered rules and accompanying doctrine. Conceptual classification of these rules in pristine categories has been the highest expression of legal reasoning. Logic has been vaunted over experience, a metaphysical, speculative approach over a utilitarian,

experimental one. Law has been regarded as immutable and static rather than a flexible instrument for shaping human affairs. (Lowenstein, 1970)

The rigidity of the curriculum has been reinforced by forces both within and outside the law schools. For example, the First Conference of Latin American Law Schools, held in 1959, warned law schools against 'overloading the curriculum with too many courses' (Declaration of Principles, 1959). Law schools, particularly the larger state-sponsored schools, are extremely bureaucratic, making any significant curricular reform difficult (Courtis, interview; Viveros, interview). And law professors who have been teaching the same required courses for many years have a vested interest in maintaining their control over those courses and their important role in the overall law school curriculum. Such professors 'tend to insulate the curriculum from fundamental change' (Lowenstein, 1970).

This is not to say that there have never been any attempts at curricular reform. Indeed, such reform was a frequent theme throughout the region during the 1960s. For example, at the Second Conference of Latin American Law Schools, in 1961, the participants concluded that:

> Law teaching should be 'active'; there should be 'an intimate copenetration between doctrinal and practical teaching, the latter meaning various aspects of professional formation, not merely procedural techniques'. The 'practical teaching' is to include, among others, orientation to legal materials, solution to practical cases and problems, and legal aid clinic work. (Mayda, 1962)

In Chile in the 1960s, there were efforts to make the curriculum more flexible and integrated with social and economic problems at large. According to Alberto Baltra Cortes, a Senator and law school professor at the time, 'We must free our teaching of its static character ... and imbue our students with the understanding that legal institutions are not eternal and immutable, but are no more than temporary structures subject to change' (Third Conference of Latin American Law Schools, 1963, 665). And former Dean Sanhueza of the University of Concepcion stated that the goal of legal education is to prepare 'lawyers in the broadest sense as people capable of giving direction to society'. (Fuenalida Pereyra, 1965).

Despite such lofty sentiments, however, there was little meaningful reform in Chilean - or Argentine - legal education through the late 1960s or early

1970s. And any hopes at reform were dashed with the military regimes that came to power in both countries during the 1970s.

Law Professors

There are certain characteristics common to most law school professors in Chile and Argentina (and, by extension, the rest of Latin America) which have impeded efforts at imbuing law schools with a social justice mission. First, most law professors have little interest in changing the status quo, both within their institutions and in society at large (Garcia, interview). This ideological pattern has been reinforced as a result of the military regimes in Chile from 1973 to 1990 and in Argentina from 1976 to 1982. These regimes either 'disappeared' progressive law professors or drove them into exile or silence. Thus, an entire generation of professors who might otherwise have fostered a sense of social justice into their pedagogy has all but disappeared from the law school landscape. As Chilean law professor Cristian Riego notes, during the Pinochet regime, progressives were not permitted to pursue academic careers, which meant that the only people teaching the nation's law students for two decades were either 'conservative or passive' (Riego, interview).

Second, most law professors work part-time for low pay and have heavy teaching schedules, as well as the demands of an outside practice; all of which discourage those professors from developing new courses or preparing new course materials (Wilson, 1989; Lowenstein, 1970). The model of the part-time professor has been historically preferred in Latin America, since it emphasizes the practical side of the profession. The first conference of Latin American Law Faculties, held in Mexico City in 1959, adopted the following basic principle:

> The appointment of full-time faculty members is considered advisable only in cases where the activity, mainly or exclusively, relates to scientific research....In all other cases, teaching shall be on a part-time basis, in order to give the instruction the benefit of the normal contact of the professor with professional atmosphere and activities. (Declaration of Principles, 1959)

There is an irony to this position, of course, since the strict confines of code memorization and the *cátedra magistral* pedagogical models would seem to leave little room for discussion of practical professional experience. In any event, historically, and unlike in the United States, part-time teaching status at Latin American law schools has been more prestigious than full-time status. Indeed, many professors resist becoming full-time members of a faculty for this reason (Wilson, 1989). As a result, the balance of power in most Chilean and Argentine law schools has rested with a veteran corps of part-time professors with little time or inclination to alter the status quo.

Lack of Legal Scholarship

One of the most important ways that law schools promote social justice is, of course, through legal scholarship. In Chile and Argentina, at least until very recently, there was virtually none of it, for a variety of reasons. As Professor Viveros notes, legal research is costly, and there is little financial support for it both within most law schools and from outside foundations (Viveros, interview). Most professors, by virtue of their part-time status, have little time for it (Wilson, 1989). Thus, in Chile for example, most legal research has consisted of approving student-produced class notes and writing relatively superficial manuals describing positive law or specific legal rules (Lowenstein, 1970). As one critic has noted, in Chilean legal scholarship:

> The attention of the researcher was directed toward the past, looking for the tracks left by the activities that had generated the law, in order to better interpret the will expressed by the legislator. Critical analysis of the existing law appeared only accidentally, as an addition to ... exposition and the efforts directed to locate the particular norm within the general normative system, or to check that norm against principles based on *a priori* rationalism. (Gesche Muller, 1967)

There has also been a dearth of legal scholarship in Argentine. According to Dezalay and Garth, Argentine legal scholarship has traditionally been little more than a collection of citations and quotes from scholars in other countries (Dezalay and Garth, 1998). This 'comparative legal tourism' has made Argentine scholarship irrelevant to issues that animate Argentine politics and society (Dezalay and Garth, 1998). Other critics see much of Argentina's legal scholarship as biased. According to Argentine law professor Martin Bohmer, since the part-time law professors who write articles are practitioners who usually have significant influence over the development of the law, they are writing in their own economic and professional self-interest (Bohmer, interview). As an example of this bias, Bohmer notes that professors sometimes hold private seminars with judges to explain why their rulings in particular cases (which went against the writings of the law professor) were inaccurate (Bohmer, interview).

The Legal Culture

Latin American law schools are part of - and operate within - a legal culture that historically has not perceived a link between law and social justice. On the contrary, most view the law more as a tool to legitimize executive and/or military repression than a means to assert rights or force decision-makers to abide by laws or constitutional provisions (Meili, 1998). According to Argentine attorney Luis Moreno Ocampo, who prosecuted military officials from the 'dirty war':

> People are not used to using the judiciary as a means of controlling power. This society never had the perception of the judiciary as an independent power. Only in 1984 when the trials started did people realize that the judiciary could be used in this way; but then you have to build up the habit and custom to do this; but the power always wants to maintain a non-independent judiciary. (Ocampo, interview)

Recent polls underscore this point: In a 1993 survey of low-income Chileans, 57 per cent believed that access to legal assistance is either difficult or impossible, and 83 per cent expressed a negative opinion about the justice system in general, frequently referring to its discriminatory character (Samway, 1996). And in Argentina, approximately half of the people believe that the judicial sector is inaccessible (Ratliff and Buscaglia, 1997) Indeed, in its platform for a second term in power, the ruling coalition in Chile (the Coalition of Parties for Democracy) noted that 'justice is still inaccessible for vast sectors of poor people' (Samway, 1996).

To the extent that it is seen as at all utilitarian, the legal system in these two countries is viewed - and has consciously been designed - as a means of resolving disputes between private individuals (almost exclusively those who can afford private counsel) rather than between individuals and the state or private corporations (Dezalay and Garth, 1998). According to Professor Felipe Viveros of Diego Portales University in Santiago:

> Lawyers are in a competitive field, where there is great pressure to be in lucrative and prestigious activities. The market determines the social and economic position of lawyers. In this respect, legal assistance for the poor and

marginalized and involvement in matters of a social and political nature does not appear to be an attractive alternative for trained graduates in accordance with a concept of success inextricably bound to status and economic power. The lawyers and centers that take part in public interest actions usually do not even have obvious clients to pay for their services. (Viveros, 1998)

For many of the reasons cited above, law schools in Latin America - particularly in Chile - generally do not attract people who view working for social justice (at least in the larger civil society sense) as a career goal. As Chilean law professor Cristian Riego puts it, those Chileans who have the most energy and interest in attacking social problems do not choose to go into law; they opt instead for more direct, political involvement with various social movements working for progressive change (womens' movements, indigenous peoples' movements, etc.). And lawyers within these same movements tend to orient themselves to sociology, anthropology and economics, rather than the application of the law, as a means of advancing the agenda of the movement. The options for effective social change through a more activist approach are far more developed and legitimate among progressives than traditional legal strategies, which are seen by the Left as overly bureaucratic, regressive, and compromised, regardless of the good intentions of the participants (Riego, interview).

While the professors hired at law schools in the two countries in the post-authoritarian period have been more progressive than those who continued teaching during the dictatorships, the students whom they teach seem to be less so. During the dictatorship, public universities, including law schools, were centers of political organizing and opposition to the governing regimes. In the aftermath of the dictatorships, most students have turned inward, focusing more on their own livelihoods than on larger social concerns (Meili 1998). As Cristian Riego puts it, 'the faculty at Universidad Diego Portales [where he teachcs] has more of an orientation toward new activism, but the students are less motivated' (Riego, interview).

Globalization

Globalization in legal education is an increasingly important phenomenon in Argentina and Chile, as well as the rest of the world (Cooper and Trubek, 1997). In many ways, such globalization has fostered social justice teaching at law schools: law professors from different countries now exchange information about human rights, environmental protection, and the rights of women and indigenous persons. And globalization is at least partially responsible for the increase in legal scholarship that focuses on social justice issues. It has also provided much of the funding to support such initiatives and exchanges. But on the other hand, while the new demands of globalization should, as Cooper and Trubek note, foster an examination by law students of the limits of the law in dealing with the myriad of problems created by a transnational economy, in some ways those demands seem to have impeded social justice training of law students. For example, in order to remain viable in the increasingly competitive legal education market, many law schools - including some which have an arguably public interest philosphy - have devoted significant resources to preparing their students for a global marketplace (Dezalay and Garth, 1998). In the past, law schools trained law students for work in firms that were not particularly competitive, and where one often obtained a job through family connections rather than skills (Riego, interview). And indeed, this is still the dominant law firm model. However, over the past decade, a few law firms have emerged with what one lawyer terms a more 'globalized' style; i.e. the attorneys speak English, frequently obtained LLMs from law schools in the United States, and the offices are more like firms in the United States. Landing graduates in positions with such firms lends credibility and, more than likely, increased financial support, to the law schools that trained them.

In addition, the prestige attached to careers with firms active in the global marketplace attracts many of the best and brightest law students, particularly at private law schools (Riego, interview). Many of these students see law school not as an end in itself, but as the means to make the all-important international contacts necessary for a career in that global marketplace (Riego, interview). This reality creates more pressure on law schools to devote the time and resources to developing and maintaining those contacts. And needless to say, it is unlikely that any of the positions coveted by students in the prestigious, global-oriented firms include social justice lawyering.

The Post-Authoritarian Social Justice Mission of Law Schools

Despite the many obstacles to the establishment of a social justice mission at law schools in Argentina and Chile, several developments in post-authoritarian society signal that some change, albeit gradual, is underway. These changes are evident in four discrete, but interrelated areas: curriculum reform, legal scholarship, clinical education, and - at least in the case of Chile - the training of judges. Each of these areas are explored below.

Curriculum Reform

While the traditional curriculum has been reformed in both countries over the past decade or so, this phenomenon seems to be more prominent in Chile, particularly in its smaller private schools. This is in part a matter of political ideology and in part a response to the increased globalization of the legal market. Efforts to reform legal education in the region include focusing less on memorization and more on the legal skills that lawyers will need to possess and use in an increasingly competitive - and global - marketplace; replacing the encyclopedic approach to legal education, manifested most dramatically in a host of mandatory courses (e.g. civil procedure, contracts, constitutional law, administrative law, commercial law, and Roman law), with a more flexible curriculum which includes electives such as government law, commercial law, family law, labor law, negotiation/mediation, and legal ethics, as well as courses in legal research and writing (Riego, interview; Courtis, interview, 12/5/99). Professor Cristian Riego of Diego Portales University provides the following market-based justification for the latter course:

> The product we are delivering is becoming more and more obsolete in relation to the requirements of the market, because now, although you can survive as a lawyer [in Chile] without doing research, generally the most advanced and important positions in the market require you to do research. You will not be an important or a well-paid lawyer if you cannot do research. (Riego, interview)

Other newly introduced courses include human rights, domestic violence, and public interest law, which until recently was never a separate category of law in either country (Viveros, interview).

The methodology of law school teaching is also undergoing change at many law schools in both Chile and Argentina. In the past, law school pedagogy consisted almost exclusively of teachers lecturing on black letter law and students taking notes. This has led to a situation in which lawyers are familiar only with textbooks, but lack a sophisticated approach to legal problems (Gonzalez, interview). Legal education reformers in Chile are suggesting that this model be altered in several ways. First, law students should be assigned a variety of mandatory reading material (i.e. in addition to traditional texts such as the Constitution and various legal codes). Examples include journal articles and legal interpretations by prestigious professors from countries like Argentina and Spain. Second, law school courses should include the study of case precedent (as in the United States and other common law countries). As Professor Felipe Gonzalez notes, 'just because case law is not legally binding does not mean that jurisprudence is unimportant' (Gonzalez, interview). In addition, students are being encouraged to focus more on legal research, although this shift in emphasis may have come too late, since most students with money travel abroad to learn legal research at law schools in the United States or Europe (Riego, interview). The situation is similar in Argentina, where upper level elective courses emphasize research papers, group projects, and class participation, as opposed to mere lecture and memorization (Courtis, interview, 5/12/99).

Although these reforms may seem - even to their designers - to have little to do with the social justice mission of law schools, deeper inspection reveals at least a subtle relationship between the two. First, these reforms are likely to make law students more creative and inquisitive as practicing attorneys than those attorneys who graduate with little more than memorized legal codes and constitutional provisions in their heads. While in most situations this distinction will merely make the former lawyers more successful in obtaining money for their clients and themselves, it will also lead to more success among those few attorneys who choose a public interest career path. It is clear that social justice advocacy in post-authoritarian Latin America will require a great deal of ingenuity and legal deftness in choosing, for example, which cases to litigate and when and how to litigate them. These decisions will require more than a routinized knowledge of legal texts, but a broader awareness of how various laws have been applied by different judges, interpreted by legal scholars, and fit within the more general context of civil society. Lawyers trained in the traditional, *càtedra magistral* method, with little emphasis on creative problem-solving or sensitivity to the interaction between law and social problems, are unlikely to meet this challenge.

Second, these reforms are likely to attract more sophisticated - and perhaps socially activist - professors who are interested in a more complex and globalized form of legal education. As Felipe Gonzalez explains, it is not as challenging to teach an encyclopedic course (Gonzalez, interview). These reforms will help law schools recruit professors who are more likely to cultivate in students an idea of how their legal education and careers as lawyers are related to various social problems and movements. In this way, the long-dominant view of law as unrelated - or even hostile - to such problems and movements may begin to subside.

Finally, another way in which reform-minded professors are subtly developing the social justice mission of law schools is through what one such professor terms as 'implicit curriculum'; i.e. encouraging a climate of pluralism, dialogue, and freedom for students to criticize authority without fear of retribution (Viveros, interview). The goal is to prevent law schools and their students from being isolated from social and political problems. This is a far cry from the traditional model of student passivity, which mirrored - and reinforced - the authoritarian nature of the larger society, particularly during periods of military dictatorship (Meili, 1998).

Legal Scholarship

Some law schools in post-authoritarian Argentina and Chile are emphasizing and encouraging independent legal research by their full-time faculty. Indeed, schools such as Diego Portales in Chile and University of Palermo in Buenos Aires have raised outside funding in order to sponsor such research (Bohmer, interview; Gonzalez, interview). The University of Palermo is actually a graduate program into which students from other law schools in Buenos Aires feed. All students in the program must either work in a clinical program (usually a placement with a public interest attorney or organization) or work on a journal.

At Diego Portales University, the emphasis is on research that goes beyond interpretations of individual judicial decisions, and focuses on more complex issues of law in the larger civil society. This development is in part a response to the demands of the global legal marketplace (a law school with journals similar to those published in the United States is likely to appear more prestigious) and a means of attracting a more sophisticated faculty (Gonzalez, interview; Riego 29/12/98 interview). A significant portion of this scholarship deals with issues of social justice, the rights of disenfranchised groups, and legal strategies for addressing problems in these areas.

Clinical Education

Perhaps the most visible and wide-ranging change in the social justice mission of law schools in post-authoritarian Argentina and Chile is in their clinical programs. This change is evident in at least two ways: the first is an expanded scope for the traditional, individual client clinical model that each country has followed for decades. In Argentina, the mandatory one year course remains in place in some of the public law schools, but the range of options for students participating in it has been increased beyond serving at a local legal aid office. Now, students can work at one of several non-governmental organizations that address issues such as human rights and childrens' rights (Courtis, interview). Such programs are similar to the for-credit externships offered by many law schools in the United States.

In Chile, some clinics in recent years have begun to emphasize a more community-based lawyering in which law students work in neighborhood centers and focus on disseminating information and training to members of the community rather than on providing direct legal assistance. An example of this model in Chile is clinical students at the University of Santa Tomar who work at neighborhood centers in a program organized by the non-profit organization FORJA (The Institute for Juridical Formation). The point of these programs is for lawyers and law students to train members of the community to act as their own advocates rather than as legal representatives who go from client to client in an attempt to solve individual legal problems. As Sebastian Cox, the Executive Director of FORJA explains, the program, which receives funding from the Ford Foundation, allows law students to see how this type of community education works (Cox, interview). Students help community organizers conduct training sessions on issues such as family law, property law, labor law, social security and retirement, and citizenship (i.e. immigration status). They also help prepare written educational materials that are distributed to the community (Cox, interview).

This kind of social justice training has something in common with 'alternative lawyering' a term used to describe lawyers who reject the legal system and traditional forms of practicing law (such as litigation and legislative advocacy) and advocate instead a more grass-roots orientation (Rojas, 1988; Ellman, 1998; Meili 1993). According to those who advocate alternative law, the role of the lawyer is more like that of a consultant to a neighborhood-based group or existing social movement, rather than as a legal advisor dictating strategy for an individual client. In this way, the role of the lawyer is de-mystified, and members of the grass roots groups are able to make choices on their own.[3]

The second way in which clinics in the two countries have changed in recent years is an increased emphasis on what some in the United States and elsewhere term 'impact litigation'. Post-authoritarian governments in both countries have passed new laws and constitutional provisions in the areas of human rights, employment discrimination, the rights of women and indigenous persons, and consumer and environmental protection. Clinics in several law schools within both countries have initiated lawsuits pursuant to these laws. Examples include suits against a Chilean department store for harassing and humiliating lower income customers, the Argentine government for approving a harmful prescription drug, and a private data bank in Argentina for invasion of privacy.

The clinics hope to achieve several objectives through this form of lawyering, which shares many characteristics with the impact litigation of the civil rights, womens', environmental and consumer movements in the United States several decades ago: One objective is to influence the scope of recently enacted laws by obtaining judicial interpretations favorable to marginalized populations. A second goal is to show the public how these laws can be used to achieve socially progressive ends. And a third aim is to encourage and develop an independent judiciary.

The efforts of these law schools have been aided significantly by the Ford Foundation, which has provided funding for annual conferences among the six law schools, as well as publications of the proceedings. These conferences provide a forum to discuss comparative legal theories and litigation strategy, as well as ethical issues. They also allow for discussion of the extent to which newly enacted statutes and constitutional provisions in each of the participating countries are being enforced by the judiciary. The conferences have also included papers by clinical faculty on topics related to the work of the individual clinics (Gonzalez, et al. 1998).

The Change in Law Student Demographics

One of the ironies of the post-authoritarian increase in the social justice activity at some law schools is that they were made possible, in part, by changes that occurred at law schools during the dictatorship periods. More specifically, the number of law schools and law students increased in both countries, particularly in Chile. Between 1945 and 1955, no more than 150 law students graduated from Chilean law schools in a given year. By 1994, that number reached 690 (Samway, 1996). This increase was the result of a large number of new private law schools established during the dictatorship, whose leaders encouraged such expansion as a sign of national modernization and professionalism, in response to the demands of an increasingly global legal marketplace. But this increase in the number of law schools also brought about changes that were most likely not intended by the ruling regimes; most significantly the diversification of the law student population. As the law schools opened themselves to students of more diverse backgrounds, they necessarily became more receptive to innovation in pedagogy and scholarship (Wilson, 1989). In addition, there was an increase in the number of progressive professors (particularly in the latter years of the dictatorship, when repression eased somewhat), and an expansion in clinical programs that sought to bring a social justice perspective to the practical training of law students. This increase in the number and diversity of law schools helped create a climate more amenable to the kind of public interest initiatives described above.

Law Schools and the Judiciary

Another way that reform-minded law schools in Chile are at least indirectly promoting social justice is by educating judges. Diego Portales University has for many years held seminars for judges on legal reasoning and judicial reform. Most of the judges who attended the seminars were 'non-mainstream' judges who are more open to new ideas and approaches. The purpose of these seminars is to introduce judges to the idea of public interest litigation and to encourage them to be more independent - not simply from the executive branch, which has long been a problem for the judiciary throughout Latin America - but also from the Superior Court, the highest court in the country which controls the judicial system in Chile (Gonzalez, interview).[4] Thus far, while a few judges have been willing to act independently, these are isolated cases. As Cristian Riego puts it, the Superior Court justices exert tremendous control over lower court judges, making it difficult for the latter to depart from the traditionally limited role of the judiciary in public interest litigation (Riego, interview, 30/12/98). Most judges adhere to the conservative notion that their function is simply to apply existing law (usually in the form of one of the explicit legal codes) to the case, rather than interpret the law in a new way because of the facts presented in a given controversy. This tradition was only strengthened during the recent Chilean military dictatorship.

Even though most judges are rather risk-averse, if they do render a decision that is publicly popular and does not infringe on any important business interests, they are not likely to be reprimanded by their superiors. Professor Cristian Riego cites decisions in discrimination cases as falling into this category. On the other hand, it is riskier for judges to side with litigants who challenge the standard economic status quo, state power, secrecy, or moral issues such as abortion (Riego, interview, 29/12/98). If there is a stronger awareness of a particular problem within a community, such as in an environmental or consumer law case, there is a greater likelihood that a public interest lawsuit will be successful, assuming it does not seek to stop an investment from being made (such as a new factory) or force an investment to be made (such as the installation of pollution control equipment).

Conclusion

One can draw at least two, intertwined conclusions, from an inquiry into the social justice mission of law schools in Argentina and Chile. The first is that schools in both countries are beginning to emphasize such a mission more than at any time in the past. Some law schools are taking steps - however modest - to revamp their curriculum more fully to integrate legal education with other forces in society. There are more scholarly journals and more full time law professors to write articles in them; articles which go beyond the recitation or summation of standard legal doctrine and focus on issues such as the law's response to the conditions and rights of marginalized groups. And the scope of law school clinical programs has enlarged beyond the traditional single client model of the past 75 years or so, moving in new directions such as community-based lawyering and impact litigation.

While this increased emphasis on social justice goals and strategies is certainly due to the recent political opening in each country following years of dictatorship, it is also a direct result of the other phenomenon influencing law schools throughout the region: globalization. The influence of the United States and Europe in these developments is unmistakable, both through their legal institutions and traditions, as well as through the financial sources which fund the social justice initiatives. For example, the law reform litigation model exemplified by the cooperative clinical effort described above is very similar to that followed by mainstream public interest groups in the United States; that is, using test case litigation as a means of either creating new law (particularly common law) or convincing a judge to interpret an existing law in a way that (at least in the eyes of the group bringing the lawsuit) will result in positive progressive change. Indeed, the post-authoritarian stage in Latin America, with its array of new laws in the areas of consumer and environmental protection and discrimination, to name a few, bears a strong resemblance to the United States in the 1960s, when a host of progressive lawyers brought lawsuits to enforce or otherwise give power to recently enacted federal and state legislation in many of the same issue areas.

In addition, many of the ideas for curricular reform came from the United States, where many of the law professors active in the nascent reform movement received at least part of their legal education. For example, according to Felipe Viveros, the concept of poverty law, which is the subject of a seminar at Universidad Diego Portales, was taken from the United States (Viveros, interview).

Moreover, the funding for many of the initiatives that have allowed this social justice mission to develop has come from the United States, in particular the Ford Foundation. While the influence of the United States is not as openly hegemonic or paternalistic as it was during the Law and Development period of the 1960s (Trubek, et al, 1993; Wilson, 1989), it is an undeniably strong force in the region. Indeed, according to Cristian Riego, 'most of the ideas [concerning public interest lawyering in Latin America] come from the United States in the 1960s' (Riego, interview 29/12/98). And Felipe Gonzalez notes that many of these ideas are attributable to 'American Airlines', a playful but nonetheless poignant reference to the significant contact and exchanges between law professors and funding sources from the United States and Latin America (Gonzalez, interview).

As we have seen, however, globalization also impedes the social justice mission of law schools in Argentina and Chile. The significant professional demands of the global legal marketplace have caused both law schools and their students to divert attention from public interest goals, and to focus instead on the practicalities of operating within an increasingly competitive market. Faced with these realities, many law schools are training students for work along a United States corporate law firm model, which leaves less time and resources for training in public interest lawyering.

Notes

1 Such programs are common throughout Latin American law schools. Wilson notes that they are 'relatively weak and of marginal importance, much the same as [they are] in the United States' (Wilson, 1989).

2 Bar Associations in some Latin American countries, most notably Brazil, have been instrumental in supporting public interest law (Junqeira, 1998; Meili, 1998).

3 Cox recognizes the parallel to alternative law, but - like many other lawyers I have interviewed in Latin America - prefers not to adopt that rather controversial term. He realizes that FORJA's work, and the way it involves law students, is different from traditional legal practice, but he prefers to focus on the work - bringing about change little by little, as he puts it, rather than be a 'big talker' about alternative law (Cox, interview).

4 One of the ways in which the Superior Court controls the careers of lower court judges is that in order for such a judge to upgrade his or her position, the judge must receive permission from the Superior Court judges (Gonzalez, interview).

References

Interviews

Martin Bohmer, University of Palermo, interview by author, tape recording, Buenos Aires, June 6, 1994.
Christian Courtis, University of Buenos Aires, interview by author, via Internet, March 15, 1999.
Christian Courtis, University of Buenos Aires, interview by author, via Internet, May 12, 1999.
Sebastian Cox, Director, Institute for Juridical Formation, interview by author, tape recording, Santiago de Chile, December 30, 1998 (translated by Leigh Payne).
Alicia Curiel, Center for the Study of Law and Society (CELS), Buenos Aires, interview by author, tape recording, Buenos Aires, July 15, 1994.
Julio Garcia, Center for Social Investigations and Popular Legal Assistance (CISALP), Buenos Aires, interview by author, tape recording, Buenos Aires, July 1, 1994 (translated by Leigh Payne).
Felipe Gonzalez, Diego Portales University, interview by author, tape recording, Santiago, de Chile, December 29, 1998.
Luis Moreno Ocampo, interview by author, tape recording, Buenos Aires, June 8, 1994.
Cristian Riego, Diego Portales University, interview by author, tape recording, Santiago de Chile, December 29, 1998.
Cristian Riego, Diego Portales University, interview by author, via telephone, Santiago de Chile, December 30, 1998.
Felipe Viveros, Diego Portales University, interview by author, Madison, Wisconsin, September 30, 1998.

Secondary Sources

Cooper, J. and Trubek, L. (1997), *Educating for Justice: Social Values and Legal Education*, Ashgate, Aldershot.
Declaration of Principles of the First Conference of Latin American Law Schools (1959), Inter-American Law Review, vol. 1, 241.
Dezalay, Y. and Garth, B. (1998), 'Argentina: Law at the Periphery and Law in Dependencies: Political and Economic Crisis and the Instrumentalization and Fragmentation of Law', *American Bar Foundation Working Paper*, 9708.
Dezalay, Y. and Garth, B. (1998), 'Chile: Law and the Legitimization of Transitions: From the Patrimonial State to the International Neo-Liberal State', *American Bar Foundation Working Paper*, 9709.
Ellman, S. (1998), 'Cause Lawyering in the Third World', in A. Sarat and S. Schiengold (eds) (1998), *Cause Lawyering: Political Commitments and Professional Responsibilities*, Oxford University Press, Oxford, 349.
Fuenalida Pereyra, J. (1965) *Un Siglo de Estudios Jurídicos en Concepción 1865-1965*, vol. 1, 108.
Gesche Müller (1967), Bernardo, *et al*, *Investigación de la Paternidad Ilegitima*, 25.
Gonzalez, F. et al, (eds) (1998) *Ciudadanía e Interés Público: Enfoques desde el derecho, la Ciencia Política y la Scoiología*, Faculty of Law, the University of Diego Portales, Santiago de Chile.
Junqueira, E. (1998) 'The Brazilian Bar Association in the Struggle for Human Rights', paper presented at the Annual Law and Society Meeting, Aspen, Colorado, June 1998.
Lowenstein, S. (1970), *Lawyers, Legal Education, and Development: An Examination of the Process of Reform in Chile*, International Legal Center, New York.
Mayda (1962), 'Second Conference of Latin-American Faculties of Law and Social Sciences', in *American Journal of Comparative Law*, vol. 11, 151.
Meili, S. (1998) 'Cause Lawyers and Social Movements: A Comparative Perspective on Democratic Change in Argentina and Brazil', in A. Sarat and S. Schiengold (eds) (1998), *Cause Lawyering: Political Commitments and Professional Responsibilities*, Oxford University Press, Oxford, 487.
Meili, S. (1993) 'The Interaction Between Lawyers and Grass Roots Social Movements in Brazil', in *Beyond Law*, vol. 3, No. 7, 61.
Ratliff, W. and Buscaglia, E. (1997), 'Judicial Reform: The Neglected Priority in Latin America' in *Annals of the American Academy of Political and Social Science*, March 1997.
Rojas, F. (1988) 'A Comparison of Change-Oriented Legal Services in Latin America with Legal Services in North America and Europe', *International Journal of the Sociology of Law*, vol. 16, 203.
Samway, M (1996), 'Access to Justice: A Study of Legal Assistance Programs for the Poor in Santiago, Chile', *Duke Journal of Comparative & International Law*, vol. 6, 347.

Third Conference of Latin American Law Schools, Facultad de Ciencias juridicas y Sociales, Universidad de Chile, (1963) 665.
Trubek, D. Dezalay, Y. Buchanan, R. and Davis, J. (1993), 'Global Restructuring and the Law: The Internationalization of Legal Fields and the Creation of Transnational Arenas', *Global Studies Working Paper No. 1*, University of Wisconsin-Madison.
Viveros, F. (1998), 'The Development of Public Interest Actions in the Extension of Access to Justice in Chile', unpublished paper, 11.
Wilson, R. (1989), 'The New Legal Education in North and South America', *Stanford Journal of International Law*, 375.

8 The Brazilian Bar Association in the Struggle for Human Rights[1]

ELIANE BOTELHO JUNQUEIRA

Introduction

The Brazilian formal democracy of the 1990s has not delivered substantial democracy. Over the last decade, law and institutions have been permanently challenged by a civic culture based on Hobbesian practices. On the one hand, the rule of law (represented by the new democratic Constitution approved in 1988) has been subverted on a daily basis by arbitrary practices of those (mainly, the police) representing the state. On the other hand, large sectors of the population (and their aspirations) have been excluded from the current economic project. The limits of Brazilian democratic projects are clear and represent a new challenge to both the government and civil society.

What has been the role played by the Brazilian Bar Association in this new situation? Much has been written about the Bar's role in organizing and defending Brazilian civil society during the authoritarian regime.[2] In fact, we have enough elements to positively answer the question raised by Terence Halliday (1987) about the influence of professional associations in the government.[3] Nevertheless, almost nothing has yet been written about the new role played by the Brazilian Bar Association after the Constitutional democratization of 1988. Unlike the 1970s and 1980s, when traditional organizations such as the Bar Association and the Catholic Church led the democratization process, in the 1990s the scene had become more complex and heterogeneous. Organizations representing Brazilian civil society are already quite well developed (as are the parties, despite their internal contradictions) and question their representative role. In the current political climate does the Bar still represent Brazilian civil society? What is the relationship between the Bar and the democratically elected government? What are the main issues confronting the Bar Association in the 1990s? Which strategies has it deployed? Is the Bar Association still the paladin for the defense of human rights in the Brazilian society? How has globalization influenced the Bar's discourse on human rights? These are the questions that I shall address.[4]

Nevertheless, unlike Halliday, who linked macro- and micro-sociological perspective in his study of the Chicago Bar Association, I shall attempt neither an analysis of the internal diversity of the Brazilian Bar in the 1990s nor an analysis of the low involvement of lawyers inside the association. Rather, from a macro-sociological standpoint, I shall consider the Bar as a collective actor - a 'collective lawyer' (Vianna, 1986) or a 'collective citizen' (Halliday, 1987) - and focus primarily on its external political activity.

The Bar Association from 1960 to 1990

Three main points require explanation concerning the Brazilian Bar Association, an institution aiming to regulate the legal profession. First, although lawyering is a liberal profession, the Bar was created by the government as a public service. This apparent paradox is related to the unique character of Brazilian liberalism, which ideologically supported both the new independent nation and the maintenance of slavery in the nineteenth century. According to Joaquim Falcão, 'liberalism penetrated Brazil mainly through government action and ... Brazilian capitalism is characterized less by the free play of market forces than by the permanent intervention in the market by the government, always on behalf of liberal ideas' (1988, 422). Second, the Brazilian Bar Association has the monopoly of representing lawyers, a crucial point in a comparative perspective. Unlike the United States, where hundreds of associations (based on ethnic, religious, gender activities etc.) share political power and increase the influence of the body,[5] we do not have in Brazil any other major lawyers' organizations besides the Bar. Third, as a creature of the revolutionary government of 1930, the Bar Association was born with an ingrained political commitment. When President Getúlio Vargas approved the legislation setting up the Bar, he was not only responding to the demands of lawyers, which dated back to 1843 and had been postponed for almost eighty years. In the political context of the early 1930s, the approval of the Bar Association clearly meant that institutional control of the profession was exchanged for the legal elite's political support to the new regime.[6]

Although the Brazilian Bar is formally part of the government, historically it has been insulated from governmental interference.[7] At different times, it has even followed the French model, which has opposed the state[8] and taken anti-government positions (Halliday and Karpik, 1997, 23). In the name of liberal principles (and despite its political commitment to the government), for example, the Brazilian Bar opposed Getúlio Vargas after 1937 when he started an authoritarian regime.

If the Bar has historically defended liberal democracy, why did it support the military *coup* of 1964? Was the Bar no longer committed to liberal ideas? Had it lost its historical autonomy? Is there any contradiction between its principles and the political position it adopted in 1964?

A deeper analysis of the Bar's discourse reveals a contradiction between its principles and its initial support of the military regime. But this contradiction is only apparent: when the Bar defended the *coup d'etat*, it acted strictly in accordance with its institutional role of defending legality. In 1964, the main motto of President Goulart's government was 'agrarian reform: using the law or using force'.[9] As the approval of legal reforms was implausible and the use of violence seemed quite widespread, the Bar assumed the defense of the rule of law which, at that time, meant supporting the *coup d'etat* against João Goulart. Some years later, in the name of the same rule of law, the Bar shifted from defending to opposing the military regime. Once again, but in a quite different position, the Bar acted on behalf of the endangered legal order when the military regime, instead of guaranteeing the legal order (as it had initially promised), suppressed basic political rights (for example, *habeas corpus*), replaced the democratic Constitution by authoritarian rules and arrested lawyers working in defense of political opponents.

Two facts explain the importance of the role played by the Bar Association in its opposition to the military regime: the dismemberment of other institutions of civil society, such as unions, political parties, students' associations etc. and the moral authority of the Bar Association (Falcão, 1988, 425). According to Falcão, 'one of the few institutions that managed to maintain its autonomy and identity was the OAB [Ordem dos Advogados do Brasil, i.e., the Brazilian Bar Association]'. Therefore, it (as well as the Catholic Church) was transformed into an institutional leader of civil society in the redemocratization of the country. It fought for human rights and the liberalization of the regime: the withdrawal of authoritarian legislation, the granting of amnesty, the restoration of *habeas corpus*, and the annulment of the national security statute' (1988, 425). At that time, using its political legitimacy, the Bar became the effective 'spokesperson' of Brazilian civil society.

A simplified schema may help foreign readers to better understand this shift from supporting to opposing the military regime. In fact, three periods can be distinguished in the recent history of the Bar Association (Linhares and Lessa, 1991): the reactive phase (1964-1980), the constructive phase (1980-1988) and the ordinary phase (starting in 1988). While the first phase was characterized by the reaction of the Bar Association to the repressive regime, in the second period the Bar participated actively in the construction of a new legal order. At that time, the Brazilian Bar moved from a procedural strategy (of protecting rights) to a substantial strategy (of conquering rights) (Halliday and Karpik, 1997, 57). In the current era, which began with the approval of the new Constitution, the Bar assumed a new political role: to monitor the legal order and pursue social justice. Nevertheless, despite this shift back to the procedural strategy of making rights effective, the Bar has now replaced the civil rights concerns of the 1970s with a concern for social and economic rights.

1964

* The Bar Association supported, in the name of legal order, the *coup d'etat* and the beginning of the military regime, which opposed the structural reforms announced by President João Goulart.[10]

1968

* The Bar Association shifted from defending to opposing the military regime, which became more authoritarian.
* The Bar's élite split into two main groups: a) some approved the modernization project undertaken by the military regime (and supported the law and development movement); b) others defended the priority of struggling for constitutional guarantees and a democratic order.[11]

1977

* After the beginning of the 'opening process', the Bar assumed the leadership of Brazilian civil society and the defense of a Democratic rule of law (*Etat de Droit Démocratique*).

1979

* The Amnesty Law permitted the return of political opponents living in exile.
* Social movements started to be reorganized.

1980

* A bomb attack on the President of the Bar Association killed his secretary.
* The Human Rights Committee of the Bar Association was created after the bomb attack.

1984

* The Bar Association led the national campaign for direct elections for President (Direct Election Now - *Diretas Já*).
* The campaign was defeated and the first civil President since 1961 was indirectly elected.

1986-7

* The Bar Association led the constitutional process.

1988

* A new democratic constitution, deeply committed to social rights, was approved.

1989

* President Collor was elected in the first direct election since 1961.

1992

* The Bar Association led the movement for the impeachment of President Collor, accused of corruption.
* After the impeachment, President Collor was replaced by his Vice-President.

1994

* The Bar Association approved its new Statute (the former dates back to 1963).
* The Bar Association approved its new Code of Ethics (the former dates back to 1934).
* A new President (Fernando Henrique Cardoso), apparently committed to left-wing ideas, was elected.

1997

* The Bar opposed the new electoral rule approved to permit the re-election of the President.

1998

* President Fernando Henrique Cardoso was re-elected.

No doubt 1977 represents the most important change in the Bar's political strategies. According to Luiz Werneck Vianna (1986), in 1977 traditional liberal ideals were revised and the Bar assumed the role of 'spokesperson' of Brazilian society. From that time onwards, the Bar asserted not only the rule of law, but a *democratic* rule of law. It no longer defended only classical liberalism, but supported the inclusion of the whole Brazilian society within the democratic project. It no longer played the role of a legal consultant of the state, but became a political actor playing a main role in the democratization of the country. In fact, the Bar's political role of the 1980s represented the beginning of a new relationship between the state and Brazilian society.

The Agenda of the 1990s

After playing a fundamental role in the struggle against the military regime and for civil rights, which guaranteed its social legitimation, the Bar Association developed new strategies of legitimation towards lawyers and civil society in the 1990s. Instead of a discourse based on political issues, a new discourse focusing on professional problems faced by lawyers and their clients seemed more appropriate to maintaining the Bar's prestige among lawyers and within society. In contrast with the early 1980s when lawyers defended the Bar's involvement in political activities and its struggle for a legitimate government, lawyers in the 1990s have been concerned primarily with professional matters and not with political agendas. In other words, while in Brazil the expansion of professional concerns clearly meant a contraction of politics, in the United States the professional legal body shifted its preoccupation with monopoly to the functioning of the state (Halliday, 1987, 22 and 347).[12]

Despite the recent strategies on behalf of the profession, the Brazilian Bar Association has not completely abandoned the political commitments assumed in the 1970s and 1980s. Two legacies of the military regime are still included in its agenda. The first legacy is represented by the bomb that killed the secretary of its President in 1980, a crime that was never punished. In an attempt to keep the case in the public eye, the Bar Association hired investigators (fifteen years after the bomb attack) to bring further evidence before the judicial process. The second legacy is related to those who died or 'disappeared' during the military regime, a problem still not completely resolved even in the 1990s. Aiming to politically support this struggle, the Bar has been party to legal actions which have tried to secure financial compensation for the family of these victims.

Stressing this political commitment, the Bar's Statutes claim that lawyers must defend the Constitution, the democratic legal order, human rights, social justice, the efficient administration of justice and progress of legal culture and legal institutions. The Code of Ethics also stresses the social responsibilities of the profession: as an instrument for humanizing social relations law must be permanently connected with citizenship (Junqueira, 1998).[13]

The defense of rights (broadly constructed) is much more institutionalized in a democratic society than in an authoritarian society, but it is also more complex. Human rights violations in the authoritarian regime were quite grave and became even more serious due to an absence of effective legal mechanisms to protect political rights. Nevertheless, those persecuted during the period of military rule were not a very large group.[14] At the present time, we have new legal and institutional tools to guarantee rights. However, a much wider population needs to be protected. In a democratic order, we no longer need to defend just political rights, but also important are social and economic rights. We are no longer concerned solely with political violence, but with all forms of violence, whether committed either by the state or by society. We need to struggle not only against political discrimination, but against all discrimination, especially where 'minority' groups are concerned. The discourse of human rights now embraces rights of all people, without distinction regarding race, sex, age, religion and social condition: the right to food, work, education, health care, housing, and the opportunity to lead a happy and peaceful existence.

New rights are strongly protected by the new Constitution. But formal democracy is meaningless when the population is unaware of either their rights or the mechanisms to defend them. In fact, a more comprehensive conception of citizenship still needs to be developed in Brazil. Trying to build a substantive democracy, different regional associations of the Bar have signed agreements with local governments to provide education on human rights (classes are taught by representatives of the Bar Association). For the same reason, the Bar has supported leftist legal activity (such as that linked to alternative legal services),[15] recognizing their importance in the struggle for human rights.

Nonetheless, the Bar's agenda for the 1990s transcends this traditional concern with civil rights. Since the approval of the new Constitution, the Bar has created committees with the task of addressing specific problems, such as environment, land reform, and judicial reform. As happened to the American Bar in the nineteenth century (Halliday, 1987, p. xii), since the 1980s the number of the Brazilian Bar's standing committees, special committees and joint committees has quickly increased. In fact, the Bar's agenda in the 1990s goes beyond human rights (understood in their strict sense) and includes international/global, national and local issues.

International/global Issues

Why should the Bar be concerned with the violation of human rights in East Timor? Why should it oppose an American law whose main target is Cuba? Or, why should it care about the Bahá'í Community?

The answer is quite simple. If the Bar cares about human rights in Brazil (as it did during the military regime and as it still does in the 1990s), it needs to oppose any violation of human rights. The struggle for human rights is no longer confined to national frontiers. Rather, the current struggle for human rights involves global organizations (NGOs, like International Amnesty and Greenpeace) and even national governments (the permanent action of the United States combating terrorism and intervening in local conflicts is the best example of this new phenomenon). For this reason, and consistent with its domestic political position in the 1970s and 1980s, the Bar Association has supported struggles in the international arena, such as of East Timor (against Indonesia), El Salvador and Cuba. For example, a representative of East Timor was invited to the International Human Rights Conference organized by the Bar Association (according to some newspapers, Fidel Castro was also invited, but he did not attend the conference). And the Rio de Janeiro branch has supported the struggle of the Bahá'í Community, a religious group under attack in Iran for defending human rights.

The struggle for human rights is not the only global phenomenon. In fact, the economy remains the main arena of globalization. For this reason, lawyers at the Brazilian Bar National Conference signed a manifesto against the American Helms-Burton law, which 'affects Brazilian enterprises and damages international peace'. Even if this law does not directly influence the legal profession in Brazil, any economic measure in the international/global arena may affect the Brazilian economy and, by consequence, increase/decrease legal demands.

In fact, the Brazilian economy and the globalization process have also been deeply criticized by the Bar, which has played a major role in the struggle against the supposedly neo-liberal economy implemented by Fernando Henrique Cardoso. In this context, the Bar opposed the privatization policy of the 1990s, which the Left considers an attack on the national sovereignty.

National Issues

In the domestic sphere, the Bar has strongly criticized the federal government's politics. For example, it condemned the electoral reform introduced by President Fernando Henrique Cardoso, who changed the law to facilitate his own re-election. The Bar has also condemned 'provisional measures', i.e, laws enacted by the Executive, without approval of the Legislative.[16] In the 1997 election for local mayor, the Bar led the campaign for *Ethics in Politics*. It has also participated in campaigns for the impeachment of state governors accused of corruption.

No doubt, the Judiciary represents the main concern of the Bar Association in the national sphere, especially in the current time, when judicial reform starts to be discussed. The law project developed by a special committee of the Bar encompasses, for example, the control of the Judiciary by civil society (which would include a representative of the Bar Association). Nevertheless, this concern with the Judiciary is, of course, clearly connected to problems faced by lawyers in the professional market. When the Bar supports mediation and arbitration, it acts on behalf of the professional market. Furthermore, when the Bar opposes the increase of court fees (which everyone must pay to commence litigation), it is primarily concerned with increasing legal demands rather than with guaranteeing poor people access to justice.[17]

Local Issues

By local issues, I refer mainly to individual and/or collective cases in which the Bar Association intervenes. For an analytical purpose, I distinguish three main areas:

1) Minorities

Strategies undertaken by the Bar Association in the protection of 'minorities' have varied. The Bar has, simultaneously, mobilized both lawyers and society in general, through the organization of seminars on specific issues, and directly intervened in specific cases. It has defended the rights of indigenous people to their land, an enduring problem in Brazil. The Bar has also provided orientation about family planning and given legal aid to battered women, divorced women and victims of sex discrimination.

Race discriminations are usually handled on a case-by-case basis, i.e., when real cases of discrimination occur. The Bar firmly criticized the American Consulate when visas were denied to black people. It even sent a letter to President Clinton complaining against this apparently discriminatory politics. The rights of disabled persons are also defended on a case-by-case basis, usually when blind people (especially lawyers) are denied the possibility of assistance in public exams.

A different strategy is used in relation to old and sick people, as well as for prisoners. Based on reports written by the representatives of its Human Rights Committees, who visit hospitals, homes for elderly and prisons, the Bar has denounced living conditions and irregularities in these establishments (whose clients are invariably poor). The Bar also gives legal support to prisoners, and exerts political pressure when prisoners die in custody.

Three aspects characterize the Bar's policies concerning children. First, it joined the United Nations in a campaign against the use of drugs by teenagers. Second, the Bar often denounces the exploitation of child labor, especially in northern Brazil. Third, the Bar has opposed some strategies to combat violence, such as a legislative proposal to reduce the age of full criminal responsibility to 16 years old.

The Bar Association also provides legal services to the 'poor' (in Brazil a disparate category), and especially those in states without public defenders. Legal services in *favelas* (slums), for example, began to be implemented in the 1980s by the Rio de Janeiro branch of the Bar and are now extended to poor suburbs of several major cities. Specific action on behalf of the poor population is also undertaken in emergency situations. For example, during floods, the Bar Association offers legal support to victims and/or participates in campaigns for collecting clothes, food etc.

2) Violence

One main consequence of the democratic culture of resistance, which developed during the military regime, was the 'discovery' that the Brazilian state is violent. In spite of its frequency in Brazilian history, violence committed by the state was not perceived as a serious problem until the 1960s, when the middle classes (mainly students, lawyers and politicians), became the principal target of state repression.

Although democratization meant an end to political violence, it did not mean the end of the historical violence committed against the working class. Arbitrary homicides (an informal death penalty) and torture persist in Brazil. Instead of trusting the police, the population still fears the police. In this context, the Bar Association has had two main tasks. Firstly, the Bar has protected and intervened in specific cases when no other resource seems available (especially when homicides or tortures are committed by the police). Secondly, the Bar has used its political influence to pressurize the government into investigating some high-profile cases. For example, in 1997, the Bar exerted political pressure against the police when the murder of an innocent man was captured on video and broadcast on all the Brazilian television networks.

Despite being mainly concerned with violence inflicted by the state, the Bar Association has also recognized the violence of Brazilian society. For example, the Bar strongly reacted when a homicide was committed by four middle-class teenagers, who burnt and killed an indigenous man sleeping in the street. The offenders justified their crime saying that the victim had been mistaken for a homeless person, as if it would not constitute a crime to burn and kill homeless people.[18] The Bar has also participated in most campaigns against criminality held in recent years (especially in big cities such as Rio de Janeiro) and it led a campaign of decommissioning firearms (collecting and destroying guns voluntarily donated by the population).

Nevertheless, the main target of the Bar's discourse remains the state violence. The state is responsible for violence not only when it kills and tortures, but also when it maintains social inequity, which is considered the major cause of violence committed against Brazilian population.[19]

3) Agrarian Reform

The paradigmatic example of the political position of the Brazilian Bar Association is the struggle by Landless Peasant Movement (*Movimento dos Sem-Terra*) for agrarian reform,[20] a historical demand of the rural population. In the name of social justice, the Bar pressurizes the federal government for agrarian reforms, publicly supports the representatives of the Landless Movement, and even participates in actions organized by the Movement. A quite important mobilization strategy of the Movement has been the symbolic trial of landlords and policemen accused of killing peasants. Representatives of civil society, religions, and human rights organizations (including representatives of the Bar) have been invited to appear in those trials, which aim mainly to attract the attention of authorities and human rights groups in the international arena.

As in the United States, where substantive justice has always been subordinated to formal justice (Halliday, 1987, 369),[21] the Brazilian Bar has supported the struggle for social justice only within the confines of law.[22] Even when defending the Landless Movement, the Bar never abandoned its main task of protecting legal order. In fact, the Bar Association has condemned violent actions committed not only against the Landless Movement, but also those committed *by* the Landless Movement. For example, while supporting the Landless Peasant Movement's goals, the Bar condemns its extra-legal strategies, e.g, the occupation of private properties.

Conclusions

It is especially difficult to transmit, to a foreign audience, all the nuances of the

Bar Association's actions. A deeper knowledge of Brazilian politics - as well as the Bar internal politics, an arena where contradictory forces and proposals dispute political space - is essential. Even so, I hope the reader can appreciate the following conclusions.

First, no other institution has so strongly defended human rights in Brazil. As Stephen Meili states (1998), the current social image of the Bar Association is the result of its progressive commitment during the military regime. Therefore, although some blunders in Brazilian democracy have justified the Bar's action in defense of the institutional order in the 1990s,[23] its political survival stems mainly from its past glory.[24]

Second, formal democracy redefined both the political role of the Bar Association and its field of action. Since 1988, political rights have been substituted by social and economic rights. Women, children, sick and elderly people, disabled persons, black and indigenous groups have all replaced political prisoners and opponents. The concern with political violence inflicted by the state has also been replaced by concern about other forms of violence.

Third, the development of civil society, the reorganization of political parties and the emergence of NGOs have transformed the Brazilian political context. Since the approval of the new Constitution, the Bar Association has shared the task of defending the demands of Brazilian civil society with other institutions. In fact, the previous Bar's action on behalf of human rights and democracy opened the way to these new institutions, which are indebted to the Bar.[25] In the 1990s, the Bar is no longer the 'spokesperson' of Brazilian civil society. It needs to establish alliances with other interest groups. When the fragile civil society was replaced by a complex associational life, the Bar also moved from 'act[ing] as spokesmen for publics they themselves help create' to 'construct[ing] political alliances' (Halliday and Karpik, 1997, 41). Nevertheless, in spite of no longer being a primary political actor, the Bar still plays a major role in facilitating this dialogue between civil society and the state.

Fourth, interventions of the Bar Association are still justified by its statutory task of defending the legal order. The Bar defended the legal order when it supported the military regime, when it condemned the military regime, and when it condemned the new electoral law. The Bar has also defended the legal order when it condemned land occupations. Therefore, legal order represents an ambiguous expression which has been used by the Bar to justify any political position.

Fifth, the Bar's commitment to the rule of law is inextricably connected to the project of political liberalism,[26] which has dramatically changed during the past three decades. Although the Bar still is strongly committed to the development of citizenship and the extension of rights, it opposes the neo-liberal economy implemented by President Fernando Henrique Cardoso, which is perceived as an obstacle for social justice.[27] In fact, the history of the Bar Association directly questions Halliday and Karpik's conclusion:

> the massive centre of the twentieth century profession protects the core of liberal institutions without venturing too far into the uncharted waters of social and economic substantive rights. Lawyers' political liberalism should not be confused with political democracy or social democracy: it is a classic or restricted liberalism (1997, 51).

No doubt, divisions within institutions make it difficult to achieve a consensus on either social and economic rights or civil rights.[28] And, no doubt, the expansion of lawyers in the 1980s and 1990s increased the internal diversity of the Brazilian Bar Association.[29] Nevertheless, the Brazilian Bar successfully overcame these internal political divisions and, despite some resistance, replaced old liberal ideals by a commitment to social problems. As Vianna points out, the struggle against the authoritarian regime helped the Bar to abandon the conservative political liberalism and incorporate demands of new social sectors in its agenda (1984, 276).

Sixth, in contrast with previous decades, the Bar now uses legal mechanisms to protect specific rights and the Constitution. Articles, official statements published in newspapers and public campaigns are no longer its sole strategy. In the 1990s, the Bar has also used litigation, political pressure and legislative lobbying to mobilize lawyers and intervene in the public arena.

Seventh, since the military regime, the Bar has established a political commitment to left-wing sectors and parties of Brazilian society. Although this left-wing position is criticized by conservative lawyers, it still influences the Bar's actions and discourse directly related to the economic order.

Eighth, the Bar has tried to maintain a good relationship with civil society, especially with different religions. As a strategy to promote this relationship, representatives of the main religious groups are often invited to seminars promoted by the Bar Association in the 1990s. This is not a new phenomenon. The alliance between the Bar Association with the Catholic Church and the Jews dates back to the military regime, when both religious organizations supported the struggle for human rights. The main difference in the 1990s is the inclusion of Protestants in this alliance.

Ninth, it is clear that visibility of the Bar in the media has decreased in recent years. The Bar is no longer on the front page of newspapers. Does this phenomenon represent a retreat of the Bar's defense of society? Of course, it does. As previously analyzed, the role of defending society is now played by multiple institutional actors. Nevertheless, it is also true that a smaller visibility of the Bar in the media represents a consequence of democracy. According to the President of the Bar Association, news about the Bar's interventions is not a positive sign, but indicates a threat to the democratic process.

Tenth, the relationship between the Bar Association and Brazilian society is now mediated by networks of leftist organizations, to whom the intervention of the Bar represents a useful 'technology of action'.[30] At the present time, there is an implicit division of labor between the Bar Association and other organizations of civil society. While common problems are solved directly by those organizations, problems requiring stronger political pressure put the Bar Association into action.

Eleventh, although concerned with international/global issues (struggles for democracy and human rights, opposition to the privatization process and to the neo-liberal economy), the Bar is not yet directly affected by this new phenomenon. Of course the Bar has taken a position in the national debate about globalization. Nevertheless, globalization will only really influence the Bar when, internally, it starts to respond to the demands of the new international law firms. In other words, the Bar will be really affected by globalization when the phenomenon promotes changes in the structure of the legal profession.

Twelfth, the Bar's defense of democracy in the national arena has not been matched by a defense of democracy within the association. First, its federal representatives are still chosen through an indirect election process, in which lawyers do not have the right to vote. Second, although the Bar defends external control over the Judiciary, it denies lay participation in its disciplinary committees.[31] Third, unlike in other jurisdictions (such as the American mosaic of organized bar associations), the Brazilian Bar maintains the monopoly of representing lawyers.

Finally, unlike in previous decades, when the Bar's actions and discourse focused on political democracy, in the 1990s the Bar has faced a new challenge. At the present time, the Bar is urged simultaneously to defend access to justice and to guarantee the professional market for lawyers (defending the monopoly of judicial representation).[32] The contradiction between these two goals is clear: whenever a translator (such as a lawyer) mediates clients' legal relations with the Court it follows that litigation becomes more expensive and justice less accessible.[33] But, as Terence Halliday reminds us, contradictions are inherent in any professional association, and it would be naïve not to take into account 'tensions between self-interest and civility, private satisfaction and public service, autonomy and accountability, prestige and wealth and the helping function'. If Halliday is right, as I think he is, the Brazilian Bar Association only represents a neat example of 'two faces of professionalism - the one monopolistic, even narcissistic, and the other benign, even altruistic' (1987, 3).

The defense of lawyers' interests above civil society's interests has clearly damaged the Bar's image among (left-wing) lawyers and the civil society. Its strategy of simultaneously building internal and external legitimacy seems hardly sustainable. According to Joaquim Falcão (1996), the Bar even lost political capital in recent years, when it began to defend the professional market.

Therefore, at the end of the 1990s, our questions are quite different from those raised ten years ago. Instead of asking about the Bar's role in the defense of the Constitution, we shall ask: How much longer will the strategy of trying to appease both lawyers and the civil society continue? How will the Bar overcome the contradiction of its current discourse? Will the Bar preserve its historical commitment to human rights? Or will this commitment give way to professional matters? How much longer will the Bar defend the indirect election of its federal representatives, a mechanism that the Bar did not accept in the national arena in the mid-1980s? How much longer will the Bar deny the participation of lay persons in its disciplinary committees? How will the Bar be affected by the globalization process? Will the Bar maintain the monopoly of representing lawyers, or will it learn with other jurisdictions (such as the American mosaic of lawyers' organizations) and allow a multiple representation of the legal profession? As history continues, answers to these questions must await the next millennium.

Notes

1 A first version of this article was presented at the Law and Society Association Annual Meeting (Aspen, 1998). I am grateful to Monica Cristine Rezende de Campos and Natalia Infante Vieira for their research assistance.

2 I commend the article by Joaquim Falcão, published in the *Lawyers in Society* volume (Abel, 1988), and the article by Linhares and Lessa (1991).

3 'Do professional associations attempt to influence government? If so, how often do they do so? Over how broad a range of matters? With what efficacy? Do they affect the policies and the administration of those institutions in which they have such a central role? Is their expertise deferred to by legislators and administrators? Do they effectively mold public policy - but out of the public eye?' (Halliday, 1987, p. xiii).

4 My research was based on news about the Bar Association published by Brazilian newspapers. Working with newspapers means that I looked at the visibility of the Bar, rather than at the role played by the institution. Nevertheless, in order to understand the relationship between the lawyers' professional association and civil society, one must analyze what the Brazilian population (at least those who read newspapers) learn about the role played by the Bar Association. Therefore, the analysis of newspapers helps explain which actions are publicized and which image of the Bar Association circulates in Brazilian society at the end of this decade.

5 See Halliday (1987), Trubek and Kransberger (1998), and Sheingold (1998).

6 At that time, the Bar represented the political elite of lawyers, a professional group recruited from the Brazilian elite. This characteristic has changed since 1970, with the democratization of legal education and the recruitment of lawyers in middle-class groups.

7 Despite some attempts by the government to control the Bar, especially during the military regime, it succeeded in maintaining its political autonomy.

8 In contrast to the English model.

9 'Reforma agrária: na lei ou na marra'.

10 President João Goulart, who was formerly the Vice-President, replaced President Janio Quadros when the latter resigned.

11 A new authoritarian Constitution, drafted by the military regime, replaced the democratic Constitution of 1946.

12 In his analysis of the Chicago Bar Association, Halliday describes this shift as a transition from a formative (concerned with market control) to an established stage of professional development (concerned with the state)

(1987, 347). In the United States, this transition corresponds to a decline in the number of committees related to professional fees, professional education and professional disciplines (1987, 351). If we remember that the number of professional committees of the Brazilian Bar Association has increased in recent years (and if we remember the important role played by its education committee in the reform of law curriculum in the early 1990s), we may conclude that legal professional associations in Brazil and in the United States have followed two different routes. We could even consider that the Brazilian Bar Association, unlike its American counterpart, shifted from an established profession (less self-protective and self-preoccupied and less collectively narcissistic) to a formative profession (more concerned with the market control) (Halliday, 1987, 353).

13 The contradiction between the Bar's discourse and its praxis is obvious. While defending a full citizenship in the national arena, the Bar maintains indirect elections which exclude lawyers from the decision about their federal representatives. This contradiction is even more serious if we remember that the Bar led the national campaign for Direct Elections Now in 1984.

14 We estimate that around 300 persons died or disappeared during the military regime in Brazil. In Chile and Argentina, these figures are much higher (a proportion of 1/10 and 1/100, respectively, comparing to Brazil).

15 For example, a main representative of the alternative legal service movement (Miguel Pressburger) was the Research Director of the Rio de Janeiro branch of the Bar in the early 1990s. Although the Research Director has no real political influence, the invitation addressed to Miguel Pressburger expressed the Bar's commitment to left-wing parties and left-wing lawyers.

16 Although this measure should be used only in emergencies, the Executive has often used it as a strategy to avoid the legislative process.

17 In fact, the Bar has justified its internal and professional concerns in the name of social justice. This is not a cynical statement. I just want to stress that the Bar, due to its public and not syndicalist character, tries to retrieve its social legitimacy from the defense of universal values, rather than from the defense of lawyers.

18 To burn homeless people is not unusual in Brazil. So, why was this case different? For three reasons: the death of the victim, the social origin of the

offenders, and the identity of the victim, an indigenous man.

19 Consistent with this perspective, the Bar defends the struggle for equity, housing, education and citizenship as more important than disarming the population.

20 The Landless Peasant Movement is the strongest social movement of the 1990s in Brazil.

21 'The often-expressed commitment to the rule of law represents not a cynical catch phrase for ideological manipulation but a sincere value commitment that bonds the profession as a distinctive community - and not infrequently pits it against contrary claims for a substantive justice unencumbered by procedural restraint, whatever its partisan label' (Halliday, 1987, 369).

22 Since the Bar is committed to legal means of struggle, the political and ideological discourse within the Bar represents only different interpretations of the rule of law.

23 I refer to the impeachment of President Collor in 1991.

24 Struggles for human rights and the bomb attack are main references in the Bar's web site.

25 The American Bar Association had also to build alliances with other civic groups in the complex mosaic of American society (Halliday and Karpik, 1997, 40).

26 Three different phases can be easily identified in the history of liberalism: classical liberalism, social liberalism, and anti-economical liberalism (Halliday and Karpik, 1997, 17).

27 As happened in other countries, Brazilian lawyers had to 'rethink the classical liberal core' (Halliday and Karpik, 1997, 17).

28 According to Halliday and Karpik, 'a strong emphasis on politics prevents commitment to the economic project' (1997, 53).

29 Halliday analyzes the consequences of diversity and heterogeneity at the Chicago Bar Association (1987, chapter 'The Contradictions of Inclusiveness'). See also Abel, 1989, 237.

30 Technology (in the meaning of 'know-how') of action means ways of action deeply known/dominated by some social actors. For example, strikes represent a technology of action whose dynamics are quite well known by syndicalist leaders. I prefer the expression 'technology of action' to 'way of action' because it stresses the fact that, in some contexts, even being conscious that their actions are not the more appropriate ones, social actors make use of them because they know/dominate their internal and external dynamics.

31 Unlike some experiences in the United States. For example, disciplinary commissions in Wisconsin and Michigan are independent of the organized Bar (Halliday, 1987, 352). See also Abel, 1989, 246.

32 The double meaning of the Bar's collective action is also perceived by Halliday and Karpik: 'for lawyer's representation, or the right of access to the judicial system, is a central component of citizenship. ... Lawyers insistently push at the frontiers of representation, ever widening both the scope of their own domain of work and the protections afforded individuals, real and fictive, from each other and the state' (1997, 43).

33 As Joaquim Falcão reminds us, the Bar must realize that the monopoly of representation of citizens in court is useless when the majority of the population has no access to the Judiciary (1988, 434).

References

Abel, R. and Lewis, P. (1988), *Lawyers in Society - The Civil Law World*, Berkeley; University of California Press, Berkeley.

Abel, R. (1989), *American Lawyers*, Oxford University Press, New York.

Falcão, J. (1988), 'Lawyers in Brazil', in R. Abel. and P. Lewis, *Lawyers in Society - The Civil Law World*, University of California Press, Berkeley.

Falcão, J. (1996), 'Advogados: passo em falso', *Monitor Público*; Rio de Janeiro.

Halliday, T. (1987), *Beyond Monopoly*, The University of Chicago Press, Chicago.

Halliday, T. and Karpik, L. (1997), 'Politics Matter: a Comparative Theory of Lawyers in the Making of Political Liberalism', in T. Halliday and L. Karpik, *Lawyers and the Rise of Western Political Liberalism*, Clarendon Press, Oxford.

Junqueira, E. (1998), 'The Teaching of Legal Ethics... in the Tropiques', in K. Economides, *Ethical Challenges to Legal Education and Conduct*, Hart, Oxford.

Linhares, L. and Lessa, R. (1991), *Consenso e Identidade: os advogados e a sua ordem*, Rio de Janeiro; OAB-RJ.

Meili, S. (1998), 'Cause Lawyers and Social Movements: A Comparative

Perspective on Democratic Change in Argentina and Brazil', in A. Sarat and S. Scheingold (eds), *Cause Lawyering*, Oxford University Press, New York.
Scheingold, S. (1998), 'The Struggle to Politicize Legal Practice', in A. Sarat and S. Scheingold (eds).
Trubek, L. and Kransberger, E. (1998), 'Social Justice and the Structures of Private Practice', in A. Sarat and S. Scheingold (eds).
Vianna, L. (1986), *Travessia: da abertura à constituinte*, Taurus, Rio de Janeiro.

9 Discussing Legal Ethics with Eastern-European Judges

LENY E. DE GROOT-VAN LEEUWEN AND
WOUTER T. DE GROOT

In 1996 the Czech Union of Judges asked a number of Dutch judges and the first author to contribute to a seminar on judicial ethics in the Czech Republic. All other participants were Czech judges. The focus of the seminar was on the latters' own moral dilemmas and conduct. During the months preceding the seminar the Czech judges had started to select and discuss a number of problematic examples of judicial behavior, and they had begun to write the first draft of a Code of Conduct. The present chapter discusses the contribution of the first author to this seminar. The seminar contribution is indented. The (unindented) main text consists of explanations and reflections.

The Czech judges were struggling with practical questions of professional ethics. Discussing these issues as an outsider would seem logically to entail bringing the practical issues in contact with more general ethical theories. It was decided not to follow this course, mainly because no clear links were visible between ethical theories and the practical problems of the seminar participants. These problems seemed to hinge around two major points: (1) how to evaluate judicial behavior in specific cases, and (2) how to draft a code of conduct for the judiciary. Much of this seemed to concern the relationship between the judiciary and society; for that reason it was finally decided to discuss the issues in a context of general sociological, not ethical, theory.

The next paragraph summarizes the introduction to the seminar. It emphasizes the intention to contribute by way of providing a practical philosophy.

> A notion exists in the legal profession - at least in the Netherlands - that ethics is 'something off in the clouds, or off in some never-ever land of Utopia' (Cohen, 1970, 160). The point of departure of my contribution today is that ethics are not only in the clouds, but also down to earth. We

never act as ethically neutral, neither inside nor outside the office. The technical and moral aspects of the work of professions are strongly interwoven. A good judge is equipped in both ways. Obviously, most of you share this idea. The Czech judiciary is now busy discussing case examples of moral problems and the process of drafting a code of conduct has begun. With this in mind, the title of my contribution is 'A *practical* philosophy for judicial ethics'. It focuses on practical aspects, such as how to make a good code in relation to discussing case examples.

The first topic then raised, was about 'closed' versus 'open' societies. The next section provides the text on this.

'Closed' versus 'open' societies

It is possible to design a society through a single logic of the common good. Every element in such a society, from bicycle to judiciary system, is then designed to be the single best performer of a function serving that common good. These kind of societies may be called 'closed' not primarily because they have a closed border, but because they have a closed *logic*: there is nothing higher than the common good, and the one party, the one type of car, or the one way to organize the police are logically the best ones.

Other societies are built more upon the idea that it is not humanely possible to define the common good in any fixed way, nor to define what is the single best performer of the various societal functions. Examples of philosophers connected to this idea are Mill, Popper and Dewey, among many others. Human fallibility is the point of departure of these philosophies, including the principles for the design of society. Since no one can claim to possess a single fixed logic of the common good, a continuous process of discussion is necessary to keep society in balance, as well as open markets, where consumers select the goods and services that best fit their circumstances. These kind of societies can be called 'open'. 'Open' again not because their border is open, but because their *logic* is open. The role of the state is not to implement the abstract total good, but to set the discussions and the markets in such a way they work best and stability is assured. For instance, because discussions tend to bring power to the intellectual elites, the one-man-one-vote principle works as a mechanism to restore the balance. Because markets have an inherent tendency to make the rich richer and the poor poorer, progressive income tax works as a mechanism to restore the balance. The latter has been called the basic principle of the 'liberal society' by Pareto: the market takes care of efficiency (that is, the collectively optimal allocation of goods), but before markets can be allowed to do this benign work, the state should install mechanisms to protect the poor and the others who have no bargaining power on the market (that is, equity). The law is one of these mechanisms. Both liberalism and social democracy work on this idea; they differ in the emphasis they put on the efficiency or the equity side of the balance.

This gradual differentiation between social-democratic and liberal ways of organizing an open society has to do with the well-known difference between 'minimum' and 'aspirational' norms. The typical liberal says: the role of the state is to organize a minimum set of strict norms to protect the poor, but. after that, let markets do the work. The typical social democrat says: no, the state should do more than that. The state should actively pursue the common good. We will come back to this dichotomy of minimum and aspirational norms later.

Crucial for all these 'open societies' are checks and balances. Also state institutions have to be accountable, that is, open to receive these checks and balances. The law, and all that comes with it, is part of these checks and balances. Often, for instance, the law is to protect people against the all-pervading power of economics (and the rich; all are equal before the law), as well as against the all-pervading power of the state.

What in these terms are judicial *ethics*? The are also a part of the checks and balances system. The judiciary is a powerful group, with members that cannot be voted away. Who will keep them on the right track? Who watches the watchmen? If the group of judges were closed, it would - as any closed group - go awry in the longer run. Small wrongdoings would go unrectified, thus setting new traditions on which more wrongdoings would feed and so on, until after many years a social crash would occur: 'Let us do away this whole corrupted system'! This would indeed be a check, but not without many years of problems and a lot of casualties. It seems much better to prevent this the 'open society way': in a system of checks and balances, organized as a permanent, open discussion, about the personal behavior of judges, about the way people are treated in the courts, and about the legal decisions themselves.

These discussions may take place on three planes of generality:

1) The level of truly general reflections. This concerns discussions on the place of the judiciary in the *trias politica*, on the degree to which judges should be active in regulations that set limits to markets and other such issues. The academic world is often a source of this type of discussions.
2) The level of more specific problems and issues, often brought forward by the press.

3) The level of even more specific complaints by individual people and organizations.

On all three levels, the open society way is not to suppress the issues but to organize a regular system and culture of exchange, e.g. a network of linkages with academia, and an independent body for the processing of complaints. One way *not* to do it seems to be exemplified by Principle 1 in your draft code of conduct, saying that 'the unjustified attack against the judge may be considered as an attack against the judiciary as a whole'. This almost automatic solidarity tends to close doors that should be open, even if you do not agree with everything that comes through it.

The point of the 'closed' versus 'open' issue is to reveal the crucial importance of judicial ethics as a system of mediation between society and the judiciary; drafting codes or discussing ethical dilemmas is not something people do, because it seems to be fashionable. The 'closed' versus 'open' issue was chosen because the closed society is still a lively memory in the Czech Republic, and the general drive must be much towards openness. On the other hand, old habits tend to die hard. Article 1 of the draft code of the Czech judiciary could be read as stating that the whole judiciary should defend any of its members coming under attack. This is typically a closed response.

Next in the presentation were examples of problems from elsewhere in Europe. This was partly because it is always nice to know that you are not the only one with worries. But mainly because it shows that it is impossible to foresee all potential problems that can arise between the judiciary and society. The next section summarizes this part of the text of the seminar.

All three levels of generality are levels of mediation between the judiciary and society. We have not yet discussed yet what kind of subjects should be or could be traded in these systems of mediation. Is there a kind of standard list of discussion topics? Let me give some examples.

Typical topics

Going through the discussions, and in the literature and the codes that I know from Europe and the United States, some ethical themes seem to appear everywhere. These are the principles, one could say, that form the stable heart of the judicial profession. They are dignity, impartiality and independence. They can also be found in the Czech oath and the law on judicial discipline. Out of these three, independence is often seen as the most fundamental. It means not only independence from the state, but also from one's own cultural and social backgrounds and even from the consensus of the media, the public and the judiciary itself. Some matters, however are more specific to particular countries:

■ In the United Kingdom, judges sometimes have a denigratory attitude or behavior towards people. Lord Bingham, Lord Chief Justice of England (1995) gives an example of a judge who, on receiving the assurance of a witness wishing to affirm that he had no religious belief, immediately added: 'And no morals either'. The solution to this is that all judges keep silent all the time, or at least as much as possible, and do not have contact with the press. Otherwise you run all kind of risks, especially that people discover how stupid you actually are! Both problem and solution might be connected to the class character of British society; the selection of judges is not very meritocratic.

■ In the Netherlands we have a very different problem, the problem of the substitute judges. These are basically attornies, practicing lawyers who sit as a judge for a few hours per week or month, for only a small financial compensation. Because of that, the substitute judge may find himself presiding over a case in which one of the litigants is a senior partner in his own law firm! Or he may be a mayor sitting also as judge in his own town. In Dutch culture (where everybody is supposed to be neutral and rational) this has been tolerated for a long time, but public opinion has been turning up the pressure and new regulations are being made.

■ In Spain recently a judge stood trial for tax fraud. Just before his case was about to be decided, he entered the office of one of the judges deciding in his case, and proposed to this judge as follows: 'Look here, I understood that you have a son with problems and no job. I offer to get him a job with a friend of mine at the national bank within two days'.

■ In a supermarket in Turkey, quite a battlefield erupted when two judges suddenly attacked each other and were joined immediately by their respective families. The riot resulted is a broken arm for one judge and some severe bruises for the other.

■ In another country (not the Czech Republic as we all know), a judge drank so much beer during a lunch meeting that he was unable to leave the court building on his own feet.

■ Some time ago in Belgium, a judge who was investigating a crime concerning abuse of children - one of the very few judges trusted by the public - visited a meeting of an organization of child protection. He had some food there and accepted a little present (a fountain pen) from the organization. He now will be taken off the case, accused of not being impartial any more.

Obviously, a wide array of potential accidents in the relationship between judiciary and society appears to exist. Should all these issues be addressed in the form of rules? Should a code of conduct be designed such that all these problems are prevented? The answer is no, for two reasons. One can be derived from the foregoing section about open society. Judicial ethics are a permanent mediation between society and judiciary, and there is no single all-pervading logic. Therefore, all-encompassing codes are impossible, and they are not necessary either. Societies change, and with them the problems that need to be mediated. These need to be addressed, and not necessarily all the possible others! In other words, designing courses of ethics or codes of ethics is a permanent, open process, that addresses current or envisaged problems.

This relates back to the open society issue. The objective of this was to indicate that it is better to work in a more or less relaxed manner towards an admittedly limited code of conduct, rather than try to fix a perfect code once and for all.

The next topic concerned the relationship between codes and the internalization of norms.

The second reason why not all possible norms need necessarily be discussed or codified is contained in the next section, and concerns more psychological and cultural aspects. That is also my second theoretical theme.

Guilt, shame and the internalization of norms

A well-known distinction between cultures is between 'cultures of guilt' and 'cultures of shame'. Although only describing simplified ideal types, the distinction is useful for the design of normative systems. In a culture of shame, an act is regarded as a mistake if it exposes the actor to lose face in the eyes of his fellow-men. For example, if you drive your car and by accident hit another car parked by the side of the road, you first look around if someone has seen it. If so, you feel ashamed. If not, you feel relieved, happy to have got away with it. In the same incident in a culture of guilt, the problem is in the act *itself.* That is because the norm is not external (in the eyes of the other), but someway internalized. The distinction between culture of shame and culture of guilt may be used, and has been used, to speculate about Catholic and Protestant ways of defining and solving problems, about Asian and European ways of doing business, and so on. More important for judicial ethics is that development psychologists such as Kohlberg and Piaget have shown, and also set as ideal, that social norms become internalized in the course of a child's development. Behind this is the idea (that you find also in many management books, dealing basically with the manipulation of people) that internalized norms are more *effective*. They work without anybody being necessary for control and sanctions.

The strongest norms are those that have become implanted without discussions. One example is the norm of safety in the education of civil engineers. There are many explicit norms about how to make the calculations that assure that bridges are safe. No engineer would come up with the idea to make a less safe bridge. For instance, to make two variants and then say to the decision-makers: 'This design is safe but costly, and this other design is less safe but cheaper, please take your pick'. Now, what would happen if someone would write in a Code Of Civil Engineers: 'All bridge designs should be safe designs'? The effect would be that civil engineers would begin to think that apparently, this norm does not go without saying. It would lift the safety norm from the realm of the fully internalized self-evident to the realm of norms that are somehow debatable. Thus, explicating the norm has in fact externalized, and thereby weakened it.

Explicating a norm, for instance in a code, is therefore not always a means to strengthen that norm. 'High' norms, lying at the heart of the profession, are especially vulnerable in this respect. Such norms, if written down at all, should be written down in a way that expresses that actually, they do not need to be written down at all.

This brings us back to the difference between 'aspirational' and 'minimal' norms, a distinction that runs parallel with Lon Fuller's distinction between the morality of aspiration and the morality of duty (Fuller, 1969; Van der Burg, 1995). The morality of aspiration is the morality of excellence. It starts at the top of human achievement. It presents us with a general idea of the perfection we ought to aim at, rather than afford us any certain and infallible directions of acquiring it. The morality of duty, on the other hand, starts at the bottom. It does not condemn men for failing to embrace opportunities for the fullest realization of their powers. Instead, it condemns men for failing to respect the basic requirements of social living.

The language used is an important 'marker' of norms that are meant to be aspirational and norms meant to be minimal. For instance, in the draft Czech code it is stated that: 'It is the honor of the judge to uphold the impartiality, independence of judgment (...) that form the heart of his profession'. It is not stated that 'A judge shall be impartial'. Other norms in the code are justifiedly put in minimalistic language, such as: 'Cases shall be dealt with in the time allotted by the law'.

For the design of codes of conduct it is useful also to distinguish 'derived' norms from minimal and aspirational ones. Derived norms are those that causally follow from the aspirational and minimal ones. An example is that if it can be shown that judges are generally not well equipped to explain decisions to the public in a way the public understands, judges should leave these discussion to specialized personnel. Such a derived norm should not necessarily find a place in a code at all, but might better be taken up in a set of organizational rules.

This again relates to the tendency of codemakers to capture everything, preferably in strict ('minimalistic') language. It also aims to raise the awareness of the participants with respect to the limitations of codes. Having a code, that is a set of external norms, may even be detrimental to the internalization of norms. Thus the text which is also prepared for the next theme which is the difference between learning through the discussion of cases versus learning through the drafting of a code.

The subject of internalization of norms, as you may imagine, has also to do with the process of how judicial ethics can be formed in the minds of judges and in the culture of the judiciary as a whole. Obviously, you cannot simply write down a number of norms and then say: That's it! Hence my next subject.

Cases and codes

In the coming days we will discuss ethical cases and a draft code. Both are vehicles for ethical progress, but in a different way.

The case study method is, one could say, the normal method of the judiciary worldwide, especially in common law countries. Cases come before a forum and are adjudicated by the forum. Wisdom, then, is connected to the jurisprudence. Wisdom consists of the 'higher' values that may be inferred through the jurisprudence. Strictly speaking, this wisdom may remain unwritten. You master it by going through the jurisprudence and debating it. The method is bottom-up, or 'inductive' as the methodologists of science say. The general ideas are inferred from the specific examples.

The other way around is more top-down ('deductive'). We try to formulate a law, an ethic, a rule etc. from a general logic, applying it in the analysis of a general problem. The cases then are only passive; they are adjudicated by subsuming them under the applicable general rules.

In shorthand, we could call these two methods 'proceeding by cases' and 'proceeding by codes'. These will be the subjects of the next two sections. We should be aware that these terms describe the *methods*, not the results. Studying and discussing cases may, of course, result in the addition or improvement of a rule in a code. And the other way around, codes may be used to formulate cases, e.g. for educational purposes.

After this technical introduction the seminar text splits in two branches, one on cases and one on codes.

Proceeding by cases

The discussion of cases may be used for various purposes. First, to test a code. The code is then used to formulate a case, and it is checked whether the interpretations and responses are what the codemakers expect them to be. Secondly, cases may be used to build up a code. Then a certain issue is taken, such as impartiality, or troublesome family members of judges, and an attempt is made to formulate a number of cases to describe this issue. After the discussions, an attempt is made to adduce one or more rules out of this. The third use of cases is to build up individual moral understanding in education. This is the transfer of culture.

Proceeding by cases has many advantages:

- everybody can participate, irrespective of position or education;
- discussing them is usually interesting enough to keep participants involved for a long time;
- it works to internalize norms;
- the discussions allow people to express feelings like insecurity, compassion and so on, which often remain hidden in more formal approaches.

There are disadvantages too, however:

- cases tend to be selected from the stories that are nice to tell. Less spectacular problems stay out of sight;
- the induction of general rules often requires special skills;

- usually, cases are supposed to be ethical cases beforehand, hence they do not train ethical awareness.

We may distinguish between five types of cases (Mink, 1996):

1 The 'shining example'

These are the stories and the myths of the great moral persons in difficult situations, like Gandhi or Havel. These stories are connected to the setting and internalization of aspirational norms. The limitation of such stories is that they are usually connected with big problems and do not give much guidance in the trivial problems of daily behavior.

2 The 'ship run ashore'

These are the stories of how a normal person can deviate from the right track and end up in a very immoral position and a lot of trouble. This kind of case gives us an illustration of causes and consequences of unethical behavior. One of such stories is in the making in the Netherlands at present. It is a story of how a nice, successful professor ended up plagiarising hundreds of pages of other peoples' books. Everybody is talking about it at present and in these discussions, everybody is investigating his own behavior and re-establishing his own norms.

3 The boundary-seeking case

The boundary-seeking case consists of seeking the point along an axis where acceptable behavior becomes problematic behavior. For example, you are a judge and your brother is the country's greatest criminal. The birthday-party of your mother is coming up, and if you go there, there is a fair chance that your brother will also be present and the local press will take pictures of you together with your brother. Will you go to the party or not? Let us assume that the answer is 'no'. The case is restated so that your brother is now only the local petty thief. Finally the case can be restated such that your brother now is a poorly dressed and smelly, weird drug addict. Somewhere along this line you will think: 'Well, my brother may not represent the greatest success story of society, but the public has to accept that there is a difference between the judge and his brother'. The purpose of the case discussion is to establish that point along the line.

4 The moral dilemma

The moral dilemma is a description of a case with two possible solutions which both may be ethically good or bad, depending on the ethical criteria and vision one applies. Its aim is to increase the level of ethical argumentation. A simple example from the Czech Republic is about the private firm that offered to sponsor the installation of a computer system for the district court. Accepting it will improve the court's capacity to deliver justice; on the other hand, its independence is likely to become questioned.

5 The Harvard case

The Harvard case is usually a rather complex real-life story in which the moral aspects are hidden. Part of the art of discussing these cases is to identify these ethical aspects, thus addressing the tendency of many professionals to deny the moral aspects of their work.

In the analysis of cases it is always good to make a distinction between qualitative and quantitative aspects.

- The qualitative aspect is: in which *terms* do we frame the problem? For instance in the case of one's brother being a criminal or a junkie, you may say: 'For me there is a big difference in my brother being a criminal or a junkie. In the first case he is a morally bad person and in the second case he is only a health failure'. This opinion expresses that bad health is morally different from bad acts, and that being addicted should be considered under the criterion of 'health' and not of 'acts'.

- The quantitative aspect is: knowing the criteria, what are the threshold values for these criteria? In the case of the criminal brother, to what degree should he be morally at fault in order for me to avoid him?

During the seminar, these types of cases were connected to examples brought forward by the participants. After that, the seminar presentation turned attention to the code-making process.

Proceeding by codes

We now focus on the second way of organising progress in the professional ethics field, i.e. the code-making process. Firstly, codes of conduct are country-specific mediations between society and the judiciary, and between the individual and collective level within the judiciary. Secondly, codes are only part of the total of these mediations; not everything needs to be encoded. Finally, codes are part of a process, within the judiciary and between the judiciary and society. This we got from the theories of the open society and of shame and guilt. It may be noted here that 'mediating between the judiciary and society' may be called a function of a code. Insight in these functions helps in organizing a process of code-making. Two more theories may be turned to in order to arrive at a full listing of code functions.

First there is the theory of the professions. This theory is interesting especially in the way that certain occupations manage to become regarded as something special, namely as a profession. Professions are occupational groups that own and protect special knowledge that you can get only by a special type of education that is controlled by the profession itself. The theory of the professions tells us that a code of ethics, and the allied disciplinary procedures are instruments to assert that a group can keep itself clean, and therefore does not need regulation by the state.

A second source for understanding the functions of codes is the theory of bureaucracy, for instance of Burke (Burke, 1988). One of the issues in this theory is how and why bureaucrats sometimes step outside of their hierarchy and tell everybody, also the press, that something is very wrong in their organization. For instance an environmental agency may have been closing its eyes for years on illegal dumping of toxic waste. When may a minor bureaucrat break the normal rules? One important factor here is always that the minor bureaucrat can appeal to certain higher norms, for example that the environmental agency aspires to serve the public to the best of its abilities. These higher norms are typically the aspirational norms of the organization. In other words, aspirations - although they sometimes may seem a bit superfluous - can have an important function to keep organizations clean. They offer protection to internal opposition that can keep organizations on the right track.

Thus distinguishing between internal and external functions, we arrive at the following list of the functions of a code of conduct.

External functions:

1 to bring the aspirations and the worries of society into the judiciary. It is a framework for discussions between society and the judiciary
2 to keep up the respectability of the judiciary
3 to protect the judiciary against state interference

Internal functions:

4 to guide decisions for the individual judge as well as for the judiciary as a whole

5 (especially the aspirational norms) a source for resistance against undue conformism.

This list may guide us in a systematic process of code-of-conduct design. Any such process has a first intuitive, unsystematic stage. Any judiciary that starts making a code will understand something of its functions, and the problems it should address on a common sense level. Any first draft code, such as the present one of the Czech judiciary, therefore already takes in the foregoing on a commonsense level. The next step then is to repeat the process, but in a more systematic manner. We may take the functions one by one, and then try to separate these into specific question and issues, e.g. in an aspirational, minimal and normative sense. Then we may address the questions whether these issues should be absorbed into a code or not. For instance, the first function is to bring the worries of society into the judiciary. This gives rise to the connected questions and issues such as:

- What does society want the judiciary to be (aspirational)? What are society's worries as to what could go wrong (minimum)? What do *we* think society *should* worry about? Connected issues are, for example: independence of the judiciary with respect to the police or to the urban elite. And answers are, for example: selection of judges not only from the urban elite.

Then, which way do we shape this into a code?

- As an aspirational norm in aspirational language? As a minimum norm in minimalistic language? Or maybe not at all? For instance, put it in a curriculum as case material? Or do we try to address the problem not by moral but by structural means (advisory committee, incentive structures etc.)? With respect to the urban elite, for instance, it may be put as an aspirational norm that the judiciary as a group aspires to comprise all cultures present in society. But the norm can also be translated into technical rules in the procedures of selecting judges.

The second function (keeping up the respectability) can be treated in the same way. Connected questions are:

- What do citizens want (individual) judges and court proceedings to be? What often goes wrong? (for example impartiality; judges do not listen) What do *we* want individual judges and court proceedings to be? From these questions follows a set of issues and from these issues follows a set of possible responses.

Then, crossing over to the practicalities,

- Which way do we put all that into a code, or some other place?

And so on, function by function. It is not as nice as discussing cases, but this way you organize a systematic process of 'proceeding by codes' which will be very useful because it counterbalances the weaknesses of 'proceeding by cases'.

Now followed a number of critical remarks on a number of articles of the Czech draft code based on the systematic typology. Rounding off, a third, more externally oriented path forward was presented.

Proceeding by contacts

Proceeding by cases and proceeding by codes should, of course, not take place in isolation. Two types of external contacts seem to be essential.

First, contact with the public. This includes the press, of course. In the Netherlands, for example, we also have a very active group of angry citizens out to purify the judiciary, actively searching for alleged cases of conflict of interest. But also social-scientific research and polls can play an important role here. Finally, a system of processing complaints of the 'clients' of the judiciary can serve as another crucial source (because it is different from the others). Complaints may be boring or hard to swallow, but they represent a free advice service at the same time!

Second, contact with other judiciaries may help much, e.g. reading and comparing their codes and case material, and attending international conferences. That way, for instance, we learn that contacts with the press are organized in very different ways in various countries. Some problems of other judiciaries may look only funny to you, others may look like your own of yesterday; but other problems may be your problems of tomorrow! This then, I hope, jointly with the discussion of cases and the drafting of a code, will support the Czech judiciary to make a step forward in professional ethics.

Final Reflection: How Very Dutch!

Looking back on this exercise we feel basically satisfied that we have been able to stay close to the participants' problems while also connecting these to a number of more general reflections and tools. In retrospect, it struck us that although we had tried to be only client-oriented and scientific, our contribution to the seminar may in fact have been much 'Dutcher', more inspired by the Dutch 'polder model' than we were aware of at the time.

According to the sociologist Ter Borg (1990), the key value of Dutch culture is 'pragmatische redelijkheid', which translates into 'pragmatic rationality' and 'pragmatic reasonableness'. As exemplified by Popper, the notion of rationality links up with the notion of the open society virtually automatically. In the words of the historian Van der Horst (1996), Dutch society is non-exclusivist; everybody is taken on board, albeit under the silent condition that everybody is supposed to be reasonable, willing to participate in the open discussions that lead to rational consensus. Dutch culture is a mainstreaming machine. The success of this style of operation may be measured, for instance, by the fact that the anti-bourgeois rebellion of the sixties was encapsulated by the bourgeois rapidly and without violence, thus changing the mainstream and silencing the rebellion (Kennedy, 1995). As explained by Kennedy, pragmatism was also part of this response; since the tide of rebellion was too high to be dammed, it was more practical to channel it.

The Netherlands is one of the oldest and most stable modern nation-states (Zahn, 1984). This long-term success has been achieved by avoiding political alliances and instead focusing on economic aims, getting rich quietly, focusing on the problems at hand rather than on high principles. Protestant work ethics have always been conducive in this respect (Schama, 1987).

Needless to say, many elements of this Dutch mindset may be found in the preceding sections.

Numerous Dutch law professors are involved at present in new lawmaking in many Eastern European countries. Many Dutch judges are involved in improving legal practice in these countries, too. We export a lot of law. It would be nice to know in which ways and to which extent Dutch culture, with all its niceties and limitations, is exported with the package.

References

Bingham, T. (1995), 'Judicial Ethics', in R. Cranston (ed.), *Legal Ethics and Professional Responsibility*, Clarendon Press, Oxford, 35.

Bovens, M. (1992), 'Beroepscodes voor beta's', *Filosofie and Praktijk*, vol. 13.

Burke, J. (1988), *Bureaucratic Responsibility*, The Johns Hopkins University Press, New York.

Cohen, F. (1970), 'Judicial Ethics', in L. Kramer-Cohen (ed.), *The Legal Conscience; Selected Papers*, Yale University Press, London, 160.

De Mink, F. (1996), 'Cases bij bedrijfsethiek', *Filosofie* vol. 6, nr. 3.

Fuller, L. (1969), *The Morality of Law*, Yale University Press, London.

Kennedy, J. (1995), *Nieuw Babylon in aanbouw; Nederland in de jaren zestig*, Boom, Meppel.

Kronman, A. (1987), 'Practical Wisdom and Professional Character', in J. Coleman and E. Frankel Paul (eds), *Philosophy and Law*, Basil Blackwell, New York, 203.

Morgan, T. (1987), *Legal Ethics*, Gilbert Law Summaries, 6th edition, Chicago.

Schama, S. (1987), *The Embarrassment of Riches: An Interpretation of Dutch Culture in the Golden Age*, Knopf, New York.

Van der Burg, W. (1995), 'Enkele hypothesen over de professionele moraal van juristen', in L. de Groot-van Leeuwen and L. Quant (eds), *Ethiek en het juridisch beroep*, Vuga, The Hague, 13.

Van der Horst, H. (1996), *The Low Sky; Understanding the Dutch*, Scriptum Books, Schiedam.

Van Luijk, H. (1993), *Om redelijk gewin; oefeningen in bedrijfsethiek*, Boom, Meppel.

Zahn, E. (1984), *Das unbekannte Holland; Regenten, Rebellen und Reformatoren*, Siedler, Berlin.

10 Transcending Borders: Escaping the confines of gender violence

LINDA A. KELLY

A border is a veil not many people can wear.[1]

Borders are a permeable creation. Yet whether dug into the physical terrain or constructed through legal theory, United States law and culture continue to insist upon them. Predictably, this attempt to enforce the unenforceable is a costly effort. And when the physical and theoretical borders intersect, the damage is magnified. For female refugees and immigrants in the United States, such a maze of borders exists in gender violence.

I am the co-director of the Immigration Clinic of St Thomas University School of Law in Miami, Florida. The challenges faced by the Clinic's clients are a constant reminder of the devastating effect legal and social attitudes can have on women. With a grant from the Law School Clinical Experience Program of the United States Department of Education, the Clinic was founded in 1992 and developed by Peter Margulies, the Clinic's Director.[2] In the early years, a principal focus of the Clinic was contributing to the effort to represent the large number of Haitian asylum seekers and other refugees held at the Krome Detention Center in Miami, Florida, by the Immigration and Naturalization Service (INS) of the United States Department of Justice. Since that time, the Clinic's commitment to international human rights work has grown. Detainees and non-detainees seeking asylum from countries throughout the world are now represented. The Clinic has also been involved in international human rights law reform through impact litigation, political lobbying and media work. In order further to respond to the changing needs of southern Florida's sizeable immigrant community, the Clinic has also expanded its areas of practice. There is now a strong commitment to representing individuals eligible for residency based upon family relationships. The Clinic assists the immediate relatives of United States citizens and lawful permanent residents, as well as abandoned children, in obtaining their residency or 'green cards'.

It is through this representation of asylum seekers and family members that the Clinic has come to represent a significant number of females and immigrants who have survived gender violence. Recent changes in the law have contributed to the Clinic's ability to represent these survivors. In asylum law, the 1996 success of *In Re Kasinga*[3] built upon earlier efforts to recognize the impact gender can have in qualifying a woman for asylum. And in the family-petitioning context, the immigration provisions of the 1994 Violence Against Women Act (VAWA)[4] finally created a means by which the battered spouse of a United States citizen or lawful permanent resident could achieve residency without having to rely upon her abuser.

Responding to these more positive developments, as well as to the severity of changes such as the 1996 Illegal Immigration Reform and Immigrant Responsibility Act,[5] the Clinic is an important resource for southern Florida's immigrants and a valuable learning tool for St Thomas's students. Each year, the Clinic enrols between 16 and 20 students. The Clinic is a full academic year commitment, and the students receive four graded credits per semester for their work. Students work in teams of two (and occasionally three). After dividing the teams between the two professors, who are both Florida-licensed practitioners, the students are given cases which are directly supervised by their assigned professor. Typically, a team manages a case load of 5-6 active cases throughout the year. In addition to each team meeting weekly for case review with its designated professor, the Clinic conducts a weekly class. Each year, these classes begin with an intensive training on substantive asylum law, the family petitioning process and the administrative agencies of the United States Department of Justice which are charged with executing United States immigration law. Throughout the year classes continue to meet in order to review immigration law, highlight political and legal developments of common interest, and analyze Clinic victories and failures. Class time is also devoted to conducting client-negotiation simulation exercises, discussing professional responsibility and hosting guest speakers who include immigration judges, congressional interns, private practitioners and domestic violence educators. It is through this clinical framework and pursuant to federal[6] and state[7] regulations, that the Clinic's students assume direct responsibility for representing indigent individuals before the federal Immigration and Naturalization Service (INS) and the Immigration Court, as well as before Florida state courts and officials.

Advocating for aliens has been a challenge since the earliest cases of

Chae Chan Ping[8] and *Fong Yue Ting*[9] awarded the federal political branches a virtually absolute power over US immigration matters.[10] The Clinic students quickly learn that, in every case, success demands hard work and sincere commitment. However, the representation of female aliens carries an additional burden. Female immigrants seeking refuge from abuse through asylum or VAWA must overcome the biases and stereotypes which confine the understanding of gender violence.

Advancing immigration law's treatment of women requires advancing the definition of gender violence. With this premise, the reform of immigration law can benefit from an examination of the treatment of gender violence in United States domestic law. Reviewing this work not only reveals a common struggle. More importantly, it emphasizes a shared need to address the negative images of women projected through law and culture. Relying on the stories of women represented by the St Thomas Immigration Clinic, this chapter examines the common problems and goals faced by women in the United States domestic law and immigration law settings. Such devices as the public/private dichotomy, which has limited protection for women in rape, sexual harassment and domestic violence law is fully evident in United States gender-related asylum law. Clinical experiences reveal how this challenge continues to confront female refugees, re-enforcing the need to overcome the public/private divide. The Clinic's work also illustrates how the changes of gender-related asylum law and VAWA prevent effective remedies as they are built upon negative images of women. Because these biases are so ingrained in legal and social thought, advocates for women, including the representatives of the St Thomas Immigration Clinic, must constantly be alert to their influence. In working to identify and destroy the negative, feminists must finally come together to instil honest and positive images of women.

The Private/Public Barrier and Limits of Asylum

The Domestic Backdrop

In United States law, the right to privacy has been the judicial mechanism through which female access to such rights as contraception[11] and abortion[12] has been granted. Relying on Fourteenth Amendment due process considerations, as well as the constitutional 'penumbras' of the First Amendment right to free speech and Fourth Amendment protection against search and seizure,[13] the Court has drawn a zone into which 'the state cannot enter'.[14] Yet notwithstanding the benefits women derive from the notion of privacy, feminists have effectively exposed how the right to privacy perpetuates the subjugation of women. The division of public and private spheres silently perpetuates female vulnerability by ignoring the gender inequality so firmly built into the patriarchal structure of private life. In so doing, the dynamics of inequality present in the private sphere are legitimized by public inaction. Such *de facto* approval is evident in the decision to allow the state to fund pregnancies while not similarly fund abortions.[15] It is this failure to destabilize the traditional male/female hierarchy which has rallied feminists such as Catherine MacKinnon to 'explode the private'.[16] For MacKinnon, the right of privacy is nothing more than 'the right of men "to be let alone" to oppress women one at a time'.[17] Outside the discussion of reproductive rights, such attacks have effectively challenged the public/private dichotomy as a barrier to the recognition and elimination of other forms of gender violence.[18] By defining distinct spheres of acceptable conduct, the dichotomy perpetuates a fiction which prevents intrusion into the private realm - even when such intrusion is intended to prevent further abuse. Rationales for maintaining such vigil guarding of the border can range from such apparently neutral arguments as the need to protect constitutional expectations of privacy to the belief that any acknowledgment of such realities as the pervasiveness of domestic violence would shatter our illusions of domestic bliss and spousal equality.[19] To combat such perceptions, the battle against domestic violence has relied upon the strategy of characterizing the violence as a public problem thereby meriting a public solution.[20]

Similar reservations about intruding into the private sphere of intimate relations have prevented an effective response to the gender violence committed through the laws governing rape. Historically, the public/private distinction immunized men from being guilty of raping their wives through explicit exemptions in rape statutes for husbands. Such exemptions simultaneously denied and accepted the violence committed by men against their wives.[21] The doctrine of interspousal tort immunity achieved similar results.[22]

Outside the home, the public/private dichotomy also presents a challenge. A critical part of the legal struggle against sexual harassment has been to convince both the lawmakers and society that harassment cannot be minimized as a 'personal' incident but is rather an attack on gender which demands a public response.[23] In so doing, the work against sexual harassment exposes the fictional distinction drawn between the public and the private. Sexual harassment, like other forms of gender violence, cannot simply be isolated as a personal event. To do so presumes a state of gender equality in the personal realm which does not exist. Reassessing sexual harassment law and extending employer liability in 1998, the Supreme Court understood that the power dynamics in the employment setting infiltrate all aspects of the employer/employee relationship.[24] Feminists have long recognized this reality, having persuasively declared 'the personal as political'.[25] Such recognition defies the liberal myth that state intervention can simply be contained within a rigidly prescribed public realm. The public/private border, like national borders, is an amorphous, man-made creation. As advances in United States laws on reproductive rights, rape, domestic violence and sexual harassment are made, this realization gains further legitimacy. Building upon these successes, immigrant advocates can better serve women seeking to cross the United States physical borders.

Facing the Public/Private Divide on the Gender-Related Asylum Law Frontier

The barrier erected by the public/private border has significant international implications. Women comprise the majority of refugees, and domestic violence and other forms of gender violence often factor into their reasons for fleeing.[26] Through its accession to the UN Convention and Protocol Relating to the Status of Refugees, the United State is legally committed to the protection of refugees.[27] However, as in domestic law, the public/private dichotomy impedes international obligations to women. Women who flee their homelands after suffering gender-related violence are frequently denied relief. Denials consistently cite the premise that the violence, whether perpetrated by a public or private actor, is neither a public act, nor an act implicitly condoned by public authorities.[28] Such distinction seems analogous to international policy that a state bears no responsibility for its officials' violations of customary international law if such acts are not approved by responsible government agents.[29] As seen in the domestic setting, it is concluded that international obligations do not contemplate the private. An understanding of gender violence which begins with the premise that societal obligations extend into the private realm would pre-empt the devastation such a distinction has wreaked for many female asylum seekers. Other formidable borders which reinforce containing the definition of gender violence also need to be overcome in asylum law. The ground breaking case of *Kasinga* illustrates the complexity of these borders.[30]

The Challenge of Kasinga

At the age of 17, Fauziya Kasinga fled her country of Togo in order to escape female genital mutilation (FGM).[31] Varying in severity, FGM entails the removal of all or part of the female genitalia. Following such procedure, the remaining wound may be sewn shut, leaving only a small passage for blood or urine. FGM is known to cause injuries which can range from psychological trauma to severe physical pain, hemorrhaging and death. Despite such dangers, legitimate concerns, which will be discussed momentarily, complicate efforts to prohibit, eradicate or even reduce the risks associated with the practice. Consequently, the ancient ritual continues in approximately 40 countries throughout the world, 28 of which are in Africa.[32]

Kasinga was a member of the Tchamba-Kunsuntu tribe which traditionally performed FGM upon its young female members. Yet because Kasinga's father opposed the practice and held an influential position in the tribe, Kasinga was prevented from being subjected to FGM during her early childhood years. However, when Kasinga was 16 years old, her father died. According to tribal custom, Kasinga's mother was driven from the home. Kasinga became the charge of her paternal aunt and was shortly thereafter forced by her aunt to enter into a polygamous marriage. Prior to the marriage's consummation, Kasinga's husband and aunt planned that Kasinga would undergo FGM. Faced with the imminent surgery, Kasinga fled. Traveling through Ghana and Germany, Kasinga arrived in the United States, surrendered herself to United States immigration officials and requested political asylum. After a prolonged detention and much publicized trial, Kasinga finally was found eligible for asylum on account of her fear of being forced to undergo female genital mutilation if required to return to Togo.[33] In establishing a claim for asylum, an applicant must satisfy the refugee standard of demonstrating 'persecution or a well-founded fear of persecution on account of race, religion, nationality, membership in a particular social group or political opinion'.[34] However, without an explicit provision for granting asylum 'on account of ' gender, which, if any, of the five statutorily articulated factors contemplates a claim tied to gender? Meeting the 'on account of' criteria proves to be one of the most difficult challenges for women seeking asylum as a result of gender violence. Prior to *Kasinga*, there had been some success in recognizing that rape could constitute persecution 'on account of' political opinion. *Matter of D-V-* awarded asylum to a Haitian woman raped by military soldiers in opposition to her support for President Jean-Bertrand Aristide.[35] Acknowledging rape as a tool of persecution utilized by government authorities against political opponents was a significant victory. However, there are limits to this success for women seeking asylum. A clear showing can still be required that acts of gender violence are 'an officially condoned reaction' to a woman's political opinion and not an abuse of power for 'personal edification'.[36] Such distinctions may be consistent with international treatment of the public/private distinction. Yet such conformity of law only further confirms the troubling truth that neither international law nor United States asylum law have progressed beyond the public/private border.

The Challenges of Clinical Education and Practice

Bridging the fictional public/private divide has been a significant challenge in the practice of the St Thomas Immigration Clinic. Part of this challenge is faced in the courtroom, where clients must provide ample evidence demonstrating the nexus between political opinion and the harm suffered. Consequently, in the case of a woman who had been imprisoned and raped in Haiti, it was critical that the client testify that throughout the rape, her rapists called her an 'Aristidist' and made other comments which clearly showed their actions were in opposition to her support for President Aristide. However, perhaps a more troubling aspect of the public/private challenge is faced in the classroom. In another case, the student representatives resisted the notion that a woman had suffered persecution by having sex with her prison guard as the condition of her release. The students reasoned the sex was voluntary and, after all, he did let her go.[37] That future advocates do not readily accept the power dynamics which exist in such stark circumstances as a prison relationship is a chilling reminder of the work that still needs to be done in destroying the public/private divide.

Other limits to addressing the gender violence inflicted against asylum seekers are also created by the confines of the statutorily protected grounds. 'Political opinion' has been held not only to include direct support for political candidates and parties, but also 'feminist' attitudes regarding the treatment of women, support of 'western values' and other beliefs.[38] Imputed political opinion also remains a relevant basis for asylum, having withstood Justice Scalia's conclusion that the 'ordinary meaning' of persecution on account of political opinion must be 'persecution on account of the victim's political opinion, not the persecutor's'.[39] Despite such possibilities, a woman fleeing gender violence may not come under the political opinion umbrella as she may be unable to link her abuse to a personally held political opinion or one that could be imputed to her. Similarly, a gender claim may simply have no discernible race, religion, or nationality component.

These difficulties are well illustrated by another case of the St Thomas Immigration Clinic. Paula was a Salvadoran woman who fled her country after she and her sister were gang-raped by six men while their brothers were held at gun point. Following the rape, the family made a futile attempt to report it to the local officials. As the clinic students' extensive research and documentation revealed, existing law in El Salvador did not accept victim testimony as admissible evidence.[40] Although the law theoretically permitted the testimony of Paula's brothers, the police refused to hear their account. Paula's testimony of being told by the police that only the police could serve as witnesses to rape is entirely consistent with El Salvador's societal resistance to acknowledging the pervasive violence against women.[41]

Immediately after going to the police, Paula and her family were repeatedly threatened. The family found their largest pig decapitated with an attached note stating, 'If you run around with a big mouth you too will end up slaughtered like the pig'. Other threatening notes were also left throughout the next several days. Paula's sister fled to Honduras. Finally, when Paula's home was under gun fire by a group of men demanding to be admitted, she fled.

In denying the claim, the immigration judge seemed to find the political opinion variable an insurmountable barrier. The judge reasoned the rape could not have been politically motivated as the applicant was not asserting that either she or the men had any political affiliation. Without looking past this determination, the judge determined the rape amounted to nothing more than a personal, albeit tragic, incident for which United States immigration law provided no relief. The limits of the political opinion category well illustrate how shortcomings in existing law and reason have driven the need to expand the social group category protected by asylum law. Although attempts to argue Paula was within a protected social group were unsuccessful, significant progress has been made in this area for female refugees.

Against the limitations of the political opinion and race, religion and nationality categories, gender-related asylum work has focused on broadening the social group category. *Kasinga* is a successful product of these efforts. However, the decision does not end the challenges facing women with gender-related claims. *Kasinga* did not extend the definition of social group to women generally. Even more damaging, through its definition of social group, *Kasinga* raised the threshold for women with gender-related claims.

Social group claims have traditionally been 'status based', requiring an individual to demonstrate an immutable characteristic she cannot or should not be required to change.[42] *Kasinga* curtailed the status based notion, by defining social group with both status and opinion dimensions.[43] *Kasinga's* social group became 'young women of her tribe who have not been, and do not wish to be, subjected to FGM'.[44]

The additional showing of personal opposition to the FGM practice in *Kasinga* is consistent with the heightened asylum standards placed upon women asserting other gender-related claims. A woman seeking asylum on account of her country's subjugation of women may also have to demonstrate that she specifically belongs to a subset of women 'who refuse to conform and whose opposition is so profound that they would choose to suffer the severe consequences of noncompliance'.[45]

Recognizing the strengths and weaknesses of *Kasinga*, the Clinic argued that Paula belonged to a social group of women who had been raped and could not seek protection as no legal recourse was available. The court's denial of our argument appeared clearly influenced by several common biases. The court's initial reaction was to express skepticism that all Salvadoran women could qualify for the protection of asylum when their country explicitly denied women protection. With such reservations, the court denied that Paula belonged to a social group deserving of relief.

Narrowing the class of women eligible for asylum based on gender may be seen as a justifiable means of preventing the theoretical possibility that half of a country might suddenly become eligible for asylum if one woman from such country was granted asylum solely on account of gender. However, concern about the potential size of a protected group has never legitimately factored into 'on account of ' determinations. As in the domestic treatment of gender-based crime, the true resistance is to believing that female immigrants are entitled to demand legal protection from rape and other crimes of intimate violence. As the INS trial attorney supporting Paula's deportation stated, her perpetrators were simply common criminals, motivated only by lust, not on account of Paula's gender. Relying upon precedent, the INS characterized the threats following the rape as retribution motivated by personal matters.[46] In Paula's case, despite Salvadoran law placing men in a position to brutalize women with immunity, the United States, through its administrative officials, failed to see clear government engagement in the crime. And in so doing, asylum law endorsed the public/private dichotomy.

Used to reinforce the gender hierarchy, the public/private dichotomy is a formidable challenge. However, naming the mechanisms of disempowerment is not sufficient. As feminist scholars have found in their efforts to reform United States domestic law, it is fundamentally the underlying attitudes about women reflected in the law which must be identified, excised and replaced with positive images.[47] For female immigrants, achieving equal protection necessitates confronting the paternalism which has created the 'good victim' bias.

The Good Victim Bias

Learning from Domestic Law

In the domestic setting, United States jurisprudence has consistently made stereotypical distinctions between female litigants, awarding relief only to those who personify the good victim. The good victim is seen as helpless, virginal, and completely without fault. Rather than conforming to this good victim image, the unsuccessful litigant is a 'tainted woman', embodying the negative female stereotype of whore or liar. The significance of these characterizations is apparent in the law and procedures governing rape, sexual harassment and domestic violence.

By restricting a victim's past sexual history from being admitted into evidence, rape shield statutes exemplify a legal effort to prevent the damage inflicted when a female victim is negatively cast as promiscuous.[48] The promiscuous woman is both a whore and a liar. By prohibiting a rape victim's sexual history from being introduced at trial, a jury may be prevented from succumbing to the stereotypical reasoning that a sexually active woman is a whore and a liar who is always willing to have sex, and therefore, the alleged victim must be lying about the rape. Rape shield statutes may be sincerely motivated by a desire to help women. Yet despite such good faith, precluding sexual history indulges the belief that only virgins can be true victims of rape.[49] As a consequence, rape shield statutes inadvertently perpetuate the same negative images they are seeking to overcome.[50]

The woman as liar or whore is also frequently sighted in sexual harassment cases.[51] Again, these imputed traits build upon societal stereotypes about women and their sexuality, working to discredit the female plaintiff. A woman alleging sexual harassment may be portrayed by the defense as the real seducer and therefore believed to have simply been 'asking for it'.[52] Alternatively, a suit may characterize the woman as a vengeful bitch, seeking payback for the rejection of her sexual advances or expectations.[53] The woman as opportunistic extortionist, overly dramatic exaggerator or delusional dreamer also effectively call a woman's credibility into question.[54]

The demand for a good victim unimpeded by such imagery is also evident in domestic violence law. Relying on the 'pushy' woman stereotype, one common defense to domestic violence charges is to argue the victim as provocateur of the violence (which she implicitly must deserve).[55] This characterization of the female as the real liar and aggressor is perhaps only rivaled in frequency by the belief that a woman alleging domestic violence is simply motivated by a 'quick fix' interest in gaining custody of the children or the home. Presumably, she will exaggerate or lie in order to get an immediate response from the court hearing her case for divorce, child custody or a domestic violence injunction.[56]

The Female Imagery of Immigration Law - The Good Victim of Asylum Law

Following the critiques of domestic United States law, it is apparent the demand for a good victim also exists in gender-related asylum law. By fleeing a practice loudly denounced by United States society and recently criminalized by law,[57] Kasinga typified the good victim. Her youth and detention by INS officials for over sixteen months made her an even more sympathetic figure, entitling her to national support and a picture on the New York Times front page.[58] Without hesitation, the BIA[59] denounced FGM, stating, 'The characteristic of having intact genitalia is one that is so fundamental to the individual identity of a young woman that she should not be required to change it... There is no legitimate reason for the practice'.[60] Indeed, despite opposing Kasinga's appeal, the INS was willing to concede that FGM constituted persecution and that it was not necessary for the persecutor to possess the punitive motive asylum law traditionally required.[61]

The BIA's response typifies the western reaction to FGM. In its extreme form, FGM is a horrifically brutal act, violating the most fundamental principles of bodily integrity and human respect. Yet awareness and sensitivity to the sexual, cultural, religious, and social justifications surrounding the practice complicate the ability to simply dismiss the practice as a tool of gender control.[62] In raising these issues, the long-standing debate is reignited between the universalists, who globally assert uniform and inalienable human rights, and the cultural relativists, who defer to the varying standards applied by local communities.[63] However, this dilemma is distorted by legitimate charges that the universalist position is more accurately a western bias against the practice of FGM.[64] Similar charges have been levied against the feminist movement for some time. Rather than representing all women, feminism has allowed the more limited gender equality demands of affluent white women to define the essential needs of all women.[65] Recognizing such shortcomings, feminism has progressed towards a multi-axis perspective which accounts for gender disparities and the pressures created by such factors as race, class and immigration status.[66] In contrast to the BIA's position of categorical rejection in *Kasinga*, the debate on FGM reflects how sensitivity to cultural concerns is critical to the ultimate goal of empowering women.[67] Outrightly denouncing FGM denies the agency of women who are committed to its practice. Consequently, condemning the practice in this absolute fashion perpetuates the same insensitivity to women that one set out to eliminate.[68]

The good victim established in asylum law limits the law's potential ability to address complex issues raised by female immigrants and recognize female autonomy. Asylum's basic premise of protecting individuals from persecution abroad provides no haven for female immigrants who experience gender violence in the United States. VAWA is the last major effort to provide refuge for female immigrants and their children who are victimized by gender violence in the United States.[69] Yet as in asylum law, the need to emulate a good victim again prevents an effective response to gender violence through VAWA.

VAWA's Good Victim

After years of legislative debate, VAWA was passed as part of the major crime bill of 1994. The immigration provisions form only a small part of the legislation. VAWA provides significant funding and remedies for victims of domestic violence, creates federal penalties for sex crimes and provides new evidentiary rules regarding sexual history in both the civil and criminal context.[70] Without question, VAWA has generated the greatest controversy through its creation of federal civil remedies for victims of violent crimes motivated by gender.[71] However, for female immigrants, the provisions creating a means of gaining lawful permanent residency are clearly the most significant.

VAWA's immigration provisions were passed with the intention of empowering undocumented women who were forced to remain in hostage-like relationships with their abusive spouses.[72] Until VAWA's passage, the right to lawful permanent residency based upon marriage could only be bestowed through a process begun with the cooperation of the lawful permanent resident or United States citizen spouse. Recognizing that abusive relationships are built upon an abuser's desire to control his mate, VAWA eliminated this power by entitling a battered spouse to initiate her request for lawful permanent residency.[73]

The introduction of VAWA's 'self-petitioning' process for battered immigrants shaped a critical focus of the St Thomas Immigration Clinic. Prior to VAWA's passage, there were scarce legal resources to serve southern Florida's immigrant community. The addition of a new form of relief with the potential of helping many women who previously had few options further strained this already overburdened system.[74] The Clinic recognized it could immediately fill the need. Our students' dual authorization to appear as advocates before federal immigration officials and state officials well-positioned the Clinic to represent battered immigrants in the various legal situations they traditionally encountered. Before state officials, students could assist clients in such critical matters as obtaining domestic violence injunctions and securing divorce.[75] Providing representation in state matters would prove not only to help ensure our clients' physical safety but also to preserve their federal immigration remedies. For example, VAWA claims must properly document the abuse. Consequently, domestic violence injunctions and the police reports, hospital records, and pictures of abuse which support them are a critical part of successful VAWA claims.[76] Additionally, as such possibilities as receiving a final valid order of dissolution of marriage prior to filing a VAWA self-petitioning claim preclude eligibility, having one source of legal advice has also proven invaluable for our clients.[77]

Despite the backing of such legal competence from the Clinic, the immediate question when VAWA became available was how to reach eligible applicants. Fortunately, a strong network between domestic violence courts, domestic violence legal service organizations, shelters, police, and other relevant agencies existed in the two counties of Broward and Dade which the Clinic principally serves. By attending various local functions and introducing the Clinic to key players ranging from the chief domestic violence judge, to court administrators, shelter counsellors and police officers, the Clinic tapped into this network. Making our services known to the agencies in the outlying counties of Monroe and Palm Beach also allowed the Clinic to reach individuals in more remote areas. As a result, when a woman is seeking the services of, for example, the local shelter, she may be referred to the Clinic if it becomes apparent at the shelter that the woman has concerns regarding her immigration status. In return, the Clinic relies strongly on the help of such social and legal agencies to address client needs beyond the scope of the Clinic. Unfortunately, developing such a strong referral system does not ensure that all potential VAWA applicants are assisted. The dynamics of power and control which surround domestic violence work to isolate its victims, thereby impairing a survivor's ability to reach out to legal and social agencies or even to friends and family for help.[78] An undocumented woman's fear of being deported if she appears in any official or public setting compounds the isolation dilemma.[79] Cultural attitudes can also prevent leaving or reporting a domestic violence relationship.[80]

Continual community education and outreach are key to reaching battered immigrants struggling with such challenges. However, such work is not only critical to making the initial contact with a battered immigrant. Developing sensitivity to the myriad of issues faced by battered immigrants has also proven to be an integral part of developing effective representatives in the St Thomas Clinic.

Diana was one of the first VAWA applicants represented by the Clinic. On one occasion Diana's student representative had called her into the Clinic to complete some necessary VAWA pleadings. However, in the course of the afternoon, it became apparent that Diana was still living with her batterer. Moreover, he was waiting downstairs while Diana was in our office. This was one of several times that Diana had returned to her husband. The student was clearly frustrated. Without hesitation, the student told me that she would no longer represent Diana if she did not permanently leave her husband. Recognizing the importance of instilling a sensitivity to domestic violence and building awareness to the difficulty of 'just leaving' the abuser, the Clinic now regularly hosts an employee of the local shelter whose main job function is to educate the community on domestic violence. These discussions bring students to understand that love, children, money, fear, shame, culture and other considerations complicate a domestic violence relationship.[81] As a result of the seminars, there has been a visible decrease in the tension between well-meaning clinical students and their battered clients.

Armed with able representatives and qualified aliens, the difficult journey toward VAWA relief begins. Like gender-related asylum law, VAWA also insists upon a good victim. VAWA's statutory and regulatory requirements demand strong documentation of abuse.[82] Proof of good moral character[83] and extreme hardship[84] if the victim or her children were required to return to the battered alien's home country are also required. Such conditions trivialize domestic violence and deny the strength of its survivors. For example, a 'strong woman' who is able to leave a violence relationship without public assistance and corroboration will have difficulty producing the necessary evidence to qualify for VAWA relief. A woman who is convicted for driving under the influence (DUI) will have difficulty demonstrating good moral character, even if her drinking was a mechanism used to cope with the physical violence.[85] Through the combination of these requirements, VAWA follows the pattern of setting a higher standard for victims of gender violence, thereby perpetuating the age-old myth of feminine goodness. Consequently, situations continually arise which call upon strong advocacy.[86]

Breaking the Barriers

As domestic and international law reveal, today's stereotypes and misconceptions limit an effective response to gender violence. For women and society at large, these beliefs have an accumulative negative impact. Meritorious cases are lost, dissuading other women who have been raped, sexually harassed, or beaten from seeking legal protection. Without effective legal redress, women become more vulnerable to attack as their assailants learn to capitalize on their impunity from punishment.[87] Beyond legal remedies, society also ignores its responsibility to otherwise address the crisis, willingly accepting the law's implication that the violence is minimal.[88]

Transcending the borders of gender violence entails moving beyond the boundaries which have been drawn. In the various domestic settings of rape, sexual harassment and domestic violence, significant work has been done to advance the understanding of gender violence. Immigration law can benefit from such progress. While continuing to struggle for the destruction of the private/public dichotomy, we must identify the negative images of women which underlie immigration law and harbor in the minds of judges, prosecutors and advocates.

In the law, adhering to the limits of the good victim allows gender violence to remain unchecked. Legal remedies must acknowledge that a 'strong' woman can be the subject of brutal attack. In VAWA, this recognition necessitates eliminating the statutory requirements of good moral character, extreme hardships and the practical need to document a lengthy subjugation to violence. In asylum law, this requires the clear acceptance that a woman can be a victim of persecution solely on account of gender. Yet more important than achieving technical changes to legal phrasing is the need to change the underlying societal attitudes regarding women.

As the work of the St Thomas Immigration Clinic reveals, legal and social resistance to female refugees and immigrants presents a more formidable challenge than the physical borders these survivors have crossed. Achieving female autonomy demands changing the law and the social stereotypes it supports. Progress in United States domestic law and scholarship continues to reinforce the need for such a dual strategy. Similarly, progress in immigration law necessitates letting down the conceptual borders created by the fictional public/private divide and the good victim bias. In so doing, women can finally cross the physical border to safety.

Notes

1 Danticat (1998), 264.

2 Approximately 84 per cent of the Clinic's funding now comes directly from the law school. In addition to employing two professors, the school also funds the Clinic's administrator and translators, and provides the Clinic with its physical location and office equipment.

3 Interim Decision, #3278 (BIA 1996).

4 Congress passed VAWA as part of the Violence Crime Control and Law Enforcement Act of 1994, Pub. L. No. 103-322, 108 Stat. 1796 (1994) (codified as amended in scattered sections of the INA, 8 USC).

5 Pub. L. No. 104-208, 110 Stat. 3009 (1996). For a discussion of IIRIRA and the harsh effects of other contemporary changes to immigration law see e.g., Perea (1997); Benson (1997); Johnson (1997); Guttentag (1997); Neuman (1998); Scaperlanda (1996).

6 8 C.F.R. §292.1(a)(2) (entitling a law school student to represent an individual providing the student is enrolled in an accredited law school clinical program, is appearing under the supervision of a law school faculty member or attorney, and is not receiving direct or indirect remuneration).

7 Florida Rules Regulating the Florida Bar, 11-1.5.

8 *Chae Chan Ping v. United States* 130 US 581 (1889) (otherwise known as the 'Chinese Exclusion Case') (establishing absolute power to exclude aliens).

9 *Fong Yue Ting v. United States* 149 US 698 (1893) (establishing absolute power to expel or deport aliens).

10 Many commentators have debated and breadth and propriety of the 'plenary power' doctrine. See e.g., Aleinikoff (1989); Hart (1953); Henkin (1985); Legomsky (1984).

11 *Griswold v. Connecticut*, 381 US 479 (1965).

12 *Roe v. Wade*, 410 US 113 (1973).

13 *Griswold v. Connecticut*, 381 US 479 (1965).

14 *Prince v. Massachusetts*, 321 US 158, 166 (1944).

15 *Harris v. McRae*, 448 US 297 (1980); MacKinnon (1987), 93.

16 MacKinnon (1987), 100.

17 MacKinnon (1987), 102, (quoting S. Warren and L. Brandeis (1890), 'The Right to Privacy', *Harvard Law Review*, vol. 4, 190).

18 Schneider (1991) (acknowledging the continuation of domestic violence as it is regarded as a private issue beyond legal interference); Siegel (1996) (charging that acceptance of domestic violence has been 'modernized' through its transformation in the legal system from an acceptable husband prerogative of chastisement to a practice protected through constitutional rights of privacy).

19 Reva Siegel (1996), 2180, suggests that the good-faith hope for 'domestic bliss' may motivate social resistance to exposing domestic violence. By contrast, Meier (1993), 1311, feels the reasons are more invidious. She explains that to accept 'this terrible reality would necessitate recognition that male domination over women is culturally conditioned and condoned; that gender injustice is real, present, and dire'.

20 See e.g., Burnstein (1995), 964; Schneider (1986), 645; Schneider (1995), 1250. Despite the strength of such an approach in discussing the problems faced by battered immigrant spouses, I have alternatively suggested there is some lingering legitimacy in the notion of privacy. See Kelly (1997), 306.

21 In varying forms, the interspousal immunity doctrine still exists in several states. For further discussion of its continuing viability see Harris *et al* (1996), 107.

22 It is only in very recent history that states have worked to eliminate the traditional spousal immunity which existed for both negligent and intentional torts. Compare e.g., *Hill v. Hill*, 415 So.2d 20 (Fla. 1982), (rejecting the abrogation of interspousal immunity citing need to protect family unity), *Waite v. Waite*, 618 So.2d 1360 (Fla. 93) (abrogating all interspousal tort immunity). See also Seymore (1996), 1070 (analyzing the tension of the spousal immunity doctrine on the private/public debate in the context of domestic violence).

23 MacKinnon (1987), 106.

24 *Burlington Indus. v. Ellerth*, 118 S. Ct. 2257 (1998); *Faragher v. City of Boca Raton*, 118 S. Ct. 2275 (1998).

25 MacKinnon (1989), 191.

26 UNHCR Executive Committee Report on the 36th Session, UN Executive Comm., 36th Sess., para. (C), UN Doc. A/AC.96/673 (1985) (reprinted in 1 *Int'l J. Refugee L.* 222 (1989)). In another estimate, women and children account for 80 per cent of refugees and displaced persons. See Boutros-Ghali (1996), 59.

27 In 1967, upon acceding to the UN Protocol, the United States indirectly acceded to the 1951 Convention. In 1980, this accession was confirmed by the enactment of domestic law, The United States Refugee Act of 1980, Pub. L. No. 96-212, 94 Stat. 102 (1980).

28 Within asylum and refugee doctrine, the alleged persecution must be perpetrated by the government or an agent the government is 'unwilling or unable to control'. INA §101(a)(42), 8 USC. §1101(a)(42).

29 Restatement (Third) of International Law §702, comment b (1987).

30 In *re Kasinga*, Int. Dec. #3278 (BIA 1996). It should be noted that immigration records and court proceedings uniformly misspelled Kasinga's name. It is properly spelled Fauziya Kassindja.

31 FGM can also be referred to as 'female genital surgery' (FGS), female circumcision or 'irua', the traditional term. For discussions on the controversy surrounding the terminology see Lewis (1995); Obiora (1997), 289. While using the term FGM throughout this article may reflect my own feelings

toward the practice, I have chosen it in order to maintain consistency with the terminology used in *Kasinga* and US legislation regarding the practice.

32 For descriptions of the realities of the practice see Obiora (1997), 284, 288; des Groseilliers (1998), 101; Sussman (1998), 196.

33 In *re Kasinga*, Int. Dec. #3278 (BIA 1996). Kasinga has published her own account of the ordeal she faced before achieving asylum. The work is co-written with the American university law school student who assisted Kasinga throughout the process. See Kassindja, F and Miller-Bashir, L (1998). Kasinga's attorney, then director of America's relevant clinical program, also contributed to *Do They Hear You* and has written separately on the case. See Musalo (1996).

34 INA §101(a)(42)(A), 8 USC. §1101(a)(42)(A); INA §208, 8 USC. 1158(b)(1).

35 Interim Decision #3252 (BIA, 1993).

36 *Angoucheva v. INS*, 106 F.3d 781, 790 (7th Cir. 1997) (Remanded).

37 The belief that women who have had sex are violated less, not more, than women who successfully refuse the action or prove to be forced at the moment of penetration is a recurring dilemma. Discussing problems encountered in sexual harassment law, Catharine MacKinnon charges, 'The sexual politics of the situation is that men do not see a woman who has had sex as victimized, whatever the conditions'. See MacKinnon (1987), 110.

38 *Fatin v. INS*, 12 F.3d 1233 (3d Cir. 1993) (support of feminism may constitute 'political opinion'). See also Kelly (1994), 817.

39 *INS v. Elias-Zacarias*, 502 US 478, 482 (1992). For a discussion of imputed political opinion see *INS* (1993).

40 Paula's rape occurred prior to 1996. Until 1998, El Salvador's codes did not allow victim testimony in rape cases. Changes to the Criminal Procedures Code taking effect in 1998 will allow victim testimony. Another law existing at the time of Paula's rape exonerated a rapist if he offered to marry the victim and she accepted. That law was repealed in 1996. US Department of State (1998).

41 United States Department of State (1998).

42 *Matter of Acosta*, 19 I and N Dec. 211, 233 (BIA 1985); *Matter of H-*, Int. Dec. 3276 (BIA 1996).

43 In *re Kasinga*, Int. Dec. #3278 at 43-50 (BIA 1996) (Rosenberg, J., concurring) (criticizing majority for imposing a dual requirement, and thereby departing from the traditional social group requirement that a claim is status based).

44 *Kasinga*, Int. Dec. $3278, at 24.

45 *Safaie v. INS*, 825 F.3d 636 (8th Cir. 1994). Cf. *Fatin v. INS*, 12 F.3d 1233 (3d Cir. 1993) (finding feminism a political opinion).

46 The INS relied upon *Matter of Pierre*, 15 I and N Dec. 461 (1975) (denying asylum to the wife of a high ranking Haitian official who was denied police protection when her husband threatened her).

47 Stressing that such reform is key to women gaining sexual autonomy, Elizabeth Iglesias urges the development of 'strategies of transformation' in the legal treatment of rape and other gender-related crimes. Iglesias (1996), 89. Other scholars have similarly discussed the negative images perpetuated and reflected in law. See e.g., Althouse (1994) (revealing gender prejudice in evidentiary standards); Meier (1993) (discussing legal and societal attitudes toward battered wives); Ronner (1997) (exploring images of 'woman as liar' in sexual harassment law).

48 Both state and federal rules of evidence contain versions of rape shield statutes. Fed. R. Evid., Rule 412. For discussion of both state and federal treatment see 29 Am. Jur. 2d Evidence §496.

49 Iglesias also notes there is risk of being seen as a virgin, as her constant refusal to have sex may not be distinguishable from times of willingness. See Iglesias (1996), 929.

50 Iglesias (1996), 929. For criticism of the treatment of rape shield statutes in law school texts see Althouse (1994), 941.

51 Ronner (1997).

52 Ronner (1997), 134.

53 Ronner (1997), 135.

54 Ronner (1997), 136.

55 Mahoney (1991), 12.

56 Mason (1997).

57 Prior to *Kasinga*, several states had legislation prohibiting FGM. Federal legislation criminalizing FGM performed on United States soil was signed several months after the BIA decided *Kasinga*. 18 USC. §116 (Sept. 30, 1996). At the same time, federal legislation was enacted requiring United States representatives to international organizations such as the World Bank to withhold funds to nations whose governments did not work to prevent the practice of FGM. 22 USC. §262K-2 (Sept. 30, 1996). For more on the state and federal legislation see Sussman (1998), 194, n. 2-7.

58 *New York Times*, Apr. 15, 1996, at A1.

59 The Board of Immigration Appeals is the Administration Agency under the United States Department of Justice which reviews trial court decision of immigration judges, with a wide range of power to amend those decisions.

60 *Kasinga*, Int. Dec. #3278, at 22-23 (BIA 1996). While there was one concurring and one dissenting judge, no opinion took issue with the majority's denunciation of FGM. *Kasinga*, Int. Dec. #3278, (Rosenberg, J., concurring), (Vacca, J., dissenting).

61 *Kasinga*, Int. Dec. #3278, at 19-20. However, in conceding that a punitive intent was not required, the INS argued for replacing punitive intent with a 'shock the conscience' test. In applying this test, the relevant 'conscience' was that of the community from which asylum was being sought. Ultimately, the BIA rejected such substantive arguments made by the INS and the issues raised by the INS relating to credibility. See *Kasinga*, Int. Dec. #3278; Musalo (1996).

62 Obiora (1997), Sussman (1998).

63 Obiora (1997), 284.

64 Obiora (1997), 298.

65 See e.g., Hooks (1984).

66 Cornell (1995), 6; Crenshaw (1991); Harris (1990).

67 See e.g., Gunning (1997); Lewis (1997); Obiora (1997).

68 Obiora (1997), 311.

69 While not explicitly stating in what territory the violence has to occur, VAWA relief does theoretically protect battered immigrants who experience violence abroad at the hands of a United States citizen or lawful permanent resident spouse or parent. However, to petition for relief, one must be physically present on US soil. INA §204(a)(1)(A)(iii), 8 USC. §1154(a)(1)(A)(iii); INA §204(a)(1)(B)(ii), 8 USC. §1154(a)(1)(B)(ii). A similar requirement exists for battered children. INA §204(a)(1)(A)(iv), 8 USC. §1154(a)(1)(A)(iv); INA §204(a)(1)(B)(iii), 8 USC. §1154(a)(1)(B)(iii). For a discussion of other congressional measures aimed at addressing the gender violence inflicted upon immigrants see Calvo (1991); Kelly (1997).

70 Codified as amended in scattered sections of 18, 28, 42 USC. See also Mincavage (1990).

71 The section falls under Title III of the act which is entitled 'Civil Rights for Women'. 42 USC. §13, 981 (1994). At the federal district level, the two earliest cases reached opposite results on Title III's constitutionality. However, an appeal of the finding of unconstitutionality was later reversed and remanded. Compare *Brzonkala v. Virginia Polytechnic Inst. and State Univ.*, 935 F. Supp. 779 (W.D. Va. 1996) (finding Title III unconstitutional), rev'd 132 F.3d 949 (4th Cir. 1997) with *Doe v. Doe*, 929 F. Supp. 608 (D. Conn. 1996) (finding Title III constitutional). Title III's constitutionality and predictions of how the Supreme Court may rule have been the subject of much legal scholarship, particularly in light of the Court's position on the *Commerce Clause in United States v. Lopez*, 514 US 549 (1995). See e.g., Hasday (1998); Leasure (1998); Mincavage (1998). Concern regarding VAWA has also resulted in the creation of a law school clinic geared solely to address controversies surrounding VAWA. See Kotkin (1997).

72 While the statutory requirements are gender neutral, the VAWA title alone reveals the statutory's intent is to assist battered wives.

73 As an alternative to this affirmative process, a battered immigrant may also assert an alternative claim for relief in deportation proceedings. VAWA created a new form of suspension of deportation. VAWA §40703. This provision was initially codified at INA §244(a)(3), 8 USC. §1254(a)(3) (1994).

However, with the passage of IIRIRA in 1996, this form of relief, while virtually intact has been recodified and renamed 'cancellation of removal'. IIRIRA §304 (codified at INA §240A, 8 USC. §1229b). The basic requirements of 'cancellation of removal' for battered immigrants are: 1) inadmissible or deportable under certain grounds; 2) battery or extreme cruelty by a citizen or permanent resident spouse or parent; 3) physical presence in the United States for a continuous period of three years; 4) good moral character for the past three years; 5) extreme hardship to the alien, alien's child or alien's parent (if the alien is a child). IIRIRA §304 (codified at INA §240A(b)(2), 8 USC. §1229b(b)(2)). While this article discusses only the affirmative 'self-petitioning' relief, to the extent the two forms of relief share similar requirements, the following discussion may prove illustrative. For further discussion of VAWA and the historical treatment of domestic violence within the context of a family-based residency petitions see Kelly (1998), 667.

74 Several years after VAWA's the Florida Immigrant Advocacy Center of Miami, Florida created a project solely dedicated to VAWA petitioners. The strong work of this project has become an invaluable resource for battered immigrants in southern Florida.

75 It should be noted that because the Clinic recognizes its strength to be representing clients in immigration matters, we have limited our state representation in divorce litigation to relatively simple divorces in which child custody and property distribution are not contested.

76 INA §204(a)(1)(A)(iii), 8 USC. §1154(a)(1)(A)(iii); INA §204(a)(1)(B)(ii), 8 USC. §1154(a)(1)(B)(iii), 8 C.F.R. § 204.2(c)(1)(i)(E), (c)(1)(vi), (c)(2)(iv) (1996); Self-Petitioning, 61 Fed. Reg. 13,061, 13,065-13,068. Similar provisions exist for alien children. See INA §204(a)(1)(A)(iv), 8 USC. §1554(a)(1)(A)(iv); INA §204(a)(1)(B)(iii), 8 USC. §1154(a)(1)(B)(iii); 8 C.F.R. §204.2(e)(1)(i)(E), (e)(1)(vi), (e)(2)(iv). For the difficulties battered immigrants encounter in providing such formal accounts of abuse see Kelly (1998), 674.

77 INA §204(a)(1)(A)(iii), 8 USC. §1154(a)(1)(A)(iii); INA §204(a)(1)(B)(ii), 8 USC. §1154(a)(1)(B)(iii), 8 C.F.R. §204.2(c)(1)(i)(E), (c)(1)(vi), (c)(2)(iv) (1996).

78 The emphasis on domestic violence not as physical battery but as a tool of power and control contrasts earlier definitions which stressed the physical aspect. Compare e.g., Mahoney (1991), 53 (focusing on the 'power and control, domination and subordination' aspects of domestic violence) with

Walker (1979), at xv (defining a battered woman as 'repeatedly subjected to any forceful physical or psychological behavior in order to coerce her'). See also Kelly (1998), 693 (outlining progress in defining domestic violence).

79 In announcing VAWA relief, INS Commissioner Doris Meissner recognized this difficulty. She acknowledged that battered immigrants 'are less likely to report the abuse or leave the abusive environment because they fear deportation or believe that only citizens and authorized immigrants can obtain legal and social services'. Self-Petitioning, 61 Fed. Reg. at 13,062 (1996). See also, Kelly (1998), 679.

80 Kelly (1998), 680.

81 For an excellent discussion of the dynamics surrounding separation see Mahoney (1991). Important work has also been done in refining a law school domestic violence clinic's ability to combine the legal and social issues. See Meier (1993).

82 See *supra* notes 75-77 and accompanying text.

83 INA §§101(f), 8 USC. §1101(f); INA §204(a)(1)(A)(iii), 8 USC. §1154(a)(1)(A)(iii).

84 INA §204(a)(1)(A)(iii)(II), 8 USC. §1154(a)(1)(A)(iii)(II); INA §204(a)(1)(B)(ii), 8 USC. §1154(a)(1)(B)(ii). For extreme hardship towards petitioning children see INA §204(a)(1)(A)(iv)(II), 8 USC. §1154(a)(1)(A)(iv)(II); INA §204(a)(1)(B)(iii)(II), 8 USC. §1154(a)(1)(B)(iii)(II).

85 An individual is prohibited from establishing good moral character if such person 'is, or was ... a habitual drunkard'. INA §101(f)(1), 8 USC. §1101(f)(1). Even by disproving that one DUI does not establish a pattern of continual drinking, overcoming the discretionary aspect of the good moral character may also be problematic. As stated by the definition, 'The fact that any person is not within any of the foregoing classes shall not preclude a finding that for other reasons such person is or was not of good moral character' INA §§ 101(f), 8 USC. § 1101(f).

86 For a detailed account of the various statutory, regulatory, and discretionary hurdles erected by VAWA for battered immigrants see Kelly (1998), 671.

87 Lisa Iglesias explains that in the context of rape, women attempt to limit their vulnerability to rape by narrowly defining rape as only a violent act committed by a stranger. See Iglesias (1996), 891.

88 Meier (1993), 1311.

References

Aleinikoff, T. (1989), 'The United States Constitution in its Third Century: Foreign Affairs: Rights - Here and There: Federal Regulation of Aliens and the Constitution', *American Journal of International Law*, vol. 83, 862.

Althouse, A. (1994), 'The Lying Woman, the Devious Prostitute, and Other Stories from the Evidence Casebook', *Northwestern University Law Review*, vol. 88, 914.

Benson, L. (1997), 'Back to the Future: Congress Attacks the Right to Judicial Review of Immigration Proceedings', *Connecticut Law Review*, vol. 29, 1411.

Boutros-Ghali, B. (1996), 'Introduction', *The United Nations and the Advancement of Women: 1945-1996*, 59. United Nations Department of Public Information, New York.

Burnstein, K. (1995), 'Naming the Violence: Destroying the Myth', *Albany Law Review*, vol 58, 961.

Calvo, J. (1991), 'Spouse-Based Immigration Laws; The Legacies of Coverture', *San Diego Law Review*, vol. 28, 593.

Cooper, J. and Trubek, L. (eds) (1997), *Educating for Justice: Social Values and Legal Education*, Ashgate Publishing, Aldershot.

Cornell, D. (1995), *The Imaginary Domain, Pornography and Sexual Harassment*, Routledge, New York.

Crenshaw, K. (1991), 'Mapping the Margins: Intersectionality, Identity Politics, and the Violence Against Women of Color', *Stanford Law Review*, vol. 43, 1241.

Danticat, (1998), *The Farming of Bones*, Soho Press, New York.

Des Groseillers, J. (1998), 'Comment, In Re Kasinga: When the Axe Came into the Forest, the Trees Said the Handle is One of Us', *New England Journal on Criminal and Civil Confinement*, vol. 24, 89.

Gunning, I. (1997), 'Uneasy Alliances and Solid Sisterhood: A Response to Professor Obiora's Bridges and Barricades', *Case Western Reserve Law Review*, vol. 47, 445.

Guttentag, L. (1997), 'The 1996 Immigration Act: Federal Court Jurisdiction - Statutory Restrictions and Constitutional Rights', *Interpreter Releases*, vol. 74, 245.

Harris, A. (1990), 'Race and Essentialism in Feminist Legal Theory', *Stanford Law Review*, vol. 42, 581.

Harris, L. *et al* (1996), *Family Law*, Little, Brown and Company, Boston.

Hart, H. (1953), 'The Power of Congress to Limit the Jurisdiction of the Federal Courts: An Exercise in the Dialectic', *Harvard Law Review*, vol. 66, 1362.

Hasday, J. (1998), 'Federalism and the Family Reconstructed', *University of California, Los Angeles Law Review*, vol. 45, 1297.
Henkin, L. (1985), 'The Constitution as Compact and Conscience: Individual Rights Abroad and at Our Gates', *William and Mary Law Review*, vol. 27, 11.
hooks, bell (1984), *Feminist Theory: from Margin to Center*, South End Press, Boston.
INS (1993) 'Legal Opinion: Continued Viability of the Doctrine of Imputed Political Opinion', (reproduced in *Interpreter Releases* (1993), vol. 70, 498).
Johnson K. (1997), 'The Antiterrorism Act, the Immigration Reform Act, and Ideological Regulation in the Immigration Laws: Important Lessons for Citizens and Noncitizens', *St Mary's Law Journal*, vol. 28, 833.
Kassindja, F. and Bashir, L. (1998), *Do They Hear You When You Cry*? Delacorte Press, New York.
Kelly, L. (1997), 'Domestic Violence Survivors: Surviving the Beatings of 1996', *Georgetown Immigration Law Journal*, vol. 11, 303.
Kelly, L. (1998), 'Stories from the Front: Seeking Refuge for Battered Immigrants in the Violence Against Women Act', *Northwestern University Law Review*, vol. 92, 665.
Kelly, N. (1994), 'Guidelines for Women's Asylum Claims', *Interpreter Releases*, vol. 71, 813.
Kotkin, M. (1997), 'The Law School Clinic: A Training Ground for Public Interest Lawyers', in Cooper, J. and Trubek, L. (eds).
Leasure, L. (1998), 'Commerce Clause Challenges Spawned by *United States* v. *Lopez* Are Doing Violence to the Violence Against Women Act (VAWA): A Survey of Cases and the Ongoing Debate over How the VAWA will Fare in the Wake of Lopez', *Maine Law Review*, vol. 50, 409.
Legomsky, S. (1984), 'Immigration Law and the Principle of the Plenary Congressional Power', *Supreme Court Review*, vol. 1984, 255.
Lewis, H. (1997), 'Between Irua and "Female Genital Mutilation": Feminist Human Rights Discourse and the Cultural Divide', *Harvard Human Rights Journal*, vol. 8, 1.
MacKinnon, C. (1987), *Feminism Unmodified*, Harvard University Press, Cambridge, Mass.
MacKinnon, C. (1989), *Toward a Feminist Theory of the State: Discourses on Life and the Law*, Harvard University Press, Cambridge, Mass.
Mahoney, M. (1991), 'Legal Images of Battered Women: Redefining the Issue of Separation', *Michigan Law Review*, vol. 90, 1.
Mason, J. (1997), 'Dr. Jekyll or Mr./Ms Hyde? Representing the Abused or the Abuser', *Til Death Do Us Part: Practical Advocacy for Domestic Violence Cases*, 3.1 (Florida Bar Continuing Legal Education Committee, ed.).
Meier, J. (1993), 'Notes from the Underground, Integrating Psychological and Legal Perspectives on Domestic Violence in Theory and in Practice', *Hofstra Law Review*, vol. 21, 1295.
Mincavage, C. (1998), Comment 'Title III of the Violence Against Women Act: Can it Survive a Commerce Clause Challenge in the Wake of *United States v. Lopez*',

Dickinson Law Review, vol. 102, 441.
Musalo, K. (1996), 'In Re Kasinga: A Big Step Forward for Gender-Based Asylum Claims', *Interpreter Releases*, vol. 73, 853.
Neuman, G. (1998), 'Habeas Corpus, Executive Detention and Removal of Aliens', *Columbia Law Review* vol. 98, 961.
Obiora, L. (1997), 'The Issue of Female Circumcision: Bridges and Barricades: Rethinking Polemics and Intransigence in the Campaign Against Female Circumcision', *Case Western Reserve Law Review*, vol. 47, 275.
Perea, J. ed. (1997), *Immigrants Out!* New York University Press, New York.
Ronner, A. (1997), 'The Cassandra Curse: The Stereotype of the Female Liar Resurfaces in *Jones* v. *Clinton*', *University of California, Davis Law Review*, vol. 31, 123.
Scaperlanda, M. (1996), 'Partial Membership: Aliens and the Constitutional Community', *Iowa Law Review*, vol. 81, 707.
Schneider, E. (1986), 'The Dialectic of Rights and Politics, Perspectives from the Women's Movement', *New York University Law Review*, vol. 61, 589.
Schneider, E. (1991), 'The Violence of Privacy', *Connecticut Law Review*, vol. 23, 973.
Schneider, E. 'Making Reconceptualization of Violence Against Women Real', *Albany Law Review*, vol. 58, 1245 (1995).
Seymore, M. (1996), 'Isn't It a Crime: Feminist Perspectives on Spousal Immunity and Spousal Violence', *Northwestern University Law Review*, vol. 90, 1032.
Siegel, R. (1996), 'The Rule of Love': Wife Beating as Prerogative and Privacy', *Yale Law Journal*, vol. 105, 2117.
Sussman, E. (1998), Note, 'Contending with Culture: An Analysis of the Female Genital Mutilation Act of 1996', *Cornell International Law Journal*, vol. 31, 193.
US Department of State (1998), 'El Salvador Country Report on Human Rights Practices for 1997', *Country Reports for 1997.*
Walker, L. (1979), *The Battered Woman*, Harper and Row, New York.

11 Learning from Communities: Lessons from India on clinical method and liberal education[1]

KENNETH S. GALLANT

Ramnagaram is a town in an agricultural area of southern India, not far from Bangalore. Here the National Law School of India University (NLSIU), in cooperation with Shakti, a women's social welfare organization, has established a mediation center cum legal aid office[2] using law student volunteers[3] under the supervision of the faculty.[4] The NLSIU students worked with many clients who neither understood the legal system, felt that their lives were part of it, nor felt that their problems could be solved within it. The following case is typical of many at the Ramnagaram center:[5]

> Umadevi, a woman of a farming community,[6] married Mahesh, went to live with him and his parents in their village, and had two girl children.
>
> Shortly after the second child was born, and with the connivance of Umadevi's parents, Mahesh also married her older sister, Sridevi, taking her also to live in his parents' home. Umadevi's parents originally opposed her marriage to Mahesh, apparently on the sole ground that they wanted him to marry their elder daughter, Sridevi, who, by custom, should have been married before the younger. When Mahesh later offered to marry Sridevi as well, they and she accepted, and the circumstances of the acceptance are worth noting. The production of invitations, especially with pictures, provided evidence (of a type usually acceptable to a court) that this marriage actually took place. No such documents were produced for Umadevi's marriage. Moreover, because of pressure from her family, Umadevi had to tell some persons that her marriage to Mahesh actually took place after her sister's.
>
> Sridevi now has a boy child. Mahesh has now married a third woman, and moved to her village. His parents have expelled Umadevi from their home. Umadevi was brought to the Shakti rural mediation center by her brother, who says that their parents simply do not have the resources to sustain her and her children. Umadevi wants support for herself and her children.

This story shows students confronted with the disconnection between official law and the society in which their clients are living.[7]

Work at Ramnagaram rapidly taught the students about how typical Umadevi's story is. First, in the limited time the students and I spent at Ramnagaram, every major element in her story (including the element of common, important life events, such as marriage, occurring in a manner unsanctioned by law) recurred at least once in another client's story. Second, none of the regular NLSIU faculty working at Ramnagaram, nor those students who were familiar with the problems of the poor in the region, were surprised or shocked by the story. The only persons who exhibited any surprise at the ready acceptance of polygamy by everyone involved were myself and a few upper class[8] students from northern India. The latters' surprise was that such a story should come from so close to a major metropolis, rather than a remote tribal area. Finally, and perhaps most importantly, while Umadevi and her brother were angered by the conduct of Mahesh and his family, neither of them indicated that the wrongs done her were beyond the tribulations that could be expected in life. Umadevi, while also angered by her own family's part in her troubles, did not indicate that their behavior was worse than could be expected.

Students at Ramnagaram learned quickly about the inability of existing law to solve the apparently legal problems of Umadevi and many of their other clients. First, the students found themselves faced with the curse of lawyers worldwide: a just cause with no way to demonstrate it. The students and faculty agreed that proving the marriage of Umadevi and Mahesh in court would be difficult, because of the documentation of the marriage with Sridevi, and her family's creation of the story that the elder daughter was married first.

Second, the remedies available at law simply could not give Umadevi what she needed. For example, a prosecution of Mahesh for bigamy would neither bring him back nor enable Umadevi to collect support. It might even result in a decision that she and the third wife were the bigamous spouses. Nor was divorce a reasonable option. It would end any obligation of Mahesh and his family to provide Umadevi with a place to live, without restoring to her any sense of belonging again to the family into which she was born. She would be thrust into the world without a family or land or hope of support for herself or her daughters.

Again, this failure of legal remedy to satisfactorily address a problem will be recognized by legal aid lawyers worldwide, and is addressed by clinical legal educators almost everywhere. Many abused women in the United States feel they have no place to go, in roughly the same way as those in India. They feel that the legal remedies of protection orders, criminal prosecution, or divorce are not what they want. Thus, many return to an abusive situation again and again.

The third and deepest failure of the law the students saw is the utter disconnection between the lives of Umadevi's community and the basic elements of the formal law of the nation-state of India. Polygamy among Hindus was outlawed in 1956, with the adoption of the Hindu Civil Code. However, Umadevi lives in a community in which it is still practiced, with sufficient frequency to be generally accepted, among the current generation of young people. The way Mahesh's multiple marriages came about described to the students the depths of polygamy's roots in the community.

Students learned about a society where the law was not merely divorced from the life of the community. The structure of the community was divorced from the law. The customary right of the wife to live with her in-laws, by which Umadevi would usually be supported (though not always well), is not enforceable in the courts. Umadevi, and not Sridevi, was expelled from her marital home because only Sridevi had produced a son. In this case, intervention by community leaders had failed to get her in-laws to accept her back. This failure of the traditional dispute resolution system led directly to her brother bringing her to the NLSIU students and to try to obtain relief from the formal system. Unfortunately, at my last contact with the Rural Mediation Clinic, there was no resolution, legal or otherwise, for Umadevi and her daughters.

The NLSIU clinic described here is not an isolated effort, and students have had similar experiences elsewhere. Others in South Asian clinical legal education have been bringing law students into situations where they see this deep disconnection, and working to help them act to remedy it. The Faculty of Law at Delhi University has operated a program in which law students work with community development in Gautam Nagar, a slum of Delhi.[9] Lucknow University brings law students to villages to provide on the spot legal aid.[10] Several law schools, coordinated by the National Law School of India University, have established a National Law Reform Competition, in which student groups live in communities with development problems, in order to create legal proposals which would bring the law into closer congruence with community needs. These programs are in part conscious efforts to help students experience and address the third, deepest kind of disconnection between the law and community life.

Lessons from India - For Professional Education

These Indian efforts suggest a few lessons for clinical legal education elsewhere.

Legal aid clinics at law schools, a predominant American system of clinical legal education, do well with introducing students to the first two difficulties with the law and its practice. They present students with opportunities to learn and reflect upon issues of professional technique, human interaction, and morality in systems that, for a significant percentage of persons, do not provide adequate or appropriate legal protections. Teachers are able to raise these issues, and subject them to extensive discussion and analysis, with almost all their students.

The Indian clinics present a model for addressing the third, deeper level of disconnection between law and society that may arise. It was only by physically going to the relevant places, and working there for extended periods of time, that the Indian students and faculty could build the trust necessary to obtain the stories that help them bring out the issues of incongruity between formal law on the one hand, and custom and daily life on the other.[11]

Beyond the issue of trust, this deep disconnection can become apparent to students and faculty only when they have some understanding of the community in which their clients live. Otherwise, the case of Umadevi, for example, may appear as an aberrational case of bigamy, rather than as an exemplification of a living tradition.

Public service may also suffer unless students and faculty understand the community context of the cases that arise at places such as Ramnagaram. Without understanding the social constraints on Umadevi, the students might have recommended, or even attempted, legal remedies that would have been harmful to her.

As Prof. Poonam Saxena points out, in India, 'The main thrust of clinical legal education ... is, not only to enable a law student to become a better lawyer, but to make it possible for him to help the community have recourse to justice, efficiently, effectively, and purposefully'.[12] This public service orientation drives Indian clinical programs to provide students with experiences that require them to re-evaluate the role of law in a given society. Usefulness to society is not defined for Indian clinical education as being limited to provision of services to a particular client, or even to provide a specific legal remedy to a group of clients. It includes bringing to students and the larger society an understanding of the legal issues facing what is known as the 'weaker sections of society'.

No one expects that knowledge of weaknesses of legal structures will automatically lead to fundamental changes, in either those structures or the structures of society outside the law. The definitions of the problems involved - such as community tolerance of polygamy or domestic violence - prohibit quick and easy answers that can be implemented by students. What Indian clinical educators hope and reasonably expect is that professional students will take the understandings that they have gained with them into their careers as lawyers and their lives as citizens. They expect at least some graduates will work for the creation of conditions in which the disconnections between the law and the lives of communities can be bridged, and in which social justice can be promoted. There are of course clinical law programs elsewhere that focus on community life.[13] The Indian clinical education movement, however, appears to be the most committed as a whole to focusing on community and social development as an explicit goal.[14] The traditional legal aid office may benefit, as a model for clinical education, by supplementation with Indian methods. This is especially true at schools where the goals of clinical education have been defined to include:

1) Usefulness to the society, at least where significant segments of that society are disconnected from the formal legal system; and

2) Teaching students about relationships between law and community life, and about the various ways in which formal law can succeed or fail in bringing order and justice to a community.

Moreover, the Indian experience demonstrates that these can usefully be made explicit goals of clinical legal education. Community-based service, in addition to its intrinsic values, can broaden and deepen the learning experiences available to law students.

Lessons from India - For both Professional and Liberal Education

Clinical education, whether in legal aid offices in the law school, field placements in law offices, or simulation-based classes, is generally conceptualized as professional education. This includes specific education in skills, such as client relationships and presentations in court. It also includes education concerning the values of the legal profession.

In India, not all law students wish to become practicing lawyers, creating dilemmas for those who wish to include skills and clinical training into the professional curriculum.[15] In this sense, India resembles much of the world. In many places, law is a common field of study for students who do not intend to practice as lawyers, but who may wish to serve in government either as civil servants or politicians, go into business, or engage in a wide variety of other pursuits.[16] For these students, law school may substitute for a general or liberal education in another college or department. In this sense, it needs to provide for some of the main goals of liberal education: broad exposure to ideas and development of the students' ability to think critically. These students do not see learning the skills of practicing lawyers and the values of the legal profession as central to their educations.

This may show other countries a way of deepening their legal education, in terms of teaching both professional values and the broader values of a general education. A deep exploration of the role of law in society is made possible by the experiences available to Indian clinical law students.

Professional legal education can for the most part be done using the law office, field placement and classroom simulation models currently in use in the United States and some other places. Students learn how to perform professional tasks. They learn how to think creatively within the legal system to solve problems for clients that have no obvious solution. They also regularly confront issues of professional ethics and other professional values. These are the issues that dominate the working life of most legal professionals, and thus deserve a central place in the teaching of legal praxis. One of the chief means of clinical legal education is reflection on problems of the legal system that are illustrated by the cases on which students work. As mentioned above, problems of the unavailability of legal remedies for client problems provide much very rich material for educators and students to use in exploring professional skills and values. They help the professional student develop skills for use in reducing or mitigating the failures of law to aid clients.

Without exploring the third level of disconnection clinical legal education will not successfully do two things. First, it will generally not be relevant to the non-professional student. Second, it will not take the professional (or non-professional) student outside the confines of currently recognized professional roles. This latter failure may lead to stagnation of thought about the proper role for law in society.

The deepest questions about the law are not the ones that arise most often for practitioners. If it were otherwise, the profession could not exist as a stable group of individuals working in a commonly understood enterprise. Some agreement on foundations is necessary for the common discourse and common understanding of actions that make the legal profession work. The deepest questions about any profession are those that challenge the everyday working foundations upon which the profession operates.

What stories from NLSIU and other Indian clinics demonstrate, however, is that clinical education is a way into foundational questions of what law is and the role that it serves in a given society or society generally. The availability of human situations that challenge the foundations of a given legal order are not wholly new to the legal academy. They have been used for some time by some legal academics in their scholarly work since the rise of legal realism.[17] What is not common in the West, however, is the use of experiences of this type in teaching students about foundational questions.

The use of such situations in teaching promotes the liberal education of students, whether seeking professional training or not. The approach to them cannot be narrowly professional, because the situations themselves disclose to both students and teachers that application of professional skills to these situations do not provide an adequate resolution of them. It is only by stepping outside of the context of the law as currently understood that progress can be made.

Progress, in the tradition of liberal education, would generally mean progress in the intellectual understanding of the way in which these situations arise and what they mean for the study of the theory of law - that is, jurisprudence. It is appropriate for all students at law colleges, regardless of their professional goals. It is particularly important in those societies in which legal education is usually an undergraduate substitute for a liberal arts degree. Here the direct experiencing and addressing of foundational questions serves the same educational function as, for example, the learning of the scientific method through laboratory work does for the majority of undergraduate science students who will never be working research scientists.

In India, clinical legal education has been 'visualized more in terms of its usefulness to the society, rather than its benefit to a law student'.[18] That is, where foundational rather than narrower professional questions are raised,[19] these situations are used in teaching in order to discover and implement means for resolving the disconnections between the life of society and the law.

Both lawyers and law graduates who choose other careers learn these lessons. As discussed above, students who enter the legal profession may work on legal changes to reduce these disconnections. Many graduates, both legal professionals and others, also come to understand the limits of law as an agent of social change. In most societies, mere changes in the substance of law do not by themselves create a deeper connection between the lives of citizens in their local communities and the overall community of the nation.[20] Indian educators expect graduates in all fields will use the knowledge and wisdom learned in their clinical experience to identify and address the non-legal issues involved in community development and social justice.[21]

Conclusion

Indian clinical legal education, despite limited resources, has developed a model for public service and education that confronts students with profound issues of law and community not often faced by students working in clinic law offices, both broadening and deepening the opportunities for learning available to students. The Indian model can provide direction for clinical programs elsewhere that wish to bring these issues into legal education.

Notes

1 An earlier version of this paper was presented to the Fourth International Conference on Clinical Legal Education, Lake Arrowhead, California, USA, October 1997. This paper refers to and draws on other papers presented at that conference, especially Poonam Saxena, 'Legal Education and Legal Aid: The Indian Perspective'; Yubaraj Sangroula, 'Increased Involvement of the Legal Profession in Community Problems: An Emerging Concept in Developing Societies'; and Jane Schukoske, 'View from the Shade of the Village Tree: Legal Literacy, Legal Aid and Development Strategies in Poor Communities in South Asia'.

2 Almost all of the clients of Ramnagaram Rural Mediation Center, as the project was called, came from the agricultural villages and areas surrounding the town of Ramnagaram, about forty kilometers southwest of Bangalore on the Mysore road. Its proximity to Bangalore is already beginning to change the rural character of the area. 'Cum' in this sentence in the main text is an Indian English usage, meaning roughly 'and,' when that word is used to bring together two descriptive designations for the same entity. It is particularly appropriate here because the Ramnagaram project began as a rural mediation center, but, given the frequent difficulty in bringing all parties to a dispute to the center, in many cases it is limited to providing advice similar to that which may be obtained at a legal aid office. Further notes will be provided where there is a significant difference between Indian English and American English uses of a word.

3 When I worked with these students, in 1995-1996, they, like Prof. Saxena's students, received neither academic credit nor pay for their efforts. The issue of academic credit was under discussion among both faculty and students, with no clear consensus having emerged from either group.

4 I wish to thank the Faculty of the National Law School of India University for inviting me to participate in the Ramnagaram project while I was a Fulbright lecturer there during the 1995-96 academic year. The faculty members who supervised the project while I was there were Prof. V. Nagaraj, Prof. Shankar Reddy, and Prof. P.J. Sampath. I also wish to thank Dr N.R. Madhava Menon, the founding Dean of NLSIU who invited me to come there as a Fulbright lecturer, and the students and clients with whom I worked.

The National Law School of India University is a free-standing unit of the Indian university system. It was established by the Bar Council of India, the Supreme Court of India, and the Government of the State of Karnataka with the purpose of becoming a model for the reform of legal education in India. Most law schools in India are not free-standing entities. Rather, most are either faculties of larger universities or are private colleges that gain their ability to grant degrees by their affiliation with an established university.

5 Names and details are changed to protect confidentiality. My knowledge of the client stories, as well as the prevalence of polygamy in this area, is generally dependent upon student translations and summaries of interviews in either Kannada, the majority language of Karnataka, or Tamil, the related majority language of the neighboring State of Tamil Nadu. Those students from northern India who worked at Ramnagaram faced similar difficulties, as the Hindustani-related languages of their region are hardly closer to the southern Indian languages than is English.

6 In Indian English usage, 'community' has meanings in addition to those in American English. It may refer to a caste (sometimes in the broad sense of a varna, or overall caste grouping, as the Brahmins, but more often in the narrower sense of a jati, generally called a sub-caste in American English), a religious group (as the Muslim community), a tribal group, a group speaking a specific language, or a group living in a particular locality. In Umadevi's case, the 'community' involved was a jati living in the area of Ramnagaram. The students could not say, based upon the information available from their work, the extent, if any, to which polygamy is practiced among members of other communities in the Ramnagaram area, or among members of Umadevi's own jati elsewhere.

7 Students facing similar issues at an urban clinical project run by the Law Faculty at the University of Delhi are described in Poonam Saxena, 'Legal Education and Legal Aid: The Indian Perspective', paper prepared for Fourth International Clinical Conference, Lake Arrowhead, California, October 1997 (hereinafter Saxena). See also Yubaraj Sangroula, 'Increased Involvement of

Legal Profession in Community Problems: An Emerging Concept in Developing Societies', paper prepared for Fourth International Clinical Conference, Lake Arrowhead, California, October 1997 (describing work of legally oriented non-governmental organizations in Nepal).

8 'Upper class' is used here in the American or British English sense, rather than the frequent Indian English sense of relatively higher caste.

9 Saxena, *supra* n. 1.

10 Schukoske, 'View from the Shade of the Village Tree: Legal Literacy, Legal Aid and Development Strategies in Poor Communities in South Asia', paper prepared for Fourth International Clinical Conference, Lake Arrowhead, October 1997.

11 See Saxena, *supra* n. 1, part VIII.

12 Saxena, *supra* n. 1, Introduction.

13 See, e.g. Barry, (1994); Bryant and Arias, (1992); Ogletree, (1995); Cruz, (1999); Sangroula, *supra* n. 7; and sources cited in Schukoske, *supra* n. 10.

14 South Africa has also had vibrant 'street law' programs.

15 Saxena, *supra* n. 1 part VIII.

16 In the United States, law is an explicitly professional post-baccalaureate field of study. Yet even here, significant and growing percentages of law students either do not intend to, or find that they will not, practice law in any sort of traditional setting. This is true even for those students who enter into clinical programs. In terms of the percentage of students who study law intending to become practicing lawyers, India probably ranks somewhere between the United States, where the percentage is very high, and some civil law countries, where the percentage is much lower.

17 See e.g. Llewellyn and Hoebel, (1941).

18 Saxena, *supra* n. 1, Introduction, parts III and IV.

19 Both professional training and the availability of professional legal services to the poor in India will be advanced by the recent notification ('bringing into force' in American legal parlance) of the Legal Services Act of 1987, which

encourages cooperation between the state legal aid authorities and law schools in providing legal aid services.

20 See generally Mark Galanter (1989). In the United States, one clear example is the distinct but very incomplete success of the federal statutes aimed at eliminating racial discrimination.

21 This can be seen as a challenge to the Western tradition of claiming political neutrality for liberal education. Indian clinical legal education, whether working on the law office model of legal aid or working with materials like the problem of polygamy in Ramnagaram, is aimed at being a means to social and economic advancement of the weaker sections of society. Students are expected to wrestle with questions of their duties as citizens.

References

Barry, M. (1994), 'A Question of Mission: Catholic Law School's Domestic Violence Clinic', *Howard Law Journal,* vol. 38, 135.

Bryant, S. and Arias, M. (1992) 'A Case Study: A Battered Women's Rights Clinic: Designing a Clinical Program which Encourages a Problem-Solving Vision of Lawyering that Empowers Clients and Community', *Journal of Contemporary Law,* vol. 42, 207.

Cruz, C. (1999) '[On the] Road Back In: Community Lawyering in Indigenous Communities', *Clinical Law Review,* vol 5, 557.

Galanter, M. (1989), *Law and Society in Modern India,* Oxford University Press, Delhi.

Llewellyn, K. and Hoebel, E. (1941), *The Cheyenne Way,* University of Oklahoma Press, Norman.

Ogletree, C. (1995) 'From Mandela to Mthwana: Providing Counsel to the Unrepresented Accused in South Africa', *Boston University Law Review,* vol. 75, 1.

12 Meaningful Exchange: Collaboration among clinicians and law teachers in India and the United States

JANE E. SCHUKOSKE[1]

For law teachers interested in experiential learning, academic exchange affords fertile ground for collaboration. Teachers become students abroad, witnessing law student work at sister schools and in unfamiliar communities. Imagine the questions that clinical law teachers from the United States might ask in order to comprehend the following Indian scene in which law students and their teacher counsel villagers seeking legal help.

> In Khajuron, a village of 200 families in Uttar Pradesh, India, eleven graduate students in law meet villagers under a large tree. Folding chairs and large tables are set in the shade of the tree. They are moved as the shade moves.
>
> Fourteen villagers met with the law students on July 22, 1997. Cases pertained to domestic violence and maintenance, termination of a widow's pension, official misconduct by land consolidation officers, enforcement of a High Court order for reinstatement and back pay for a discharged Peon, and a dispute about whether a tenant who planted trees on Gram Sabha (village-owned) land had a right to keep use of the land.
>
> The law students worked in groups of three or four, interviewing the villagers. A crowd of villagers stood around listening to the exchanges. Students drafted documents by hand on the spot for government benefit applications and Family Court disputes. A law teacher reviewed the drafts and participated in discussions of strategy.[2]

Clinicians[3] might be curious about the goals of the teacher; the class work that supports this case work; the coordination between the teacher; students and supervising advocate; case development and documentation; legal ethics; law practice norms; and whether the students and clients spoke the same languages, as a start. Curiosity would likely extend to the students' understanding of the problems of the community members (because of language, backgrounds, and the difference between village life and their life at the university), and to how their lawyering skills and advice relate to local practice norms. Aspects of the context that are important to discover include the laws both generally and applying to specific problems; the legal aid system; the courts and other dispute resolution systems; the health, education and occupations of the residents; the village economy, local governance and politics; literacy among and education of the residents; the religions of the residents; and the bearing that these features may have on the problems that people voice and on how they will be handled.

Witnessing such a context in which legal education and service occur in India has prompted me to consider what study would further my ability to collaborate effectively with Indian colleagues interested in teaching students in community contexts. The widespread use of the English language in the legal profession, the common British legal heritage, and similarities in constitutional law facilitate interaction among colleagues from India and the United States (Cunningham, 1991, 777). Resources on basic features of the Indian legal system and legal education system are readily available in the United States.[4] Even after consulting such resources, a United States clinician may face substantial challenges in grasping their operation and relevance in Indian society. As with any foreign exchange, differing terminology often confounds a visitor, who must realize the necessity of questioning assumptions down to the very word.[5]

Law school clinics like those operating in the United States to provide court representation to low income clients are not presently possible in India, even where Indian law faculties wholeheartedly embrace clinical method. Universities generally prohibit full-time law teachers from appearing as advocates (lawyers). Rules of the Bar Council of India, which regulates advocates, prohibit an advocate from being a full-time salaried employee of any entity (Code 1996 Rule 49). There is no authority permitting law practice by students (Menon, 1998, 23).

This chapter briefly examines current literature about the Law and Development movement, which criticizes an 'export' approach taken by some legal professionals as they consult abroad about legal change and legal education. It then describes the Indian legal and educational contexts in which law students and teachers work, and concludes with a discussion of possible themes and goals for comparative study and collaboration for clinicians from India and the United States. Collaboration with foreign colleagues on legal education activities in communities provides opportunities for rethinking one's own culture as well as learning about others and about interconnections between cultures. The paradigm of collaboration, which connotes interaction, effort and mutual benefit, contrasts with that of outside expertise on or export of clinical legal education methodology. Interaction between law teachers in the United States and India may beneficially affect the teachers' work at home and abroad.

The Law and Development Movement in the United States

The central premise of the Law and Development movement in the United States in the 1960s was that strengthening of the legal system and the legal profession in developing countries would lead to equitable social change there.[6] Essential to this instrumental vision of law were changes in legal education (at that time, to increase the reading of cases and use of Socratic method) and promotion of the model of lawyers as social engineers (Merryman, 1977, 461). The intellectual origins of the movement have been described as

> 'the idea of progress, the movement for law reform, the emergence of an interest in 'law and society' and its various components..., the notion of social engineering through law, and the US post-World War II commitment to foreign assistance'. (Merryman, 1977, 461)

The intellectual style of the movement was said to be action-oriented, impatient with theory, and unconcerned with quantitative analysis (Merryman, 1977, 473). Action-orientation was to be expected since the movement's scholars and activists were funded in part by the Ford Foundation and the United States Agency for International Development to bring about change rather than merely to conduct comparative study.

Clinics, still an innovation in the early 1970s, appeared in the Law and Development literature as one of the vehicles in the United States for raising social welfare issues (Franck, 1972, 796). Predicting a role for law school exchange between the United States and developing countries, one scholar observed that

> '...[n]ew developments at law schools in the United States - the discovery of America's poor, the development of clinical programs, the training of nonlawyers, the emphasis on quasi-legal, non-adversary processes, and the discovery or rediscovery of social and behavioral science and social policy as lawyers' tools - could bring a few of our most progressive law schools closer

to the needs of the most promising law faculties in developing countries'. (Franck, 1972, 796)

Critics berated the movement as ethnocentric, imposing on developing nations ill-fitting American liberal legalist views about the potency of law to bring about progressive social change.[7] Feeling 'estranged' from the Law and Development movement, leading academics moved on to other theories and the movement stalled in the mid-1970s.[8]

The intervening decades allowed additional experience and perspective on legal exchange to accrue.[9] During the decades of the 1960s to the 1990s, most developing nations accepted foreign assistance as they attempted to build law and manage problems created by colonial and other previous transplantations of law and institutions (Tamanaha, 1995, 474).

The 'New' Law and Development Movement

Since the 1970s, political changes, market expansion and the rise of human rights NGOs have led to renewed discussion of western study and interaction with scholars and lawyers in developing countries. Lawyer and journalist Carol V. Rose, examining commercial legal reform in Vietnam, asserts that perceptions of cross-cultural collaboration are different from those reported earlier (Rose, 1998, 130). She has observed that the 'New' Law and Development Movement, peopled by government-supported and foundation-supported professors and lawyers consulting in developing nations, possesses characteristics which may be summarized as follows:

(1) the United States is not dominant, but is one of many foreign influences,

(2) recipient governments are skeptical of foreign legal assistance and seek regional ideas and models,

(3) there is awareness of the benefits that accrue to elites in a developing nation through foreign-funded projects,

(4) developing nations gather diverse perspectives of academics, government, international organizations, judicial and bar associations, and lawyers, and

(5) theoretical debates in the legal academy may enrich discussion and understanding in the United States of cross-cultural work. Examples

are Law and Economics and Critical Legal Studies, including critical race and feminist theory. (Rose, 1998, 135)

Rose states four continuing concerns about consulting in developing countries: (1) ethnocentrism by Western lawyers and protectionism (such as excluding foreign lawyers from practice) by foreign hosts, (2) essentialization (stereotyping) by collaborating lawyers of both the host culture and of United States culture and consequent magnification of cultural gaps, (3) reinforcement of authoritarian legal structures, and (4) neo-liberal market hegemony (Rose, 1998, 130). Even where collaborators seek legal reform appropriate to the culture, she notes that market economy itself 'exacerbates the gap between rich and poor' (Rose, 1998, 135).[10]

Approaching Cross-Cultural Work

Two of the above concerns seem particularly important for clinical law teachers to bear in mind in academic exchange work.[11] First, essentialization, or oversimplification of a group based on stereotypes, is an inherent risk when one enters unfamiliar settings. Cultural study and work with foreign colleagues and their communities over time may reduce the frequency of this mistake. Secondly, ethnocentrism at least partially underlies proposals by United States educators that education models used in the United States be adopted abroad. Such proposals comes from a belief that the system in the United States is effective and would work well in other cultural contexts. One scholar has noted that two post-modern insights deflate the problem of ethnocentrism: that it is inevitable that people interpret situations using their views and values, and that there are no ultimate standards to determine superior views (Tamanaha, 1995, 483). While convinced of the value of clinical legal education methodology, United States clinicians surely agree that decisions about adoption and development of adaptations to the method to fit the local context reside with educators in a host country.

For example, a United States clinician might be tempted to advocate that a law teacher supervise student legal work for individuals in a community. But this would be based on assumptions, which may not be accurate or consonant with the local context, that the teacher had authority to practice law, practical expertise in client representation, and time free from other obligations to competently do so. Legal educators who are interested in this general clinical approach may devise interim steps or alternative methods to adapt it for use in the current system. In India, for example, legal educators sometimes use teams of practitioners and teachers to provide skills instruction and client representation. Even though professors are permitted to practice law in the United States, many United States law schools also use a variety of practitioner/professor team approaches. Dialogue about Indian and United States experience with 'practical training' (skills) courses and legal aid clinics can stimulate thinking productive for both Indian and United States contexts.

Two-way exchange and participatory development have been suggested as ways to approach cross-cultural legal consulting (Rose, 1998, 135). Before moving to discussion of these ideas in the Indian legal context, it is useful to look at basic features of Indian law and dispute resolution, aspects of legal education, and selected strategies for social change being used in the South Asian region.

Basic Features of Indian Law and Dispute Resolution

India's laws are an amalgam of its Constitution, statutes and regulations, customary law, and case law (Mahr, 1990, 109). Personal laws apply to domestic relations, adoption, guardianship and inheritance according to the religion of the parties (David, 1984, 9). Under some of these laws, women receive different treatment from men (Sehgal, 1988, 297). Real property law reflects the historically communal, rural, agricultural[12] character of the country.

The Constitution of India, which came into effect in 1950, provides for a federal system of national and state governments, for an independent judiciary, democratic election of members of parliament and state legislatures, and cabinet systems of government at the national and state levels (David, 1984, 9). The Constitution provides for a system of high courts in the states and lower courts in districts and local areas capped by one federal court, the Supreme Court of India (David, 1984, 9). The apex court, as it is known, has appellate, original and advisory jurisdiction. Backlog and delay in the courts are said seriously to undermine access to civil justice in India (Chodosh, 1997-98, 49). At the initiative of former Chief Justice A.M. Ahmadi of the Supreme Court of India, a team of Indian and United States researchers have studied the conditions in the civil litigation system and proposed reforms (Chodosh, 1997-98, 55). The reforms are directed at court administration, case management and consensual dispute resolution.

The Constitution of India not only sets out the government structure but also provides for basic freedoms called 'fundamental rights', including protection included in the United States Bill of Rights (Mahr, 1990, 109). It also contains 'Directive Principles of State Policy', such as the right to work, to education and to a living wage, which are unenforceable in courts but are to be considered in law-making (Constitution of India Art. 36-51). These principles have been given force in anti-poverty[13] programs, including the ambitious Integrated Rural Development Programme designed to raise income above the poverty level (Baxi, 1988a, xxiv-xxix). Land reform law provides for redistribution of land to scheduled castes[14] (Baxi, 1988a, xxii-xxix; Gordon and Lindsay 1990, 722).

Legal aid to the poor is recognized as a directive principle in the Constitution of India, which provides that

> '[t]he State shall secure that the operation of the legal system promotes justice, on a basis of equal opportunity, and shall, in particular, provide free legal aid, by suitable legislation or schemes in any other way, to ensure that opportunities for securing justice are not denied to any citizen by reason of economic or other disabilities'. (Constitution of India Art. 39A)

Statutes create state Legal Aid Boards to provide delivery of legal aid to the poor by advocates in private practice. The Code of Ethics for Advocates articulates a 'duty to render legal aid ... within the limits of an Advocate's economic condition' (Menon, 1998, 309). Most advocates are sole practitioners, with the exception of a small number of law firms operating in urban areas (Gordon and Lindsay, 1990, 715).

Community education and mediation are widespread methods of assisting villagers and slum-dwellers with disputes. Law school outreach efforts are often modelled on the work of area non-governmental organizations (NGOs). NGOs promote 'legal awareness training' (community legal education) to increase 'legal literacy' in communities. Legal literacy is 'the process of acquiring critical awareness about rights and the law, the ability to assert rights, and the capacity to mobilize for change' (Schuler and Kadirgamar-Rajasingham, 1992, 2). NGOs conduct 'legal aid camps', during which a group of legal advisors make themselves available at a community site to counsel the often large number of people who attend. Alternative dispute resolution occur at Lok Adalats ('People's Courts') at which selected civil cases are conciliated (Bloch and Ishar (1990), Menon (1998), and Shah (1998)). Non-lawyers such as social workers, journalists and NGOs, have successfully commenced 'social action litigation' before the Supreme Court of India under Court decisions relaxing standing requirements in view of the urgent social needs in the country (Baxi, 1988b, 396).

Legal Education

Three types of institutions provide legal education in India: free-standing law colleges, multi-faculty (department) colleges having a law department, and universities (Dayal, 1978, 163). A five-year program of law study, including two years of social science study, has broadened the traditional three-year LLB program (Menon, 1998, 20; Cottrell, 1986). Historically, most law graduates have not joined the legal profession (Dayal, 1978, 165).

By statute, the Bar Council of India regulates legal education, setting Standards of Legal Education and Recognition of Degrees in Law (Mahr, 1990, 116). In 1995, the Bar Council of India mandated a one-year, uncompensated apprenticeship for law graduates seeking to become advocates (Menon, 1998, 297). This apprenticeship rule was successfully challenged in the Supreme Court of India in three cases, decided together as *V. Sudeer v. Bar Council of India*, 1999 (2) S.C. 141 (12 and 15 March 1999), on the grounds that the Advocates Act did not authorize Bar Council to issue the rule (Kumari, 1999, 1). The Supreme Court suggested ways for training to occur pending amendment of the Act.

The Bar Council has also mandated that law schools offer certain courses (called 'papers') on skills and legal aid as of the 1998-99 academic year (Bar Council, 1997, 2). Under this Bar Council rule, the curriculum must include, inter alia, papers on Moot Court, Pretrial Preparation and Participation in Trial Proceedings; Drafting, Pleading and Conveyancing; and Public Interest Lawyering, Legal Aid and Para Legal Services, which may

> be taught partly through class room instructions including simulation exercises and partly through extension programmes like Lok Adalat, Legal Aid Camp, Legal Literacy and Para Legal Training. The course should also contain lessons on Negotiations and Counselling, use of Computer in legal work, legal research in support of Public Interest Litigation, writing of case comments, editing of Law Journals and Law Office Management. (Bar Council, 1997, 5)

Full-time law teachers, who do not practice law, sometimes affiliate practitioners to team-teach skills courses to tap their expertise.[15]

These innovations contrast with traditional classroom courses which follow a fixed syllabus and in which law students are evaluated by examination. Examinations are often written and evaluated by teachers other than the classroom teacher due to university rules and convention (Dayal, 1978, 168, 173) intended to insure competency in knowledge of a subject and objectivity in grading. In these circumstances, teachers necessarily focus on preparing students for examinations. A scholar in Delhi reports that many Indian law teachers feel that skills training is relevant at the point of entry into the profession, rather than during university education (Saxena, 1997a, 45).

National Law School of India University (NLSIU) in Bangalore has pioneered clinical teaching methods in India. Students must take two compulsory clinics, the Client Interviewing and Alternate Dispute Resolution Clinic in which law students provide advice at legal aid camps and participate in resolution of consumer disputes at Lok Adalats, and the Trial Advocacy and Appellate Advocacy Clinic, a simulation course. In addition, they must choose one Special Clinic, such as Labour Law or Constitutional Litigation. Students may also participate in moot court competitions, work in a Legal Services Clinic in conjunction with the Karnataka State Legal Aid Board, and write policy papers for a Community-Based Law Reform Competition (Menon, 1998, 238).[16] The movement for practical training and clinical legal education in India has been championed by Dr N. Madhava Menon, the first Director of the NLSIU. NLSIU has sponsored conferences on clinical legal education for law teachers from the South Asian region with participation by Western law professors.[17] Legal aid clinics were established as an extracurricular activity of law teachers and students at Delhi University and a few others law departments in the 1960s (Menon, 1998, 18).

Academic credit has been awarded for community legal work, such as the village visit described at the beginning of this chapter, undertaken in the Post Graduate Diploma in Criminal Practice and Advocacy Programme (PGDCPA) at Lucknow University, since 1994 (Chauhan, 1997, 2) In Khajuron, graduate law students in this program administered a 'legal awareness' survey to the villagers, conducted legal aid visits to the village, and notified district government officials of their visits to the village so that they could be present to respond to requests and complaints. The officials cooperated by appearing, and thereby facilitated official responses (Chauhan, 1997, 9).

The Lucknow University students also surveyed residents of an encampment of urban poor in Lucknow that was known for criminal activity, and gradually won resident trust there. They then educated residents about bail and how to seek relief from police abuse while in custody (Chauhan, 10). For more than 10 years, people had lived in this encampment without a nearby supply of drinking water because the area did not fit the legal definition of community that would have imposed a requirement on the municipality to provide it with wells. After the intervention of students and teachers from the Lucknow University Faculties of Law and Sociology, the municipal Department of Social Work arranged for five wells with hand-pumps to be dug to provide drinking water to this community.

Some Indian law teachers and students perform volunteer work in communities as public service (Bloch and Ishar 1990). Dr Poonam Saxena of Delhi University has worked with Karmika, a social welfare NGO in the Gautam Nagar slum in Delhi on Saturdays for several years to provide service and also to supplement classroom learning in her class on Family Law. Dr Saxena has seen direct benefits: 'The need for social and gender sensitisation ... cannot come sitting in a class room, it comes only with direct exposure to the people who can be easily exploited. Earlier in the class room, a debate on gender issues has always resulted in ... passionate and offensive outbursts ...The same discussion after their field visits was much more mature ...' (Saxena, 1997b, 14). Dr Saxena and her students, legal practitioners, and family counsellors met with residents about their legal problems. She has observed that the pressure created from regular student visits to the 400-family community prompted better police response and acted as a deterrent to violent husbands (Saxena, 1997b, 13). Besides exposure to gender issues such as domestic violence and economic dependence, the students learned about researching real life problems (regarding motor vehicle law, narcotics law, and insurance, for example) and how to apply rules to a real situation (Saxena, 1997b, 14).

From these selected Indian clinical legal education efforts come many interesting ideas. The implementation of a criminal practice program that is community-based, such as the one at Lucknow University, bears resemblance to civil representation and community development clinics in the United States. By design, it provides future prosecutors and defenders with social exposure relevant to the criminal legal work as a complement to criminal law and procedural studies. One Lucknow student, for example, visited an encampment known for prostitution and suddenly realized the desperate effect of economic need. He exclaimed, 'These are just mothers and sisters'.

At Delhi University, student volunteer involvement in Lok Adalats and legal literacy campaigns reinforces a message of professional obligation to the public and provides students with community fora in which they must translate technical legal language into clear statements. The volunteer work done in Gautam Nagar has formed a base of experience which a classroom teacher has cultivated and used in sensitising her students about gender issues and legal problems of the poor.

Beyond community service activities in which law teachers and students have been involved, activists in the South Asian region have approached social change in innovative ways. A selection are described in the next section to provide social context.

South Asian Legal and Organizing Strategies

Some South Asian lawyers, activists and judges are using creative strategies to address urgent social issues. Profiles of activists in this section are drawn from the network of Ashoka fellows, selected by a global, non-profit organization that finds and supports individuals with ideas for far-reaching social change.[18]

The problem of child labor, which often deprives youth of health and education, is an important focus of activism. Mandatory education laws exist, but census data indicate that many school-age (ages 6 to 14) children do not attend school, especially in rural areas (Sainath, 1996, 25). The attendance rate is lower for girls than boys. The Constitution prohibits employment of children below the age of 14 in any factory, mine, or hazardous employment, such as the production of glass, brass, locks, gems, matches, fireworks, slates, tiles, carpets and bidis (cigarettes) (Constitution Art. 24). However, child labor in hazardous employment is so widespread that the International Labour Office has targeted it as a priority in its plan for India (International Labour Conference, 1996, 102).

Various approaches to reduce child labor have been implemented. Indian activist Kailash Satyarthi, of the South Asian Coalition Against Child Servitude, monitors carpet factories, certifies by a 'Rugmark' emblem the products of businesses that follow child labor laws, and seeks punishment for violators (Bonbright, 1997, 237). Indian activist Damodar Acharya has organized workers' unions of children and a children's 'panchayat' (a local council of elected village officials) to empower children to influence parents to seek educational opportunities and child-centered programs (Visick, 1998, 85). In Nepal, an NGO headed by attorney Yubaraj Sangroula has conducted extensive community organizing and legal training to stem trafficking in children for prostitution from Nepal to India (Sangroula, 1997).

Advocacy for low-wage factory workers, agricultural workers, and small farmers is critically important in view of the large numbers of people in these occupations. Indian activist Haushala Prasad Mishra has organized textile workers and formed an NGO to secure better working conditions in mills to prevent byssinosis ('brown lung disease'), to improve processing of insurance claims, and to negotiate for a public occupational health center in Ahmedabad (Bonbright, 1997, 225). Indian activist Jagdish Pradhan promotes use of traditional methods of irrigation enhanced with new technology in hilly regions of Kalahandi and Western Orissa, and advocates for policies in support of community-based irrigation and against large-scale irrigation projects (Bonbright, 1997, 404). Abdul Hakim Khoso, an activist who has organized small farmers to secure access to irrigation water, has argued a case based on a provision of the Pakistani constitution and won a judgment in a Pakistani court holding that small farmers have the right to access irrigation water (Visick, 1998, 89).

Activists have been constructing infrastructure for the women's human rights movement in India. Soma Sengupta, through an organization she formed called Sahita, has begun setting up a national gender information and communications bureau to collect and disseminate information to local women's groups (Bonbright, 1997, 94). Anuradha Kapoor has formed an organization called Swayam to provide comprehensive services to victims of domestic violence through a corps of volunteers, and to partner in publishing a directory of specialty organizations. Swayam also arranges workshops on self-employment skills and employment training for clients, and works in combination with 40 advocacy groups for women in West Bengal to address policy issues (Bonbright, 1997, 157). Activist Anu V. Wakhlu has founded the Pragati Foundation to help middle-aged housewives and female students strengthen work skills, pursue education, make career choices, and receive peer support (Bonbright, 1997, 491).

Judicial activism has been an important force for social change in India. In the 1980s, the Supreme Court of India began accepting cases referred to as 'public interest litigation' or 'social action litigation', which address problems of impoverished people. The Supreme Court relaxed requirements for standing to sue, accepting letters and newspaper articles as sufficient to invoke its jurisdiction (Baxi, 1988b, 396). The Court has ruled to protect the fundamental rights of bonded laborers, prisoners, pavement dwellers, and minimum wage workers, among other impoverished groups (Cassels, 1991, 132; Cunningham, 1987; Gordon and Lindsay, 1990, 756; Sussman, 1994; Sripati, 1998, 443).

Two-way Exchange and Broader Collaboration

A growing body of work evidences the evolving legal academic and clinical exchanges between India and the United States. This section features a few examples of long-term study of India and clinical legal education projects jointly undertaken by Indian and United States law teachers. Two-way exchange between India and the United States occurs along with growing regional (LeBrun, 1998) and global legal education efforts.[19]

Professor Marc Galanter, a critic of the Law and Development movement, conducted in-depth studies of Indian law and legal structures which can serve as a model for lawyers learning about another country (Galanter, 1984, 1989). Indian scholar Rajeev Dhavan's introduction and response to Professor Galanter's *Law and Society in Modern India* create a lively debate about the limits on the role of law in India.[20] The book sparked thought-provoking reviews.[21]

Much collaboration between India and the United States has occurred on the roles of clinics and legal aid. Law teachers have compared clinical teaching with the goal of public service (Bloch and Ishar, 1990). Indian legal workers have shared their approaches with law professors in the United States on methods of representing the impoverished (Ellmann, 1998, 378). Two practicing attorneys from the United States studied 'structures of dominance' in a village primarily through caste interactions (Gordon and Lindsay, 1990, 655). Their detailed analysis emphasizes the importance of access to land and credit through government programs to the well-being of villagers, and recommends greater access to the legal aid system that exists (Gordon and Lindsay, 1990, 770). Indian colleagues have invited United States and other foreign clinicians to plan workshops on learning from experience, to demonstrate clinical teaching techniques such as evaluation of moot court performances, and to consult about clinic and legal education administration.[22] Indian law teachers interested in clinics have presented papers and visited clinics in the West.[23]

Substantive law comparisons, with implications for clinics, have also been conducted. Public interest litigation in the United States and in India have been compared as to standing to sue, non-adversarial litigation, and the relationship of rights and remedies (Cunningham, 1987). Alternative approaches to remedying past discrimination on the basis of race and caste in India, South Africa and the United States have been explored (Cunningham, 1997). During academic visits in the late 1990s, Indian colleagues have sought interaction about research topics (medical waste disposal law, means of combatting corruption among police, death penalty for juvenile offenders, creation of battered women's shelters, and civil protection orders, for example) and access to research resources (books, listservs, websites[24]).

A Sampling of Areas for Increased Collaboration

International legal education exchange in South Asia offers a number of fertile areas for collaboration. Future interaction can expand the efforts already underway of observing Indian community lawyering and teaching, reading Indian scholarship and responding to it, co-authoring, and seeking input from foreign colleagues on community lawyering, teaching and scholarship.

Much of the interaction which has occurred in the last ten years has centered upon use of clinical education methodology in India. In sharing the few specific ideas that follow, I suggest that United States clinicians not only continue to discuss clinical education and community service issues, but also seek ways to convey Indian legal perspectives to United States students and colleagues.[25]

Collaboration on Clinical Legal Education Issues. Some United States and Indian law teachers may choose to collaborate on pedagogical issues such as structuring experiential learning, designing role plays for skills training, preparing for fieldwork, debriefing on interactions with clients, or on clinical scholarship. Clinician organizations should continue to increase involvement of Indian and other law teachers from developing countries in conferences on clinical legal education.

'Training of trainers' workshops, in which a range of clinical methodology is demonstrated to and practiced by law teachers, are regularly held in the South Asian region and may provide a useful introduction to exchange work. Indian teachers and practitioners generally must take the lead in setting goals, selecting disputes to use in role plays and defining the 'best practices' sought to be taught to make sure that the exercises are locally appropriate. Indian and foreign clinicians then may jointly plan other aspects and conduct the workshops. Also, Indian law departments may seek United States visitors to facilitate discrete teaching discussions, such as design and delivery of role plays or the process of fairly evaluating student performance in moot court performances.

Collaboration on clinical scholarship might take the form of writing on clinical education method, community service provision or clinical theory (e.g.,

Bloch and Ishar, 1990; Menon 1998). Cross-cultural skills comparisons (e.g., Cunningham 1999) may also emerge from this work.

Comparative legal education scholarship on United States and Indian law school clinics across subject matter would also prove intriguing. Women's rights clinics analyses (e.g. White 1998) may lend themselves to this study. Clinics serving migrant laborers and immigrant workers (Dubin, 1998; Gordon, 1995) may find interesting comparisons in Indian labor efforts.

Community lawyering Clinics built upon community-based legal services models to work for organizational clients on environmental justice (Babcock, 1995) and on community development (Jones, 1997; Lehman and Lento, 1992; Pitegoff, 1995) may benefit from study of community organizing models in India. South Asian gatherings, such as Lok Adalats and legal aid camps, and methods such as 'legal literacy' campaigns provide ideas on ways to educate impoverished communities.

Field work with Indian colleagues and their clients may be feasible on extended exchange visits. 'Participatory development' which emphasizes the involvement of impoverished communities in change strategies has been used and studied in South Asia (Mathur, 1995; Rahman, 1993) and in developing countries in other regions (Hall, and Fretz, 1990 p.786) and may offer insights to clinicians working with communities. AWARE[26] is an Indian organization following this theory (Ellmann, 1998, 378). Socio-legal studies conducted by South Asian students provide a model for community-based policy development (Schukoske, 1997). Such collaboration with client communities parallels effort under study in the United States.[27]

Rethinking representation strategies for low-income groups in the United States in light of other legal services experience and perspective may provide important insights. In the United States, restrictions on the use of the federal funding for legal services has limited attention to certain issues, such as group representation, public protest, and certain categories of cases.[28]

Sharing perspectives on the roles of NGOs, both grass-roots client organizations and intermediary organizations, in community development has promise as an important area for international collaboration.[29] In India, for example, lively debate occurs about acceptance of foreign aid, the significance of and leadership of women in NGOs, and NGO ties to political parties and social movements (Eldrich and Ratan, 1996, 76). This work may offer insight into parallel concerns in Western contexts (e.g., acceptance of government aid, foundation aid or corporate support rather than foreign aid).

South Asian and international NGO strategies to organize and channel resources into disadvantaged communities may stimulate thought about parallel problems and opportunities in the United States (Oliver, 1997). An example is microlending, the lending of amounts smaller than usual commercial loan levels, to individuals in low income communities as a way of stimulating 'microenterprise' (very small business) formation (Jones, 1997, 196). Microlending, begun at the Grameen Bank in Bangladesh, spread to India where women in 'loan circles' pooled their savings to lend to each other (White, 1998, 330). Microlending and microenterprise strategies are now used in the United States, where local, state and national microenterprise funding and technical assistance programs are receiving national recognition (Edson and Lane, 1999, 669) and cautious attention as economic development initiatives for women (White, 1998).

Raising United States student awareness of conditions and substantive legal activity in South Asia Study abroad in India exposes students to the urgent needs of the region and perspective on the role of law in society.[30] Since relatively few United States students will actually study in India, teachers interested in India face the challenge of incorporating awareness of this region into courses and clinics in the United States.

Indian NGOs or law school clinics might seek participation by a United States clinic on an international human rights or environmental law topic. Collaboration on cases readily occurs among lawyers and NGOs working in the fields of human rights (Ellmann, 1998; Rekosh, 1998) and international environmental law (Wirth, 1991). International human rights clinics representing foreign clients on civil and political rights have involved students on cases.[31] In such efforts, there may be controversies about whether rights are viewed as universal or culturally relative. Gross disparities in social, economic and political power are cited as evidence that international human rights claims reinforce the existing balance of power among nations rather than universal values (Otto, 1997, at 34). In working against child labor, for example, activists might choose an incremental approach involving schooling and work under safe conditions rather than an abrupt halt to underage employment, to balance dual concerns about child protection and family economic need.

Collaboration may spark ideas for topics for research by teachers and students in comparative law and human rights courses. The labor activism undertaken by South Asian activists described above may inspire possible assignments for law students in India. Likewise, United States law teachers may suggest topics that would involve students in support of such projects. Teachers could suggest research on legal aspects of other serious problems in India, such as illiteracy and lack of sanitation in Bihar; pavement housing and choking pollution in Delhi; custodial violence in jails in Uttar Pradesh; the scrapping of international freighters on the beaches of Gujarat; the loss of rural work due to displacement by dam projects; trafficking of girls for prostitution from Nepal to India; and other issues which Indian activists identify.

Comparative law studies can be interwoven even in courses and clinics which have a primarily domestic content through participation by visiting scholars and reading assignments. Fulbright scholars in law from India have team taught with law professors in the United States to provide cross-cultural perspective.[32] A teacher may assign readings about Indian scholars and lawyers to educate students about Indian social problems and legal strategies.[33] *Pro bono* projects addressing problems which plague South Asia may naturally arise from engagement with colleagues there.[34]

Problems to which the United States directly contributes warrant particular attention. Child labor, for example, is encouraged by United States consumer purchase of goods made by children. Collaboration among Indian and United States. students, teachers and activists in international human rights, labor law and business could lead to approaches that meet the educational, health and economic needs of the children involved in production of goods. As described earlier, Indian activists have taken innovative steps to form child panchayats for involvement of children in identifying and addressing their needs and to initiate programs to label products made with child labor.[35] Collaborators could consider 'fair practices' codes for employers for wages and working conditions in apparel factories that United States companies use or operate anywhere in the world, such as one proposed by a presidential task force (Fox, 1998, 900). Comparison of strategies used in representation of workers against unfair labor practices in India and in the United States may be fruitful.[36]

Raising awareness of our own laws, systems and cultures The child labor example above illustrates how cross-cultural work can provide insights about values and the role law plays in the United States. Work within a foreign legal culture may help a person learn tobecome more aware of her cultural preconceptions and legal acculturation:

> 'The understanding of, respect for and engagement of foreign legal systems rather than their mere tolerance will not only facilitate discussions with

foreign counsel or clients but will also allow us to respect cultural, gender-based, religious, and legal differences at home to a greater extent. In that respect, comparative law could live up to its promise of providing a domestic as much as a foreign perspective'. (Demleitner, 1998, 665)

Questions from colleagues from another culture force us to discuss policy, history and implications which one may otherwise not think through. Indian colleagues are apt to question important policy matters ranging from economic sanctions imposed by the United States on India (Wall, 1998, 588) to imposition of the death penalty on juveniles in the United States.[37] United States legal scholars seeking to apply international human rights standards to conditions in the United States may benefit from sharing perspectives of and theorizing with scholars from developing countries.[38]

The material disparity between India and the United States demands that exchange participants recognize resource maldistribution. South Asia's lack of resources contrasts so sharply with resources in the United States that the returning visitor reevaluates the routine wasting of resources (electricity, paper, water) and consumer consumption in the United States Resource distribution is an important issue for teachers and students to discuss.

Conclusion

Exchange visits and conference interactions offer opportunities for cross-cultural learning. Strong ties have been established between law teachers in India and in the United States as a result of such connections. Optimism in the potential power of law and legal education, which characterized the Law and Development movement, also underlies current clinical collaboration efforts. Lessons from that movement about the weaknesses of the 'export' model warrant attention by clinicians and others participating in international legal exchange.

With globalization occurring at a rapid pace, opportunities for collaboration and comparative law study in India and other developing countries are burgeoning. Clinicians, open to learning from experience while assisting impoverished clients, have an important role to play in identifying issues for our students at home as well as in sharing information, resources and scholarly debate with colleagues abroad.

Notes

1 I thank Clinton Bamberger, Balraj Chauhan, Clark D. Cunningham, Kenneth S. Gallant, Ved Kumari, N.R. Madhava Menon, Yubaraj Sangroula, Poonam Pradhan Saxena, and N. Selvakkumaran for teaching me about South Asian legal education and fieldwork during visits I made to India, Nepal and Sri Lanka in 1995-1998. Also, I thank Paula Baig, Clark D. Cunningham, Kenneth S. Gallant, Odeana R. Neal, Michael Meltsner, and Leah Wortham for their comments on an earlier draft of this chapter.

2 Balraj Chauhan, Reader in Law and Course Director, Post Graduate Diploma in Criminal Practice and Advocacy Programme (PGDCPA), and his students conducted the interviews. PGDCPA is a one year program started by the Faculty of Law, Lucknow University in 1994 for the students who want to enter the legal profession after completing their LLB degree (Chauhan, 1997, 2). The program is discussed within this chapter under the section, 'Legal Education'. The social structure and status of women in the village of Khajuron is discussed in Bumiller (1990, 75).

3 'Clinician' in this article includes law teachers who teach law, lawyering skills and values through simulation or student work in real world settings involving education of the public, advice to clients, and resolution of disputes through negotiation or a formal process (court, agency, etc.).

4 Resources for learning basic features of Indian law are readily available for the reader in the United States. A basic overview of Indian law and law libraries appears in Mahr (1990); of the Constitution of India in Flanz (1997) and Sripati (1998); of the legal system in David (1984) and Redden and Schlueter (1990), of the court system in Chodosh (1997-98), of the legal education system in Dayal (1978) and Menon (1998). A collection of essays exploring Indian poverty law in-depth is found in Baxi (1988a). A seminal collection of articles on law in Indian society by Professor Marc Galanter from the United States. with a substantive critique by Indian Rajeev Dhavan is Galanter (1989). A book which serves both as a textbook and a resource for practitioners of environmental law is Rosencranz, Divan and Noble (1991). A key periodical is the Journal of the Indian Law Institute. Law review articles on other aspects of Indian law appear throughout this article.

5 Terminology confounds not only when the word is unfamiliar (a news article proclaiming the success of vaccination of 22 lakh children may baffle until one learns that 'lakh' means 100,000), but especially when familiar words

have different meanings (a colleague asked me for recent cases in the United States about 'processions', by which he meant labor demonstrations).

6 The movement was based on the liberal legalism paradigm that the state is the primary agent of social change and control, that it will use law as an instrument to change society and will act within legal limits; that law would change behavior; that legal professions would serve the public interest; that changes in legal education would ultimately reform the profession (Trubek and Galanter, 1974, 1075).

7 Scholars theorized about the liberal realist underpinnings of the law and development movement, examined liberal realist assumptions, and called for a critical legal approach to the study of the role of law in developing countries (Trubek and Galanter 1974). A former Ford Foundation officer described the law and development movement in Latin America and concluded that the movement's endeavor and legal models were flawed (Gardner, 1980, 239). Legal services lawyers discussed the ethnocentrism of the attempted export of American legal education, and the evolution of the Movement towards clinical legal education and legal assistance to the poor (Hall and Fretz, 1990, 782).

8 Scholars categorized post-legal-liberalist camps as isolationism, a-legal developmentalism, pragmatic problem solving, positivistic pure science, and eclectic critique (Trubek and Galanter, 1974, 1096). This article, 'Scholars in Self-Estrangement' has been recognized as a piece of critical legal scholarship (published by one of the founders (Trubek) of the movement just prior to its birth (Tamanaha, 1995, 474). A comparative law scholar called for maturation of the Law and Development movement to one of 'comparative law and social change', and urged that academics pay more attention to inquiry rather than technical assistance when venturing into the social, cultural and legal contexts of developing countries (Merryman, 1977).

9 Opining that the Law and Development movement was a 'Western academic conversation', scholar Brian Z. Tamanaha examined political development theories: modernization theory, with which legal liberalism resounds, and dependency theory, which contributed to the development of critical legal studies (Tamanaha 1995). Tamanaha summarized the lessons about the role of law as follows: 'Modern law is necessary, though not sufficient, for economic development... The appearance of the rule of law is helpful, though not sufficient, for political development... Beyond these minimums, law is not of primary importance. The center of gravity in each society rests on its unique historical, cultural, economic, political and material (population, natural resources, technology base, and so forth) mix... Developing countries

will benefit - that is, the quality of life of their citizens will improve - if they develop their own variants of the minimum content of the rule of law... The minimum content of the rule of law can best be established through efforts oriented to legal development...' (Tamanaha, 1995, 484). Dr Rajeev Dhavan, in his introduction to *Law and Society in Modern India* takes issue with the charge that instrumentalism in law is a western notion. He asserts that in India it derives from Nehru's Soviet-inspired system of Five Year Plans for the country (Galanter, 1989, lxv).

10 Professor Amy L. Chua has noted that special problems flow from efforts to transplant commercial law from a nation with a market economy to one with an economy that has been less market-based. She has examined the fundamental tension in developing countries when democracy empowers an impoverished majority group against a market-dominating minority. She posits that in a democracy in which markets benefit only an elite minority group, the majority often responds with ethnic backlash (Chua 1998). This analysis partially explains why transplantation of market-based legal models may fail to significantly boost development in some settings.

11 Rose's points about reinforcement of legal structures and market structures are important ones and are beyond the scope of this chapter. They relate to a distinction drawn by Professor Upendra Baxi between poverty and impoverishment: '... people are not naturally poor but are made poor, that *impoverishment is a dynamic process of public decision-making in which it is considered just, right and fair that some people may become, or stay impoverished*', (Baxi, 1988a, vi) (emphasis in original).

12 India is predominantly agricultural. The labor force in India in 1990 was 64 per cent agricultural and 16 per cent industrial; 32 per cent of it was female in 1995 (World Bank 1997 220). In most Indian states, there are no laws regulating working conditions, annual leave, and employee benefits for agricultural workers (Srivastava, 1988, 222).

13 The United Nations Development Programme defines poverty as 'denial of choices and opportunities for living a tolerable life' which include adequate food and water, health care, and education (UNDP, 1997, 3). UNDP's Human Poverty Index Ranking for Developing Countries reports that 36.7 per cent of India's population lives in human poverty defined by the three indicators : longevity (expected to die before age 40), knowledge (illiteracy) and decent living standard (access to health care, safe drinking water, and percentage of malnourished children under age 5) (UNDP, 1997, 18). UNDP has reported that 53 per cent of India's populations live in income poverty defined as less

than $1/day/person (UNDP, 1997, 55). See also poverty indicators in World Bank, 224.

14 'Scheduled castes, scheduled tribes and other backward classes' are groups historically discriminated against due to their occupations and castes, or lack of stature within the caste system (Singh, 1988, 132; Baxi, 1988c, 165; Baxi, 1988d, 186).

15 Dr Ved Kumari, a full-time law teacher at Delhi University who has participated in clinical training for law teachers in India and has visited as a Fulbright scholar at law school clinics in the United States, team-taught a course entitled 'Clinical Legal Education and Practical Training for the Profession of Law' with an adjunct teacher/practitioner at Delhi University in 1998-99. She reports:

> 'Lectures were delivered by in-house faculty and guest lawyers on court structure; stages in a civil and criminal case; management of files; general documents like bail bond, affidavits, etc.; Public Interest Litigation; Legal Aid; colloquial terminology in court proceedings; professional ethics; and legal research. The students were also placed with lawyers for three weeks. We did not succeed in placing the students with judges for a week. We did simulations of client interviewing and counselling, negotiation, examination and cross-examination. The students got the chance to practice their negotiation skills in real life situation by participating in a Lok Adalat held in the Faculty by the Legal Aid Board. We prepared role plays for clients, respondents and witnesses for three mock trials on family, criminal and rent matters. The students were divided in groups of four each to take up the case on each side and do all the work a lawyer would be required to do for their clients in those circumstances. They interviewed their clients, counselled them and determined the case strategies. They then prepared petitions, written statements and replications with necessary stamps, etc., filed the papers in the appropriate courts. On the trial date, they examined and cross-examined witness and presented their arguments.
>
> The problem in doing most of these activities was that I had no first hand knowledge of the ground realities in practice. My exposure to all these class activities being more from the west, I suspected that certain things may be alien to the Indian court culture and scenario. At the preparation stage I needed an honest and professional feedback on how close to reality and practice our simulation exercises were - what was good, what was bad, what

needed improvement, what was completely idealistic and impracticable. My part-time colleague cooperated fully in what I planned but she was new in teaching and had no clue about simulation exercises. She had been enrolled but had little practical experience in reality. The end result was that we learnt about suggestions and different ways of formulating questions in cross-examination only during the mock trial when the students were being evaluated. I felt very bad at not knowing about those little things before and at not having briefed the students about it earlier.

Despite its shortcomings, I have got a very positive feedback from my students and I have a feeling that the number is going to far exceed our capacity to deal with that. This time there were 23 of them and it was quite a task to give individual time to them...' . (Kumari, 1999, 2)

16 An example of a case that students at NLSIU encountered at the Ramanagaram Rural Mediation Centre is eloquently discussed in Gallant (1999), chapter 11 of this volume.

17 In 1995, National Law School of India University in Bangalore held a Refresher Course on Clinical Legal Education involving participants from Australia, Bangladesh, India, Nepal, Sri Lanka, U.K. and United .States. Dr Menon thereafter served as editor of a collection of essays entitled *Clinical Legal Education* (1998). He serves on the steering committee for an international conference to be held in Trivandrum, India in December, 1999 inaugurating an organization of law professors, the Global Alliance for Justice Education (GAJE) which is focusing on legal skills training and other clinical and social justice issues.

18 Indian Ashoka Fellows' work is listed on the Ashoka Foundation website at <http://www.ashoka.org/html/asia.html#India >(viewed June 15, 1999).

19 The Global Alliance for Justice Education (GAJE) is an international organization dedicated to the promotion of socially relevant legal education. Dr N.R. Medhava Menon is one of its founders.

20 Dr Rajeev Dhavan wrote a substantive introduction and critique of the 1989 book noting the origins and shape of controversies in India about the role of law and taking issue with Professor Galanter's optimism about the power of law in modern India. See Galanter (1989).

21 Galanter's book provided grist for further reflection on the limits of legal change, legal pluralism and 'compensatory discrimination' (the parallel to 'affirmative action' in India) (Cunningham, 1991, 792). One scholar examined Professor Galanter's comparative legal study of India and notes that in India's political and economic context, modern law may reinforce the status quo to the advantage of the elite, the capitalist and land-owning classes (Cassels, 1991, 120, 136).

22 For example, a Refresher Course for Law Teachers on Clinical Legal Education sponsored by the University Grants Commission, New Delhi, was held at National Law School of India University in Bangalore, November 13 - December 3, 1995. The Course involved participants from Australia, Bangladesh, India, Nepal, Sri Lanka, U.K., and United States. Four of the U.S. faculty had connections to South Asia as Fulbright scholars (Frank Bloch, Clark D. Cunningham, Kenneth Gallant, and Jane Schukoske).

The Australian government sponsored a conference, 'New Horizons in Legal Education', in New Delhi in 1996, and the Australia-India Council sponsored 'Training-the-Legal-Trainer Workshop' at National Law School of India University in October, 1997 (LeBrun 1998).

Numerous workshops on clinical topics have been held at South Asian universities. The Ford Foundation in India Human Rights Project (1996 - 1998, directed by Clark D. Cunningham) sponsored faculty exchange visits between India and the United States, which included the offering of workshops in India. The Faculty of Law of the University of Colombo, Sri Lanka, held 'Workshops on Clinical Legal Education Methods' in May and June, 1996, see Atapattu, Schukoske, and Selvakkumaran (1996). As this chapter goes to press, plans are underway for a clinical/poverty law conference to be sponsored by the Global Alliance for Justice Education in Trivandrum, India in December, 1999.

23 For example, the American Association of Law Schools Clinical Section Conference, in May, 1996 in Miami, Florida involved panellists from Bangladesh, India, and Nepal, and post-conference visits to a number of United States law schools. The Law and Society Association conference, 'Globalization and the Quest for Justice', held in Glasgow, Scotland in July, 1996, involved panellists from Sri Lanka and India, among other developing countries. The Fourth International Clinical Conference 'Conceptual Paradigms in Clinical Legal Education', held in Lake Arrowhead, California in October, 1997, had a panel involving two participants from India.

V. Nagaraj of NLSIU in 1994 and Ved Kumari of Delhi University in 1997 have visited clinics at Vanderbilt University School of Law. Dr Poonam Saxena visited at University of Baltimore School of Law in 1998.

24 The Global Alliance for Justice Education (GAJE), an organization forming to serve as a clearinghouse for law teaching methods and materials, operates a discussion list with Indian and other international participants. The GAJE website is found at <http://ls.wustl.edu/Academics/Faculty/Activities/Global> (viewed June 15, 1999). The Public Interest Library Clinical Legal Education website, <http://www.pili.org/library/cle> (viewed June 15, 1999), posts articles of interest to clinicians working internationally, and maintains a listserv available through the website. Although many universities in South Asia have no or limited access to electronic mail, some, such as University of Delhi, India, NLSIU, and University of Colombo, Sri Lanka, do. Increasingly, law teachers in India have access to electronic mail at home.

25 Clinical law teachers who also teach non-clinical courses may accomplish this more easily than those who do not.

26 Action for Welfare and Awakening in Rural Environment.

27 See Cruz (1999); Eagly (1998, 433 note 1); Marisco (1995); White (1994, 157).

28 Federal legal services statutes and regulations have channelled legal services staff to handle cases for individuals, primarily disputes that would be resolved through negotiation, agency action or litigation. Group client representation has historically tended to fit the dispute model: litigation on behalf of a group client or class. Federal law has also prohibited representation on labor issues, voting rights issues, non-therapeutic abortion rights and school desegregation issues, among others. 42 U.S.C. Section 2996f (1997). Legal services workers, as other federal employees, are restricted in engaging in political activity. Free criminal and civil representation has been divided among separate offices in most places in the United States. That bifurcation may have lead to less than complete aid and referral for individuals and a loss of a community perspective.

29 The International Center for Not-For-Profit Law, funded by the Charles Stewart Mott Foundation and the Rockefeller Brothers Fund, is an international organization that assists in providing 'creation and improvement of laws and regulatory systems that permit, encourage, and regulate the NGO sector in countries around the world' <http://www.icnl.org> (viewed June 15, 1999). Cross-cultural studies identify the role NGOs play between the market and the state (Salamon and Anheier, 1998, 2).

30 Since 1996, Touro Law School and South Texas School of Law have operated a summer abroad program for United States law students in Shimla, India. Other law schools in the United States are funding law student work overseas after the first and second year of law school. See, e.g., Ishar (1999).

31 These clinics include, for example, St. Mary's (Texas, United States) International Human Rights Clinic's work on asylum cases and law reform projects (Dubin, 1998) and American University (Washington, D.C., United States) International Human Rights Law Clinic's work in asylum cases and human rights litigation before the Inter-American Human Rights Commission (Wilson, 1996).

32 See, e.g., De La Vega (1994 and 1997); De La Vega and Brown (1998); Hernandez-Truyol (1996 and 1997); Stark (1992 and 1995).

33 Dr Ved Kumari of Delhi University taught in the Juvenile Justice Clinic at Vanderbilt University School of Law (Tennessee, United States) with Clinical Professor Susan Brooks in fall, 1997. Dr. Poonam Saxena of Delhi University taught in the Family Law Clinic at University of Baltimore School of Law (Maryland United States) with Professors Jane C. Murphy and Barbara Babb and in a Domestic Relations class with Professor Murphy in fall, 1998.

34 For example, in a Law and Social Reform seminar, which is primarily domestic in content, I assigned students at University of Baltimore in spring, 1999, readings from Bonbright (1997) discussing legal strategies used in several developing countries and asked students to discuss the similarities and dissimilarities between them and the law reform approaches in the United States that we had studied.

35 See Daly, (1996, 297), envisioning students satisfying a future mandatory *pro bono* requirement in a foreign country.

36 The website of the International Labour Organization, <http://www-ilo-mirror.who.or.jp/public/english/child/index.htm>(viewed June 15, 1999), lists labelling efforts designed to discourage purchase of goods made with child labor.

37 Such representation occurs at a clinic at St. Mary's University (Dubin, 1998, 1461) and at The Workplace Project in New York (Gordon 1995).

38 The execution of juvenile offenders in the United States is an issue which has been raised repeatedly by Indian law teachers during my visits to India. For

further information on this issue, see De La Vega and Brown (1998) and Hernandez-Truyol (1996).

References

Aggarwal, N. (1998) *Campus Law Centre Faculty of Law Annual Report* 1997-98, Delhi University, Delhi.

Atapattu, S., Schukoske, J. and Selvakkumaran, N. (eds) (1996) 'Reading Materials for Workshops on Clinical Legal Education Methods', (Presented at workshops on Clinical Legal Education Methods at University of Colombo, Sri Lanka, May/June 1996).

Babcock, H. (1995), 'Environmental Justice Clinics: Visible Models of Justice', *Stanford Environmental Law Journal*, vol. 14, 3.

Bar Council of India (1997), *Revised Curriculum for Three and Five Year Law Course for Implementation by the Academic Year 1998-1999*, LE Cir. No. 4.

Baxi, U. (ed.) (1988a), *Law and Poverty - Critical Essays*, vi, N.M. Tripathi Private Limited, Bombay.

Baxi, U. (1988b), 'Taking Suffering Seriously: Social Action Litigation in the Supreme Court of India', in Baxi, U. (ed.) (1988a).

Baxi, U. (1988c), 'Untouchability: Constitution, Law and Plan', in Baxi, U. (ed.)(1988a).

Baxi, U. (1988d), 'Untouchable's Access to Water: Two Moralities of Law Enforcement', in Baxi, U. (ed.) (1988a).

Bloch, F.S. and Ishar, I.S. (1990), 'Legal Aid, Public Service, and Clinical Legal Education: Future Directions from India and the United States', *Michigan Journal of International Law*, vol. 12, 92.

Bonbright, D. (ed.) (1997), *Leading Public Entrepreneurs*, 227, Ashoka: Innovators for the Public, Arlington, Virginia.

Bumiller, E. (1990) *May You Be The Mother of a Hundred Sons,* 75-100, Penguin Books India (P)Ltd, New Delhi.

Carty, A. (1992), *Law and Development*, vol. 2, Dartmouth Publishing Co, Aldershot.

Cassels, J. (1991) 'Bitter Knowledge, Vibrant Action: Reflections of Law and Society in Modern India', *Wisconsin Law Review* 109.

Chauhan, B. (1997), 'Training Lawyers for Radical Practice', (Working paper prepared for Fourth International Conference on Clinical Legal Education and Scholarship, October, 1997) (on file with the author).

Chodosh, H. Mayo, S.A. Ahmadi, A.M., Singhu, A.M. (1997-98) 'Indian Civil Justice Reform: Limitation and Preservation of the Adversarial Process', *New York University Journal of International Law and Politics*, vol. 3, 1.

Cottrell, J. (1986), '10+2+5: A Change in the Structure of Indian Legal Education', *Journal of Legal Education*, vol. 36, 331.

Chua, A. (1998), 'Markets, Democracy and Ethnicity: Towards a New Paradigm for

Law and Development', *Yale Law Journal*, vol. 108, 1.
Cooper, J. and Trubek, L. (eds) (1997), *Educating for Justice: Social Values and Legal Education*, Ashgate Publishing, Aldershot.
Cruz, C. (1999), '[On the] Road Back In: Community Lawyering in Indigenous Communities', *Clinical Law Review*, vol. 5, 557.
Cunningham, C. (1999) 'Evaluating Effective Lawyer-Client Communication: An International Project Moving from Research to Reform', *Fordham Law Review*, vol. 67, 1959.
Cunningham, C. (1987), 'Public Interest Litigation In the Indian Supreme Court: A Study In Light of the American Experience', *Journal of Indian Law Institute*, vol. 29, 494.
Cunningham, C. (1991), 'Why American Lawyers Should Go to India: Retracing Galanter's Intellectual Odyssey', *Journal of the American Bar Foundation*, vol. 16, 777.
Cunningham, C. (ed) (1997), 'Symposium: Rethinking Equality in the Global Society', *Washington University Law Quarterly*, vol. 75.
Daly, M. (1996) 'Thinking Globally: Will National Borders Matter to Lawyers a Century from Now?', *Journal Institute Study of Legal Ethics*, vol. 1, 297.
David, R. (ed.) (1984) 'The Legal System of the Republic of India', *The Legal Systems of the World, Their Comparison and Unification*, vol. 2, 9.80.5-9.80.37 Martinus Nijhoff Publishers, Boston, Massachusetts.
Dayal, S. (1978) 'Legal Profession and Legal Education', Joseph Minattur (ed.), *The Indian Legal System*, 148, Oceana Publications, Inc., Dobbs Ferry, New York.
De La Vega, C. (1997), 'Civil Rights During the 1990's: New Treaty Law Could Help Immensely', *University of Cincinnati Law Review*, vol. 65, 423.
De La Vega, C. (1994), 'Protecting Economic, Social and Cultural Rights', *Whittier Law Review*, vol. 15, 471.
De La Vega, C. and Brown, J. (1998), 'Can A United States Treaty Reservation Provide A Sanctuary for the Juvenile Death Penalty?', *University of San Francisco Law Review*, vol. 32, 735.
Demleitner, N. (1998) 'Challenge, Opportunity and Risk: An Era of Change in Comparative Law', *American Journal of Comparative Law*, vol. 46, 647.
Dubin, J. (1998), 'Clinical Design for Social Justice Imperatives', *Southern Methodist University Law Review*, vol. 51, 1461.
Eagly, I. (1998), 'Community Education: Creating A New Vision of Legal Services Practice', *Clinical Law Review*, vol. 4, 433.
Edson, C. and Lane, B. (eds) (1999) 'Clinton Announces Second Round Of Microenterprise Awards', in Current Developments in Housing, Community Development, Finance and Taxation, *Housing and Development Reporter*, vol. 26, 669.
Eldrich, P. and Ratan, N. (1996), *Non Governmental Organizations and Social Action Groups in India*, 76-81, Syndicate Publications, Patna.
Ellmann, S. (1998), 'Cause Lawyering in the Third World' in Sarat, A. and Scheingold, S. (eds), 349.

Flanz, G. (ed.) (1997), *Constitutions of the Countries of the World,* Constitution of India (1950 as amended), pt. IV, art. 39A, Oceana Publications, Inc., Dobbs Ferry, New York.
Fox, E. (1998) 'Globalization and Its Challenges for Society', *Loyola University Chicago Law Journal*, vol. 29, 891.
Franck, T. (1972), 'The New Development: Can American Law and Legal Institutions Help Developing Countries?', *Wisconsin Law Review*, 767.
Galanter, M. (1984), *Competing Equalities: Law and the Backward Classes in India,* University of California Press, Berkeley, California.
Galanter, M. (1989), *Law and Society in Modern India,* Oxford University Press, Delhi.
Gallant, K. (1999), *Learning from Communities: Lessons from India For Legal Education*, chapter 11 of this volume.
Gardner, J. (1980), *Legal Imperialism*, 239, University of Wisconsin Press, Madison.
Gordon, J. (1995), 'We Make the Road by Walking: Immigrant Workers, the Workplace Project, and the Struggle for Social Change', *Harvard Civil Rights-Civil Liberties Law Review*, vol. 30, 407.
Gordon Jr., R. and Lindsay, J.M. (1990), 'Law and the Poor in Rural India: The Prospects for Legal Aid', *American University Journal of International Law and Policy*, vol. 5, 655.
Hall, G. and Fretz, B. (1990), 'Legal Services in the Third World', *Clearinghouse Review*, 784.
Hernandez-Truyol, B. (1996), 'Building Bridges: Bringing International Human Rights Home', *La Raza Law Journal*, vol. 9, 69.
Hernandez-Truyol, B. (1997), 'International Law, Human Rights, and LatCrit Theory: Civil and Political Rights - An Introduction', *University of Miami Inter-American Law Review*, vol. 28, 223.
International Labour Conference, (1996), *Child Labour: Targeting the Intolerable*, 102, International Labour Office, Geneva.
Ishar, I. (ed) (1999), 'Global Public Service Law Project', *GlobaLaw*, no. 3, 7.
Jones, S. (1997), 'Small Business and Community Economic Development: Transactional Lawyering for Social Change and Economic Justice', *Clinical Law Review*, vol. 4, 195.
Kumari, V. (1999) Electronic mail messages on *V. Sudeer v. Bar Council of India* and on 'Clinical Legal Education and Practical Training for the Profession of Law' at Delhi University Campus Law Centre to Jane Schukoske (on file with the author).
Le Brun, M. (1998), 'Regionalising Legal Education through Staff Development Initiatives and Institutional Co-operation: Lessons from Experience', (paper presented at Law Asia: Regionalising Legal Education, Bangkok, Thailand, November 16-18, 1998).
Lehman, J.S. and Lento, R.E. (1992), 'Law School Support for Community-Based Economic Development in Low-Income Urban Neighborhoods', *Washington University Journal of Urban and Contemporary Law*, vol.42, 65.

Mahr, T.A. (1990), 'An Introduction to Law and Law Libraries in India', *Law Library Journal*, vol. 82, 91.
Marsico, Richard D. (1995), 'Working for Social Change and Preserving Client Autonomy: Is There a Role For Facilitative Lawyering?', *Clinical Law Review*, vol. 1, 439.
Mathur, H. (1995), 'The Role of Social Actors in Promoting Participatory Development at Local Level: A View From India', in Schneider, H. with Libercier, M.-H. (eds), *Participatory Development from Advocacy to Action* 153, Organisation for Economic Co-operation and Development, Paris.
Menon, N. (1998), *Clinical Legal Education*, Eastern Book Co., Lucknow.
Menon, N.R.M. (1988), 'Legal Aid and Justice for the Poor', in Baxi, U. (ed.) (1988a).
Merryman, J.H. (1977), 'Comparative Law an Social Change: On the Origins, Style, Decline and Revival of the Law and Development Movement', *American Journal of Comparative Law*, vol. 25, 457.
Oliver, M. (1997), 'Building Assets: Another Way to Fight Poverty', *Ford Foundation Report*, vol. 28, 8.
Otto, D. (1997), 'Rethinking the "Universality" of Human Rights Law', *Columbia Human Rights Law Review*, vol. 29, 1.
Patel, M. (1992), 'Paralegals and Labor Organizing in India: The Self-Employed Women's Association', in Schuler, M. and Kadirgamar-Rajasingham, S. (eds), *Legal Literacy*, PACT Communications, New York.
Pitegoff, P. (1995), 'Law School Initiatives in Housing and Community Development', *Boston University Public Interest Law Journal*, vol. 4, 275.
Rahman, M. (1993), *People's Self-Development*, Zed Books, Atlantic Highlands, New Jersey.
Redden, K. and Schlueter, L. (eds) (1990),'India', *Modern Legal Systems Cyclopedia*, vol. 9A, W. Hein, Buffalo, New York.
Rekosh, E. (1999), 'Supporting Human Rights NGOs' (Prepared for Conference on Identifying Objectives to 2010 for the Human Rights Movement in the OCSE Area) (paper on file with the author).
Rose, C. (1998), 'The "New" Law and Development Movement in the Post-Cold War Era: A Vietnam Case Study', *Law and Society Review*, vol. 32, 93.
Rosencranz, A. Divan, S. and Noble, M. (1991), *Environmental Law and Policy in India,* N.M. Tripathi Private Ltd, New Delhi.
Sainath, P. (1996), *Everybody Loves a Good Drought*, 25, Penguin Books, New Delhi.
Salamon, L. and Anheier, H. and Assoc. (1998), *The Emerging Sector Revisited,* 2, Johns Hopkins University, Baltimore.
Sangroula, Y. (1997), *Increased Involvement of the Legal Profession in Community Problems: An Emerging Concept in Developing Societies* (Working paper prepared for Fourth International Conference on Clinical Legal Education and Scholarship, October, 1997) (on file with the author).

Sarat, A. and Scheingold, S. (eds) (1998), *Cause Lawyering,* Oxford University Press, New York.
Saxena, P. (1997a), 'Legal Education and Legal Aid: The Indian Perspective', *Indian Journal of Contemporary Law*, vol. 1, 33.
Saxena,P. (1997b), 'Legal Education and Legal Aid: The Indian Perspective', (Working paper prepared for Fourth International Conference on Clinical Legal Education and Scholarship, October, 1997) (on file with the author).
Schukoske, J. (1997), 'Facing Realities: Socio-Legal Study in Sri Lanka', in Cooper, J. and Trubek, L. (eds), 194.
Schuler, M. and Kadirgamar-Rajasingham, S. (eds) (1992), *Introduction* in *Legal Literacy: A Tool for Women's Empowerment,* PACT Communications, New York.
Sehgal, N. (1988) 'Women and the Law: A General Survey', in Baxi, U. (ed.), *Law and Poverty - Critical Essays*, 297-309, N.M. Tripathi Private Limited, Bombay.
Shah, D.S. (1998), *Courts, Legal Literacy, and the Role of Community Participation in Indian Legal Aid* (unpublished paper on file with the author).
Singh, P. (1988), 'The Scheduled Castes and the Law', in Baxi, U. (ed.) (1988a).
Singh, S. (1998), *Sulabh Sanitation Movement*, 19, Sulabh International Social Service Organisation, New Delhi.
Sripati, V. (1998), 'Towards Fifty Years of Constitutionalism and Fundamental Rights in India: Looking Back to See Ahead', *American University International Law Review*, vol. 14, 413.
Srivastava, S. (1988),'Organized Rural Labour and the Law', in Baxi, U. (ed.) (1988a).
Stark, B. (1992), 'Economic Rights in the United States and International Human Rights Law: Towards an "Entirely New Strategy",' *Hastings Law Journal*, vol. 44, 79.
Stark, B. (1995), 'International Human Rights Law, Feminist Jurisprudence and Nietzsche's "Eternal Return": Turning the Wheel', *Harvard Women's Law Journal,* vol. 19, 164.
Sussman, S. (1994), 'Distant Voices in the Courts of India: Transformation of Standing in Public Interest Litigation', *Wisconsin International Law Journal*, vol. 13, 57.
Tamanaha, B. (1995), 'Book Review and Note: Law and Development', *American Journal of International Law*, vol. 89, 470.
Trubek, D. and Galanter, M. (1974), 'Scholars in Self-Estrangement: Some Reflections on the Crisis in Law and Development Studies in the United States', *Wisconsin Law Review*, 1062.
Ul Hoque, R. (1997), 'Social Values Through Litigation: the Case of Bangladesh, in Cooper, J. and Trubek, L. (eds).
United Nations Development Programme, (1997), *Human Development Report*, vol. 2, 18-21, Oxford University Press, New York.
Visick, J. (ed.) (1998), *Leading Public Entrepreneurs*, 85-89, Ashoka: Innovators for the Public, Arlington, Virginia.
Wall, C. (1998), 'Human Rights and Economic Sanctions: The New Imperialism', *Fordham International Law Journal*, vol. 22, 588.

White, L. (1994), 'Collaborative Lawyering in the Field? On Mapping the Paths from Rhetoric to Practice', *Clinical Law Review*, vol. 1, 157.
White, L. (1998) 'Feminist Microenterprise: Vindicating The Rights of Women in the New Global Order?', *Main Law Review*, vol. 50, 327.
Wilson, R. (1996), 'Clinical Legal Education as a Means To Improve Access to Justice in Developing and Newly Democratic Countries', (viewed June 15, 1999) <http://www.pili.org/library/cle/index.html>
Wirth, D. (1991), 'Legitimacy, Accountability, and Partnership: A Model for Advocacy on Third World Environmental Issues', *Yale Law Journal*, vol. 100, 1.
World Bank, (1997), *World Development Report*, 224, OUP, New York.